THE WILL TO BELIEVE

and other essays in popular philosophy

HUMAN IMMORTALITY

two supposed objections to the doctrine

by William James

Dover Publications, Inc., New York

Published in Canada by General Publishing Company, Ltd., 30 Lesmill Road, Don Mills, Toronto, Ontario.
Published in the United Kingdom by Constable and Company, Ltd., 10 Orange Street, London WC 2.

This Dover edition, first published in 1956, is an unabridged and unaltered republication of the first edition of *The Will to Believe and Other Essays in Popular Philosophy* as originally published by Longmans, Green & Co. in 1897 and of the second edition of *Human Immortality,* which first appeared in 1898 and was originally published by Houghton Mifflin & Co.

Standard Book Number: 486-20291-7
Library of Congress Catalog Card Number: 59-8984

Manufactured in the United States of America
Dover Publications, Inc.
180 Varick Street
New York, N. Y. 10014

THE WILL
TO BELIEVE

and other essays in popular philosophy

by William James

Dover Publications, Inc., New York

To

My Old Friend,

CHARLES SANDERS PEIRCE,

To whose philosophic comradeship in old times
and to whose writings in more recent years
I owe more incitement and help than
I can express or repay.

PREFACE.

———•———

AT most of our American Colleges there are Clubs formed by the students devoted to particular branches of learning; and these clubs have the laudable custom of inviting once or twice a year some maturer scholar to address them, the occasion often being made a public one. I have from time to time accepted such invitations, and afterwards had my discourse printed in one or other of the Reviews. It has seemed to me that these addresses might now be worthy of collection in a volume, as they shed explanatory light upon each other, and taken together express a tolerably definite philosophic attitude in a very untechnical way.

Were I obliged to give a short name to the attitude in question, I should call it that of *radical empiricism*, in spite of the fact that such brief nicknames are nowhere more misleading than in philosophy. I say 'empiricism,' because it is contented to regard its most assured conclusions concerning matters of fact as hypotheses liable to modification in the course of future experience; and I say 'radical,' because it treats the doctrine of monism itself as an hypothesis, and,

unlike so much of the half-way empiricism that is
current under the name of positivism or agnosticism
or scientific naturalism, it does not dogmatically affirm monism as something with which all experience
has got to square. The difference between monism
and pluralism is perhaps the most pregnant of all the
differences in philosophy. *Primâ facie* the world is
a pluralism; as we find it, its unity seems to be that
of any collection; and our higher thinking consists
chiefly of an effort to redeem it from that first crude
form. Postulating more unity than the first experiences yield, we also discover more. But absolute unity,
in spite of brilliant dashes in its direction, still remains
undiscovered, still remains a *Grenzbegriff*. "Ever not
quite" must be the rationalistic philosopher's last confession concerning it. After all that reason can do
has been done, there still remains the opacity of the
finite facts as merely given, with most of their peculiarities mutually unmediated and unexplained. To
the very last, there are the various 'points of view'
which the philosopher must distinguish in discussing
the world; and what is inwardly clear from one point
remains a bare externality and datum to the other.
The negative, the alogical, is never wholly banished.
Something — "call it fate, chance, freedom, sponta-
neity, the devil, what you will" — is still wrong and
other and outside and unincluded, from *your* point of
view, even though you be the greatest of philosophers.
Something is always mere fact and *givenness;* and
there may be in the whole universe no one point of
view extant from which this would not be found to
be the case. "Reason," as a gifted writer says, "is

but one item in the mystery; and behind the proudest consciousness that ever reigned, reason and wonder blushed face to face. The inevitable stales, while doubt and hope are sisters. Not unfortunately the universe is wild, — game-flavored as a hawk's wing. Nature is miracle all; the same returns not save to bring the different. The slow round of the engraver's lathe gains but the breadth of a hair, but the difference is distributed back over the whole curve, never an instant true, — ever not quite." [1]

This is pluralism, somewhat rhapsodically expressed. He who takes for his hypothesis the notion that it is the permanent form of the world is what I call a radical empiricist. For him the crudity of experience remains an eternal element thereof. There is no possible point of view from which the world can appear an absolutely single fact. Real possibilities, real indeterminations, real beginnings, real ends, real evil, real crises, catastrophes, and escapes, a real God, and a real moral life, just as commonsense conceives these things, may remain in empiricism as conceptions which that philosophy gives up the attempt either to 'overcome' or to reinterpret in monistic form.

Many of my professionally trained *confrères* will smile at the irrationalism of this view, and at the artlessness of my essays in point of technical form. But they should be taken as illustrations of the radically empiricist attitude rather than as argumentations for its validity. That admits meanwhile of be-

[1] B. P. Blood: The Flaw in Supremacy: Published by the Author, Amsterdam, N. Y., 1893.

ing argued in as technical a shape as any one can
desire, and possibly I may be spared to do later a
share of that work. Meanwhile these essays seem
to light up with a certain dramatic reality the attitude itself, and make it visible alongside of the higher
and lower dogmatisms between which in the pages of
philosophic history it has generally remained eclipsed
from sight.

The first four essays are largely concerned with
defending the legitimacy of religious faith. To some
rationalizing readers such advocacy will seem a sad
misuse of one's professional position. Mankind, they
will say, is only too prone to follow faith unreason-
ingly, and needs no preaching nor encouragement in
that direction. I quite agree that what mankind at
large most lacks is criticism and caution, not faith.
Its cardinal weakness is to let belief follow recklessly
upon lively conception, especially when the conception
has instinctive liking at its back. I admit, then, that
were I addressing the Salvation Army or a miscella-
neous popular crowd it would be a misuse of opportunity to preach the liberty of believing as I have in
these pages preached it. What such audiences most
need is that their faiths should be broken up and ven-
tilated, that the northwest wind of science should get
into them and blow their sickliness and barbarism
away. But academic audiences, fed already on science, have a very different need. Paralysis of their
native capacity for faith and timorous *abulia* in the
religious field are their special forms of mental weakness, brought about by the notion, carefully instilled,
that there is something called scientific evidence by

waiting upon which they shall escape all danger of shipwreck in regard to truth. But there is really no scientific or other method by which men can steer safely between the opposite dangers of believing too little or of believing too much. To face such dangers is apparently our duty, and to hit the right channel between them is the measure of our wisdom as men. It does not follow, because recklessness may be a vice in soldiers, that courage ought never to be preached to them. What *should* be preached is courage weighted with responsibility, — such courage as the Nelsons and Washingtons never failed to show after they had taken everything into account that might tell against their success, and made every provision to minimize disaster in case they met defeat. I do not think that any one can accuse me of preaching reckless faith. I have preached the right of the individual to indulge his personal faith at his personal risk. I have discussed the kinds of risk; I have contended that none of us escape all of them; and I have only pleaded that it is better to face them open-eyed than to act as if we did not know them to be there.

After all, though, you will say, Why such an ado about a matter concerning which, however we may theoretically differ, we all practically agree? In this age of toleration, no scientist will ever try actively to interfere with our religious faith, provided we enjoy it quietly with our friends and do not make a public nuisance of it in the market-place. But it is just on this matter of the market-place that I think the utility of such essays as mine may turn. If reli-

gious hypotheses about the universe be in order at
all, then the active faiths of individuals in them,
freely expressing themselves in life, are the experimental tests by which they are verified, and the only
means by which their truth or falsehood can be
wrought out. The truest scientific hypothesis is that
which, as we say, 'works' best; and it can be no
otherwise with religious hypotheses. Religious history proves that one hypothesis after another has
worked ill, has crumbled at contact with a widening
knowledge of the world, and has lapsed from the
minds of men. Some articles of faith, however,
have maintained themselves through every vicissi-
tude, and possess even more vitality to-day than ever
before: it is for the 'science of religions' to tell us
just which hypotheses these are. Meanwhile the free-
est competition of the various faiths with one another,
and their openest application to life by their several
champions, are the most favorable conditions under
which the survival of the fittest can proceed. They
ought therefore not to lie hid each under its bushel,
indulged-in quietly with friends. They ought to live
in publicity, vying with each other; and it seems to
me that (the régime of tolerance once granted, and
a fair field shown) the scientist has nothing to fear for
his own interests from the liveliest possible state of
fermentation in the religious world of his time. Those
faiths will best stand the test which adopt also his hypotheses, and make them integral elements of their
own. He should welcome therefore every species of
religious agitation and discussion, so long as he is willing to allow that some religious hypothesis *may* be

true. Of course there are plenty of scientists who would deny that dogmatically, maintaining that science has already ruled all possible religious hypotheses out of court. Such scientists ought, I agree, to aim at imposing privacy on religious faiths, the public manifestation of which could only be a nuisance in their eyes. With all such scientists, as well as with their allies outside of science, my quarrel openly lies; and I hope that my book may do something to persuade the reader of their crudity, and range him on my side. Religious fermentation is always a symptom of the intellectual vigor of a society; and it is only when they forget that they are hypotheses and put on rationalistic and authoritative pretensions, that our faiths do harm. The most interesting and valuable things about a man are his ideals and over-beliefs. The same is true of nations and historic epochs; and the excesses of which the particular individuals and epochs are guilty are compensated in the total, and become profitable to mankind in the long run.

The essay 'On some Hegelisms' doubtless needs an apology for the superficiality with which it treats a serious subject. It was written as a squib, to be read in a college-seminary in Hegel's logic, several of whose members, mature men, were devout champions of the dialectical method. My blows therefore were aimed almost entirely at that. I reprint the paper here (albeit with some misgivings), partly because I believe the dialectical method to be wholly abominable when worked by concepts alone, and partly because the essay casts some positive light on the pluralist-empiricist point of view.

The paper on Psychical Research is added to the volume for convenience and utility. Attracted to this study some years ago by my love of sportsmanlike fair play in science, I have seen enough to convince me of its great importance, and I wish to gain for it what interest I can. The American Branch of the Society is in need of more support, and if my article draws some new associates thereto, it will have served its turn.

Apology is also needed for the repetition of the same passage in two essays (pp. 59–61 and 96–7, 100–1). My excuse is that one cannot always express the same thought in two ways that seem equally forcible, so one has to copy one's former words.

The Crillon-quotation on page 62 is due to Mr. W. M. Salter (who employed it in a similar manner in the ' Index ' for August 24, 1882), and the dream-metaphor on p. 174 is a reminiscence from some novel of George Sand's — I forget which — read by me thirty years ago.

Finally, the revision of the essays has consisted almost entirely in excisions. Probably less than a page and a half in all of new matter has been added.

HARVARD UNIVERSITY,
CAMBRIDGE, MASSACHUSETTS,
December, 1896.

CONTENTS.

———◆———

Contents.

the will to believe

and other essays in popular philosophy

ESSAYS

IN

POPULAR PHILOSOPHY.

———•———

THE WILL TO BELIEVE.[1]

IN the recently published Life by Leslie Stephen of
his brother, Fitz-James, there is an account of a
school to which the latter went when he was a boy.
The teacher, a certain Mr. Guest, used to converse
with his pupils in this wise: "Gurncy, what is the
difference between justification and sanctification? —
Stephen, prove the omnipotence of God!" etc. In
the midst of our Harvard freethinking and indifference we are prone to imagine that here at your good
old orthodox College conversation continues to be
somewhat upon this order; and to show you that
we at Harvard have not lost all interest in these vital
subjects, I have brought with me to-night something
like a sermon on justification by faith to read to you,
— I mean an essay in justification *of* faith, a defence
of our right to adopt a believing attitude in religious
matters, in spite of the fact that our merely logical

[1] An Address to the Philosophical Clubs of Yale and Brown
Universities. Published in the New World, June, 1896.

intellect may not have been coerced. 'The Will to Believe,' accordingly, is the title of my paper.

I have long defended to my own students the lawfulness of voluntarily adopted faith; but as soon as they have got well imbued with the logical spirit, they have as a rule refused to admit my contention to be lawful philosophically, even though in point of fact they were personally all the time chock-full of some faith or other themselves. I am all the while, however, so profoundly convinced that my own position is correct, that your invitation has seemed to me a good occasion to make my statements more clear. Perhaps your minds will be more open than those with which I have hitherto had to deal. I will be as little technical as I can, though I must begin by setting up some technical distinctions that will help us in the end.

I.

Let us give the name of *hypothesis* to anything that may be proposed to our belief; and just as the electricians speak of live and dead wires, let us speak of any hypothesis as either *live* or *dead*. A live hypothesis is one which appeals as a real possibility to him to whom it is proposed. If I ask you to believe in the Mahdi, the notion makes no electric connection with your nature, — it refuses to scintillate with any credibility at all. As an hypothesis it is completely dead. To an Arab, however (even if he be not one of the Mahdi's followers), the hypothesis is among the mind's possibilities: it is alive. This shows that deadness and liveness in an hypothesis are not intrinsic properties, but relations to the individual thinker. They are measured by his willingness to act. The maximum of liveness in an hypothesis means willingness to act irrevocably. Practically, that means belief; but there is some believing tendency wherever there is willingness to act at all.

Next, let us call the decision between two hypotheses an *option*. Options may be of several kinds. They may be — 1, *living* or *dead*; 2, *forced* or *avoidable*; 3, *momentous* or *trivial*; and for our purposes we may call an option a *genuine* option when it is of the forced, living, and momentous kind.

1. A living option is one in which both hypotheses are live ones. If I say to you: "Be a theosophist or be a Mohammedan," it is probably a dead option, because for you neither hypothesis is likely to be alive. But if I say: "Be an agnostic or be a Christian," it is otherwise: trained as you are, each hypothesis makes some appeal, however small, to your belief.

2. Next, if I say to you: "Choose between going out with your umbrella or without it," I do not offer you a genuine option, for it is not forced. You can easily avoid it by not going out at all. Similarly, if I say, "Either love me or hate me," "Either call my theory true or call it false," your option is avoidable. You may remain indifferent to me, neither loving nor hating, and you may decline to offer any judgment as to my theory. But if I say, "Either accept this truth or go without it," I put on you a forced option, for there is no standing place outside of the alternative. Every dilemma based on a complete logical disjunction, with no possibility of not choosing, is an option of this forced kind.

3. Finally, if I were Dr. Nansen and proposed to you to join my North Pole expedition, your option would be momentous; for this would probably be your only similar opportunity, and your choice now would either exclude you from the North Pole sort of immortality altogether or put at least the chance of it into your hands. He who refuses to embrace a unique opportunity loses the prize as surely as if he tried and failed. *Per contra*, the option is trivial when the opportunity is not unique, when the stake is insignificant, or when the decision is reversible if it later prove unwise. Such trivial options abound in the scientific life. A chemist finds an hypothesis live enough to spend a year in its verification: he believes in it to that extent. But if his experiments prove inconclusive either way, he is quit for his loss of time, no vital harm being done.

It will facilitate our discussion if we keep all these distinctions well in mind.

II.

The next matter to consider is the actual psychology of human opinion. When we look at certain facts, it seems as if our passional and volitional nature lay at the root of all our convictions. When we look at others, it seems as if they could do nothing when the intellect had once said its say. Let us take the latter facts up first.

Does it not seem preposterous on the very face of it to talk of our opinions being modifiable at will? Can our will either help or hinder our intellect in its perceptions of truth? Can we, by just willing it, believe that Abraham Lincoln's existence is a myth, and that the portraits of him in McClure's Magazine are all of some one else? Can we, by any effort of our will, or by any strength of wish that it were true, believe ourselves well and about when we are roaring with rheumatism in bed, or feel certain that the sum of the two one-dollar bills in our pocket must be a hundred dollars? We can *say* any of these things, but we are absolutely impotent to believe them; and of just such things is the whole fabric of the truths that we do believe in made up, — matters of fact, immediate or remote, as Hume said, and relations between ideas, which are either there or not there for us if we see them so, and which if not there cannot be put there by any action of our own.

In Pascal's Thoughts there is a celebrated passage known in literature as Pascal's wager. In it he tries to force us into Christianity by reasoning as if our concern with truth resembled our concern with the stakes in a game of chance. Translated freely his words are these: You must either believe or not believe that God is — which will you do? Your human reason cannot say. A game is going on between you and the nature of things which at the day of judgment will bring out either heads or tails. Weigh what your gains and your losses would be if you should stake all you have on heads, or God's existence: if you win in such case, you gain eternal beatitude; if you lose, you lose nothing at all. If there were an infinity of chances, and only one for God in this wager, still you ought to stake your all on God; for though you surely risk a finite loss by this procedure, any finite loss is reasonable, even a certain one is reasonable, if there is but the possibility of infinite gain. Go, then, and take holy water, and have masses said; belief will come and stupefy your scruples, — *Cela vous fera croire et vous abêtira.* Why should you not? At bottom, what have you to lose?

You probably feel that when religious faith expresses itself thus, in the language of the gaming-table, it is put to its last trumps. Surely Pascal's own personal belief in masses and holy water had far other springs; and this celebrated page of his is but an argument for others, a last desperate snatch at a weapon against the hardness of the unbelieving heart. We feel that a faith in masses and holy water adopted wilfully after such a mechanical calculation would lack the inner soul of faith's reality; and if we were ourselves in the place of the Deity, we should probably take particular pleasure in cutting off believers of this pattern from their infinite reward. It is evident that unless there be some pre-existing tendency to believe in masses and holy water, the option offered to the will by Pascal is not a living option. Certainly no Turk ever took to masses and holy water on its account; and even to us Protestants these means of salvation seem such foregone impossibilities that Pascal's logic, invoked for them specifically, leaves us unmoved. As well might the Mahdi write to us, saying, "I am the Expected One whom God has created in his effulgence. You shall be infinitely happy if you confess me; otherwise you shall be cut off from the light of the sun. Weigh, then, your infinite gain if I am genuine against your finite sacrifice if I am not!" His logic would be that of Pascal; but he would vainly use it on us, for the hypothesis he offers us is dead. No tendency to act on it exists in us to any degree.

The talk of believing by our volition seems, then, from one point of view, simply silly. From another point of view it is worse than silly, it is vile. When one turns to the magnificent edifice of the physical sciences, and sees how it was reared; what thousands of disinterested moral lives of men lie buried in its mere foundations; what patience and postponement, what choking down of preference, what submission to the icy laws of outer fact are wrought into its very stones and mortar; how absolutely impersonal it stands in its vast augustness, — then how besotted and contemptible seems every little sentimentalist who comes blowing his voluntary smoke-wreaths, and pretending to decide things from out of his private dream! Can we wonder if those bred in the rugged and manly school of science should feel like spewing such subjectivism out of their mouths? The whole system of loyalties which grow up in the schools of science go dead against its toleration; so that it is only natural that those who have caught the scientific fever should pass over to the opposite extreme, and write sometimes as if the incorruptibly truthful intellect ought positively to prefer bitterness and unacceptableness to the heart in its cup.

> It fortifies my soul to know
> That, though I perish, Truth is so —

sings Clough, while Huxley exclaims: "My only consolation lies in the reflection that, however bad our posterity may become, so far as they hold by the plain rule of not pretending to believe what they have no reason to believe, because it may be to their advantage so to pretend [the word 'pretend' is surely here redundant], they will not have reached the lowest depth of immorality." And that delicious *enfant terrible* Clifford writes: "Belief is desecrated when given to unproved and unquestioned statements for the solace and private pleasure of the believer. . . . Whoso would deserve well of his fellows in this matter will guard the purity of his belief with a very fanaticism of jealous care, lest at any time it should rest on an unworthy object, and catch a stain which can never be wiped away. . . . If [a] belief has been accepted on insufficient evidence [even though the belief be true, as Clifford on the same page explains] the pleasure is a stolen one. . . . It is sinful because it is stolen in defiance of our duty to mankind. That duty is to guard ourselves from such beliefs as from a pestilence which may shortly master our own body and then spread to the rest of the town. . . . It is wrong always, everywhere, and for every one, to believe anything upon insufficient evidence."

III.

All this strikes one as healthy, even when expressed, as by Clifford, with somewhat too much of robustious pathos in the voice. Free-will and simple wishing do seem, in the matter of our credences, to be only fifth wheels to the coach. Yet if any one should thereupon assume that intellectual insight is what remains after wish and will and sentimental preference have taken wing, or that pure reason is what then settles our opinions, he would fly quite as directly in the teeth of the facts.

It is only our already dead hypotheses that our willing nature is unable to bring to life again But what has made them dead for us is for the most part a previous action of our willing nature of an antagonistic kind. When I say 'willing nature,' I do not mean only such deliberate volitions as may have set up habits of belief that we cannot now escape from, — I mean all such factors of belief as fear and hope, prejudice and passion, imitation and partisanship, the circumpressure of our caste and set. As a matter of fact we find ourselves believing, we hardly know how or why. Mr. Balfour gives the name of 'authority' to all those influences, born of the intellectual climate, that make hypotheses possible or impossible for us, alive or dead. Here in this room, we all of us believe in molecules and the conservation of energy, in democracy and necessary progress, in Protestant Christianity and the duty of fighting for 'the doctrine of the immortal Monroe,' all for no reasons worthy of the name. We see into these matters with no more inner clearness, and probably with much less, than any disbeliever in them might possess. His unconventionality would probably have some grounds to show for its conclusions; but for us, not insight, but the *prestige* of the opinions, is what makes the spark shoot from them and light up our sleeping magazines of faith. Our reason is quite satisfied, in nine hundred and ninety-nine cases out of every thousand of us, if it can find a few arguments that will do to recite in case our credulity is criticised by some one else. Our faith is faith in some one else's faith, and in the greatest matters this is most the case. Our belief in truth itself, for instance, that there is a truth, and that our minds and it are made for each other, — what is it but a passionate affirmation of desire, in which our social system backs us up? We **want to have** a truth; we want to believe that our

experiments and studies and discussions must put us
in a continually better and better position towards it;
and on this line we agree to fight out our thinking
lives.   But if a pyrrhonistic sceptic asks us *how we
know* all this, can our logic find a reply? No! certainly it cannot.   It is just one volition against another, — we willing to go in for life upon a trust or
assumption which he, for his part, does not care to
make.[1]

As a rule we disbelieve all facts and theories for
which we have no use.   Clifford's cosmic emotions
find no use for Christian feelings.   Huxley belabors
the bishops because there is no use for sacerdotal-
ism in his scheme of life.   Newman, on the contrary,
goes over to Romanism, and finds all sorts of reasons
good for staying there, because a priestly system is
for him an organic need and delight.   Why do so few
'scientists' even look at the evidence for telepathy,
so called?   Because they think, as a leading biologist,
now dead, once said to me, that even if such a thing
were true, scientists ought to band together to keep
it suppressed and concealed.   It would undo the
uniformity of Nature and all sorts of other things
without which scientists cannot carry on their pursuits.   But if this very man had been shown something which as a scientist he might *do* with telepathy,
he might not only have examined the evidence, but
even have found it good enough.   This very law which
the logicians would impose upon us — if I may give
the name of logicians to those who would rule out
our willing nature here — is based on nothing but
their own natural wish to exclude all elements for

[1] Compare the admirable page 310 in S. H. Hodgson's "Time and
Space," London, 1865.

which they, in their professional quality of logicians, can find no use.

Evidently, then, our non-intellectual nature does influence our convictions. There are passional tendencies and volitions which run before and others which come after belief, and it is only the latter that are too late for the fair; and they are not too late when the previous passional work has been already in their own direction. Pascal's argument, instead of being powerless, then seems a regular clincher, and is the last stroke needed to make our faith in masses and holy water complete. The state of things is evidently far from simple; and pure insight and logic, whatever they might do ideally, are not the only things that really do produce our creeds.

IV.

Our next duty, having recognized this mixed-up state of affairs, is to ask whether it be simply reprehensible and pathological, or whether, on the contrary, we must treat it as a normal element in making up our minds. The thesis I defend is, briefly stated, this: *Our passional nature not only lawfully may, but must, decide an option between propositions, whenever it is a genuine option that cannot by its nature be decided on intellectual grounds ; for to say, under such circumstances, " Do not decide, but leave the question open," is itself a passional decision, — just like deciding yes or no, — and is attended with the same risk of losing the truth.* The thesis thus abstractly expressed will, I trust, soon become quite clear. But I must first indulge in a bit more of preliminary work.

V.

It will be observed that for the purposes of this discussion we are on 'dogmatic' ground, — ground, I mean, which leaves systematic philosophical scepticism altogether out of account. The postulate that there is truth, and that it is the destiny of our minds to attain it, we are deliberately resolving to make, though the sceptic will not make it. We part company with him, therefore, absolutely, at this point. But the faith that truth exists, and that our minds can find it, may be held in two ways. We may talk of the *empiricist* way and of the *absolutist* way of believing in truth. The absolutists in this matter say that we not only can attain to knowing truth, but we can *know when* we have attained to knowing it; while the empiricists think that although we may attain it, we cannot infallibly know when. To *know* is one thing, and to know for certain *that* we know is another. One may hold to the first being possible without the second; hence the empiricists and the absolutists, although neither of them is a sceptic in the usual philosophic sense of the term, show very different degrees of dogmatism in their lives.

If we look at the history of opinions, we see that the empiricist tendency has largely prevailed in science, while in philosophy the absolutist tendency has had everything its own way. The characteristic sort of happiness, indeed, which philosophies yield has mainly consisted in the conviction felt by each successive school or system that by it bottom-certitude had been attained. "Other philosophies are collections of opinions, mostly false; *my* philosophy

gives standing-ground forever," — who does not recognize in this the key-note of every system worthy
of the name? A system, to be a system at all, must
come as a *closed* system, reversible in this or that
detail, perchance, but in its essential features never!

Scholastic orthodoxy, to which one must always
go when one wishes to find perfectly clear statement,
has beautifully elaborated this absolutist conviction
in a doctrine which it calls that of ' objective evidence.' If, for example, I am unable to doubt that
I now exist before you, that two is less than three, or
that if all men are mortal then I am mortal too,
it is because these things illumine my intellect irre-
sistibly. The final ground of this objective evidence
possessed by certain propositions is the *adæquatio
intellectûs nostri cum rê*. The certitude it brings involves an *aptitudinem ad extorquendum certum assensum* on the part of the truth envisaged, and on the
side of the subject a *quietem in cognitione*, when once
the object is mentally received, that leaves no possibility of doubt behind ; and in the whole transaction
nothing operates but the *entitas ipsa* of the object
and the *entitas ipsa* of the mind. We slouchy modern thinkers dislike to talk in Latin, — indeed, we dislike to talk in set terms at all ; but at bottom our own
state of mind is very much like this whenever we
uncritically abandon ourselves : You believe in objective evidence, and I do. Of some things we feel
that we are certain : we know, and we know that we
do know. There is something that gives a click inside of us, a bell that strikes twelve, when the hands
of our mental clock have swept the dial and meet
over the meridian hour. The greatest empiricists
among us are only empiricists on reflection : when

left to their instincts, they dogmatize like infallible popes. When the Cliffords tell us how sinful it is to be Christians on such 'insufficient evidence,' insufficiency is really the last thing they have in mind. For them the evidence is absolutely sufficient, only it makes the other way. They believe so completely in an anti-christian order of the universe that there is no living option: Christianity is a dead hypothesis from the start.

VI.

But now, since we are all such absolutists by instinct, what in our quality of students of philosophy ought we to do about the fact? Shall we espouse and indorse it? Or shall we treat it as a weakness of our nature from which we must free ourselves, if we can?

I sincerely believe that the latter course is the only one we can follow as reflective men. Objective evidence and certitude are doubtless very fine ideals to play with, but where on this moonlit and dream-visited planet are they found? I am, therefore, myself a complete empiricist so far as my theory of human knowledge goes. I live, to be sure, by the practical faith that we must go on experiencing and thinking over our experience, for only thus can our opinions grow more true; but to hold any one of them — I absolutely do not care which — as if it never could be reinterpretable or corrigible, I believe to be a tremendously mistaken attitude, and I think that the whole history of philosophy will bear me out. There is but one indefectibly certain truth, and that is the truth that pyrrhonistic scepticism itself leaves stand-

ing, — the truth that the present phenomenon of
consciousness exists.   That, however, is the bare
starting-point of knowledge, the mere admission of
a stuff to be philosophized about.   The various philosophies are but so many attempts at expressing
what this stuff really is.   And if we repair to our
libraries what disagreement do we discover!   Where
is a certainly true answer found?   Apart from abstract propositions of comparison (such as two and
two are the same as four), propositions which tell
us nothing by themselves about concrete reality, we
find no proposition ever regarded by any one as evidently certain that has not either been called a falsehood, or at least had its truth sincerely questioned
by some one else.   The transcending of the axioms
of geometry, not in play but in earnest, by certain
of our contemporaries (as Zöllner and Charles H.
Hinton), and the rejection of the whole Aristotelian
logic by the Hegelians, are striking instances in
point.

No concrete test of what is really true has ever
been agreed upon.   Some make the criterion external to the moment of perception, putting it either
in revelation, the *consensus gentium*, the instincts of
the heart, or the systematized experience of the race.
Others make the perceptive moment its own test, —
Descartes, for instance, with his clear and distinct
ideas guaranteed by the veracity of God; Reid with
his ' common-sense; ' and Kant with his forms of
synthetic judgment *a priori*.   The inconceivability
of the opposite; the capacity to be verified by sense;
the possession of complete organic unity or self-rela-
tion, realized when a thing is its own other, — are
standards which, in turn, have been used.   The much

lauded objective evidence is never triumphantly there;
it is a mere aspiration or *Grenzbegriff*, marking the
infinitely remote ideal of our thinking life. To claim
that certain truths now possess it, is simply to say
that when you think them true and they *are* true,
then their evidence is objective, otherwise it is not.
But practically one's conviction that the evidence
one goes by is of the real objective brand, is only
one more subjective opinion added to the lot. For
what a contradictory array of opinions have objective evidence and absolute certitude been claimed!
The world is rational through and through, — its existence is an ultimate brute fact; there is a personal God, — a personal God is inconceivable; there
is an extra-mental physical world immediately known,
— the mind can only know its own ideas; a moral imperative exists, — obligation is only the resultant of
desires; a permanent spiritual principle is in every
one, — there are only shifting states of mind; there
is an endless chain of causes, — there is an absolute
first cause; an eternal necessity, — a freedom; a
purpose, — no purpose; a primal One, — a primal
Many; a universal continuity, — an essential discontinuity in things; an infinity, — no infinity. There is
this, — there is that; there is indeed nothing which
some one has not thought absolutely true, while his
neighbor deemed it absolutely false; and not an
absolutist among them seems ever to have considered that the trouble may all the time be essential,
and that the intellect, even with truth directly in its
grasp, may have no infallible signal for knowing
whether it be truth or no. When, indeed, one remembers that the most striking practical application
to life of the doctrine of objective certitude has been

the conscientious labors of the Holy Office of the Inquisition, one feels less tempted than ever to lend the doctrine a respectful ear.

But please observe, now, that when as empiricists we give up the doctrine of objective certitude, we do not thereby give up the quest or hope of truth itself. We still pin our faith on its existence, and still believe that we gain an ever better position towards it by systematically continuing to roll up experiences and think. Our great difference from the scholastic lies in the way we face. The strength of his system lies in the principles, the origin, the *terminus a quo* of his thought; for us the strength is in the outcome, the upshot, the *terminus ad quem*. Not where it comes from but what it leads to is to decide. It matters not to an empiricist from what quarter an hypothesis may come to him: he may have acquired it by fair means or by foul; passion may have whispered or accident suggested it; but if the total drift of thinking continues to confirm it, that is what he means by its being true.

VII.

One more point, small but important, and our preliminaries are done. There are two ways of looking at our duty in the matter of opinion, — ways entirely different, and yet ways about whose difference the theory of knowledge seems hitherto to have shown very little concern. *We must know the truth;* and *we must avoid error,* — these are our first and great commandments as would-be knowers; but they are not two ways of stating an identical commandment, they are two separable laws. Although it may indeed happen that when we believe the truth *A,* we escape

as an incidental consequence from believing the falsehood *B*, it hardly ever happens that by merely disbelieving *B* we necessarily believe *A*. We may in
escaping *B* fall into believing other falsehoods, *C* or
D, just as bad as *B*; or we may escape *B* by not
believing anything at all, not even *A*.

Believe truth! Shun error! — these, we see, are
two materially different laws; and by choosing between them we may end by coloring differently our
whole intellectual life. We may regard the chase
for truth as paramount, and the avoidance of error as
secondary; or we may, on the other hand, treat the
avoidance of error as more imperative, and let truth
take its chance. Clifford, in the instructive passage
which I have quoted, exhorts us to the latter course.
Believe nothing, he tells us, keep your mind in suspense forever, rather than by closing it on insufficient
evidence incur the awful risk of believing lies. You,
on the other hand, may think that the risk of being in
error is a very small matter when compared with the
blessings of real knowledge, and be ready to be duped
many times in your investigation rather than post-
pone indefinitely the chance of guessing true. I
myself find it impossible to go with Clifford. We
must remember that these feelings of our duty about
either truth or error are in any case only expressions
of our passional life. Biologically considered, our
minds are as ready to grind out falsehood as veracity,
and he who says, " Better go without belief forever
than believe a lie! " merely shows his own prepon-
derant private horror of becoming a dupe. He may
be critical of many of his desires and fears, but this
fear he slavishly obeys. He cannot imagine any one
questioning its binding force. For my own part, I

have also a horror of being duped; but I can believe that worse things than being duped may happen to a man in this world : so Clifford's exhortation has to my ears a thoroughly fantastic sound. It is like a general informing his soldiers that it is better to keep out of battle forever than to risk a single wound. Not so are victories either over enemies or over nature gained. Our errors are surely not such awfully solemn things. In a world where we are so certain to incur them in spite of all our caution, a certain lightness of heart seems healthier than this excessive nervousness on their behalf. At any rate, it seems the fittest thing for the empiricist philosopher.

VIII.

And now, after all this introduction, let us go straight at our question. I have said, and now repeat it, that not only as a matter of fact do we find our passional nature influencing us in our opinions, but that there are some options between opinions in which this influence must be regarded both as an inevitable and as a lawful determinant of our choice.

I fear here that some of you my hearers will begin to scent danger, and lend an inhospitable ear. Two first steps of passion you have indeed had to admit as necessary, — we must think so as to avoid dupery, and we must think so as to gain truth; but the surest path to those ideal consummations, you will probably consider, is from now onwards to take no further passional step.

Well, of course, I agree as far as the facts will allow. Wherever the option between losing truth and gaining it is not momentous, we can throw the chance of *gaining truth* away, and at any rate save ourselves from any chance of *believing falsehood*, by not making up our minds at all till objective evidence has come. In scientific questions, this is almost always the case; and even in human affairs in general, the need of acting is seldom so urgent that a false belief to act on is better than no belief at all. Law courts, indeed, have to decide on the best evidence attainable for the moment, because a judge's duty is to make law as well as to ascertain it, and (as a learned judge once said to me) few cases are worth spending much time over: the great thing is to have them decided on *any* acceptable principle, and got out of the way. But in our dealings with objective nature we obviously are recorders, not makers, of the truth; and decisions for the mere sake of deciding promptly and getting on to the next business would be wholly out of place. Throughout the breadth of physical nature facts are what they are quite independently of us, and seldom is there any such hurry about them that the risks of being duped by believing a premature theory need be faced. The questions here are always trivial options, the hypotheses are hardly living (at any rate not living for us spectators), the choice between believing truth or falsehood is seldom forced. The attitude of sceptical balance is therefore the absolutely wise one if we would escape mistakes. What difference, indeed, does it make to most of us whether we have or have not a theory of the Röntgen rays, whether we believe or not in mind-stuff, or have a conviction about the causality of conscious states? It makes no difference. Such options are not forced on us. On every account it is better not to make them, but still keep weighing reasons *pro et contra* with an indifferent hand.

I speak, of course, here of the purely judging mind. For purposes of discovery such indifference is to be less highly recommended, and science would be far less advanced than she is if the passionate desires of individuals to get their own faiths confirmed had been kept out of the game. See for example the sagacity which Spencer and Weismann now display. On the other hand, if you want an absolute duffer in an investigation, you must, after all, take the man who has no interest whatever in its results: he is the warranted incapable, the positive fool. The most useful investigator, because the most sensitive observer, is always he whose eager interest in one side of the question is balanced by an equally keen nervousness lest he become deceived.[1] Science has organized this nervousness into a regular *technique*, her so-called method of verification; and she has fallen so deeply in love with the method that one may even say she has ceased to care for truth by itself at all. It is only truth as technically verified that interests her. The truth of truths might come in merely affirmative form, and she would decline to touch it. Such truth as that, she might repeat with Clifford, would be stolen in defiance of her duty to mankind. Human passions, however, are stronger than technical rules. "Le cœur a ses raisons," as Pascal says, "que la raison ne connaît pas;" and however indifferent to all but the bare rules of the game the umpire, the abstract intellect, may be, the concrete players who furnish him the materials to judge of are usually, each one of them, in love with some pet ' live hypothesis ' of his own. Let us agree, however, that wherever there is no forced option, the

---

[1] Compare Wilfrid Ward's Essay, "The Wish to Believe," in his *Witnesses to the Unseen*, Macmillan & Co., 1893.

dispassionately judicial intellect with no pet hypothesis, saving us, as it does, from dupery at any rate, ought to be our ideal.

The question next arises: Are there not somewhere forced options in our speculative questions, and can we (as men who may be interested at least as much in positively gaining truth as in merely escaping dupery) always wait with impunity till the coercive evidence shall have arrived? It seems *a priori* improbable that the truth should be so nicely adjusted to our needs and powers as that. In the great boarding-house of nature, the cakes and the butter and the syrup seldom come out so even and leave the plates so clean. Indeed, we should view them with scientific suspicion if they did.

IX.

Moral questions immediately present themselves as questions whose solution cannot wait for sensible proof. A moral question is a question not of what sensibly exists, but of what is good, or would be good if it did exist. Science can tell us what exists; but to compare the *worths*, both of what exists and of what does not exist, we must consult not science, but what Pascal calls our heart. Science herself consults her heart when she lays it down that the infinite ascertainment of fact and correction of false belief are the supreme goods for man. Challenge the statement, and science can only repeat it oracularly, or else prove it by showing that such ascertainment and correction bring man all sorts of other goods which man's heart in turn declares. The question of having moral beliefs at all or not having them is decided by

our will. Are our moral preferences true or false,
or are they only odd biological phenomena, making
things good or bad for *us*, but in themselves indifferent? How can your pure intellect decide? If
your heart does not *want* a world of moral reality,
your head will assuredly never make you believe in
one. Mephistophelian scepticism, indeed, will satisfy
the head's play-instincts much better than any rigorous idealism can. Some men (even at the student
age) are so naturally cool-hearted that the moralistic
hypothesis never has for them any pungent life, and
in their supercilious presence the hot young moralist
always feels strangely ill at ease. The appearance of
knowingness is on their side, of *naïveté* and gullibility
on his. Yet, in the inarticulate heart of him, he clings
to it that he is not a dupe, and that there is a realm
in which (as Emerson says) all their wit and intellectual superiority is no better than the cunning of
a fox. Moral scepticism can no more be refuted or
proved by logic than intellectual scepticism can.
When we stick to it that there *is* truth (be it of either
kind), we do so with our whole nature, and resolve to
stand or fall by the results. The sceptic with his
whole nature adopts the doubting attitude; but which
of us is the wiser, Omniscience only knows.

Turn now from these wide questions of good to a
certain class of questions of fact, questions concerning
personal relations, states of mind between one man
and another. *Do you like me or not ?* — for example.
Whether you do or not depends, in countless instances, on whether I meet you half-way, am willing
to assume that you must like me, and show you trust
and expectation. The previous faith on my part in
your liking's existence is in such cases what makes

your liking come. But if I stand aloof, and refuse to budge an inch until I have objective evidence, until you shall have done something apt, as the absolutists say, *ad extorquendum assensum meum*, ten to one your liking never comes. How many women's hearts are vanquished by the mere sanguine insistence of some man that they *must* love him! he will not consent to the hypothesis that they cannot. The desire for a certain kind of truth here brings about that special truth's existence; and so it is in innumerable cases of other sorts. Who gains promotions, boons, appointments, but the man in whose life they are seen to play the part of live hypotheses, who discounts them, sacrifices other things for their sake before they have come, and takes risks for them in advance? His faith acts on the powers above him as a claim, and creates its own verification.

A social organism of any sort whatever, large or small, is what it is because each member proceeds to his own duty with a trust that the other members will simultaneously do theirs. Wherever a desired result is achieved by the co-operation of many independent persons, its existence as a fact is a pure consequence of the precursive faith in one another of those immediately concerned. A government, an army, a commercial system, a ship, a college, an athletic team, all exist on this condition, without which not only is nothing achieved, but nothing is even attempted. A whole train of passengers (individually brave enough) will be looted by a few highwaymen, simply because the latter can count on one another, while each passenger fears that if he makes a movement of resistance, he will be shot before any one else backs him up. If we believed that the whole car-full would rise

at once with us, we should each severally rise, and
train-robbing would never even be attempted. There
are, then, cases where a fact cannot come at all unless
a preliminary faith exists in its coming. *And where
faith in a fact can help create the fact,* that would be
an insane logic which should say that faith running
ahead of scientific evidence is the ' lowest kind of
immorality' into which a thinking being can fall. Yet
such is the logic by which our scientific absolutists
pretend to regulate our lives!

X.

In truths dependent on our personal action, then,
faith based on desire is certainly a lawful and possibly an indispensable thing.

But now, it will be said, these are all childish human cases, and have nothing to do with great cosmi-
cal matters, like the question of religious faith. Let
us then pass on to that. Religions differ so much
in their accidents that in discussing the religious
question we must make it very generic and broad.
What then do we now mean by the religious hypothesis? Science says things are; morality says some
things are better than other things; and religion says
essentially two things.

First, she says that the best things are the more
eternal things, the overlapping things, the things in
the universe that throw the last stone, so to speak,
and say the final word. " Perfection is eternal," —
this phrase of Charles Secrétan seems a good way of
putting this first affirmation of religion, an affirmation
which obviously cannot yet be verified scientifically
at all.

The second affirmation of religion is that we are better off even now if we believe her first affirmation to be true.

Now, let us consider what the logical elements of this situation are *in case the religious hypothesis in both its branches be really true.* (Of course, we must admit that possibility at the outset. If we are to discuss the question at all, it must involve a living option. If for any of you religion be a hypothesis that cannot, by any living possibility be true, then you need go no farther. I speak to the 'saving remnant' alone.) So proceeding, we see, first, that religion offers itself as a *momentous* option. We are supposed to gain, even now, by our belief, and to lose by our non-belief, a certain vital good. Secondly, religion is a *forced* option, so far as that good goes. We cannot escape the issue by remaining sceptical and waiting for more light, because, although we do avoid error in that way *if religion be untrue,* we lose the good, *if it be true,* just as certainly as if we positively chose to disbelieve. It is as if a man should hesitate indefinitely to ask a certain woman to marry him because he was not perfectly sure that she would prove an angel after he brought her home. Would he not cut himself off from that particular angel-possibility as decisively as if he went and married some one else? Scepticism, then, is not avoidance of option; it is option of a certain particular kind of risk. *Better risk loss of truth than chance of error,* — that is your faith-vetoer's exact position. He is actively playing his stake as much as the believer is; he is backing the field against the religious hypothesis, just as the believer is backing the religious hypothesis against the field. To preach scepticism to us as a duty until

'sufficient evidence' for religion be found, is tanta-
mount therefore to telling us, when in presence of the
religious hypothesis, that to yield to our fear of its
being error is wiser and better than to yield to our
hope that it may be true. It is not intellect against
all passions, then; it is only intellect with one passion laying down its law. And by what, forsooth,
is the supreme wisdom of this passion warranted?
Dupery for dupery, what proof is there that dupery
through hope is so much worse than dupery through
fear? I, for one, can see no proof; and I simply
refuse obedience to the scientist's command to imi-
tate his kind of option, in a case where my own stake
is important enough to give me the right to choose
my own form of risk. If religion be true and the
evidence for it be still insufficient, I do not wish, by
putting your extinguisher upon my nature (which
feels to me as if it had after all some business in this
matter), to forfeit my sole chance in life of getting
upon the winning side, — that chance depending, of
course, on my willingness to run the risk of acting
as if my passional need of taking the world religiously
might be prophetic and right.

All this is on the supposition that it really may
be prophetic and right, and that, even to us who are
discussing the matter, religion is a live hypothesis
which may be true. Now, to most of us religion
comes in a still further way that makes a veto on
our active faith even more illogical. The more perfect and more eternal aspect of the universe is represented in our religions as having personal form.
The universe is no longer a mere *It* to us, but a *Thou*,
if we are religious; and any relation that may be
possible from person to person might be possible

here. For instance, although in one sense we are passive portions of the universe, in another we show a curious autonomy, as if we were small active centres on our own account. We feel, too, as if the appeal of religion to us were made to our own active good-will, as if evidence might be forever withheld from us unless we met the hypothesis half-way. To take a trivial illustration: just as a man who in a company of gentlemen made no advances, asked a warrant for every concession, and believed no one's word without proof, would cut himself off by such churlishness from all the social rewards that a more trusting spirit would earn, — so here, one who should shut himself up in snarling logicality and try to make the gods extort his recognition willy-nilly, or not get it at all, might cut himself off forever from his only opportunity of making the gods' acquaintance. This feeling, forced on us we know not whence, that by obstinately believing that there are gods (although not to do so would be so easy both for our logic and our life) we are doing the universe the deepest service we can, seems part of the living essence of the religious hypothesis. If the hypothesis *were* true in all its parts, including this one, then pure intellectualism, with its veto on our making willing advances, would be an absurdity; and some participation of our sympathetic nature would be logically required. I, therefore, for one, cannot see my way to accepting the agnostic rules for truth-seeking, or wilfully agree to keep my willing nature out of the game. I cannot do so for this plain reason, that *a rule of thinking which would absolutely prevent me from acknowledging certain kinds of truth if those kinds of truth were really there, would be an irrational rule.* That for me ıs the long and short of the formal logic of the situation, no matter what the kinds of truth might materially be.

I confess I do not see how this logic can be escaped. But sad experience makes me fear that some of you may still shrink from radically saying with me, *in abstracto*, that we have the right to believe at our own risk any hypothesis that is live enough to tempt our will. I suspect, however, that if this is so, it is because you have got away from the abstract logical point of view altogether, and are thinking (perhaps without realizing it) of some particular religious hypothesis which for you is dead. The freedom to ' believe what we will ' you apply to the case of some patent superstition; and the faith you think of is the faith defined by the schoolboy when he said, " Faith is when you believe something that you know ain't true." I can only repeat that this is misapprehension. *In concreto*, the freedom to believe can only cover living options which the intellect of the individual cannot by itself resolve; and living options never seem absurdities to him who has them to consider. When I look at the religious question as it really puts itself to concrete men, and when I think of all the possibilities which both practically and theoretically it involves, then this command that we shall put a stopper on our heart, instincts, and courage, and *wait* — acting of course meanwhile more or less as if religion were *not* true [1] —

---

[1] Since belief is measured by action, he who forbids us to believe religion to be true, necessarily also forbids us to act as we should if we did believe it to be true. The whole defence of religious faith hinges upon action. If the action required or inspired by the religious hypothesis is in no way different from that dictated by the

till doomsday, or till such time as our intellect and
senses working together may have raked in evidence
enough, — this command, I say, seems to me the
queerest idol ever manufactured in the philosophic
cave. Were we scholastic absolutists, there might be
more excuse. If we had an infallible intellect with
its objective certitudes, we might feel ourselves dis-
loyal to such a perfect organ of knowledge in not
trusting to it exclusively, in not waiting for its releasing word. But if we are empiricists, if we believe that
no bell in us tolls to let us know for certain when
truth is in our grasp, then it seems a piece of idle
fantasticality to preach so solemnly our duty of waiting for the bell. Indeed we *may* wait if we will, — I
hope you do not think that I am denying that, — but
if we do so, we do so at our peril as much as if we
believed. In either case we *act*, taking our life in
our hands. No one of us ought to issue vetoes to
the other, nor should we bandy words of abuse. We
ought, on the contrary, delicately and profoundly to
respect one another's mental freedom : then only shall
we bring about the intellectual republic ; then only
shall we have that spirit of inner tolerance without
which all our outer tolerance is soulless, and which is
empiricism's glory ; then only shall we live and let
live, in speculative as well as in practical things.

I began by a reference to Fitz James Stephen ; let
me end by a quotation from him. " What do you think

naturalistic hypothesis, then religious faith is a pure superfluity,
better pruned away, and controversy about its legitimacy is a piece
of idle trifling, unworthy of serious minds. I myself believe, of
course, that the religious hypothesis gives to the world an expression
which specifically determines our reactions, and makes them in a
large part unlike what they might be on a purely naturalistic scheme
of belief.

of yourself? What do you think of the world? . . .
These are questions with which all must deal as it
seems good to them. They are riddles of the Sphinx,
and in some way or other we must deal with them.
. . . In all important transactions of life we have to
take a leap in the dark. . . . If we decide to leave the
riddles unanswered, that is a choice; if we waver in
our answer, that, too, is a choice: but whatever choice
we make, we make it at our peril. If a man chooses
to turn his back altogether on God and the future,
no one can prevent him; no one can show beyond
reasonable doubt that he is mistaken. If a man
thinks otherwise and acts as he thinks, I do not see
that any one can prove that *he* is mistaken. Each
must act as he thinks best; and if he is wrong, so
much the worse for him. We stand on a mountain
pass in the midst of whirling snow and blinding mist,
through which we get glimpses now and then of paths
which may be deceptive. If we stand still we shall
be frozen to death. If we take the wrong road we
shall be dashed to pieces. We do not certainly know
whether there is any right one. What must we do?
'Be strong and of a good courage.' Act for the best,
hope for the best, and take what comes. . . . If
death ends all, we cannot meet death better." [1]

---

[1] Liberty, Equality, Fraternity, p. 353, 2d edition. London, 1874.

IS LIFE WORTH LIVING?[1]

WHEN Mr. Mallock's book with this title appeared some fifteen years ago, the jocose answer that "it depends on the *liver*" had great currency in the newspapers. The answer which I propose to give to-night cannot be jocose. In the words of one of Shakespeare's prologues, —

> " I come no more to make you laugh; things now,
>   That bear a weighty and a serious brow,
>   Sad, high, and working, full of state and woe, " —

must be my theme. In the deepest heart of all of us there is a corner in which the ultimate mystery of things works sadly; and I know not what such an association as yours intends, nor what you ask of those whom you invite to address you, unless it be to lead you from the surface-glamour of existence, and for an hour at least to make you heedless to the buzzing and jigging and vibration of small interests and excitements that form the tissue of our ordinary consciousness. Without further explanation or apology, then, I ask you to join me in turning an attention, commonly too unwilling, to the profounder bass-note of life. Let us search the lonely depths for an hour together, and see what answers in the last folds and recesses of things our question may find.

---

[1] An Address to the Harvard Young Men's Christian Association. Published in the International Journal of Ethics for October, 1895, and as a pocket volume by S. B. Weston, Philadelphia, 1896.

I.

With many men the question of life's worth is answered by a temperamental optimism which makes them incapable of believing that anything seriously evil can exist. Our dear old Walt Whitman's works are the standing text-book of this kind of optimism. The mere joy of living is so immense in Walt Whitman's veins that it abolishes the possibility of any other kind of feeling: —

" To breathe the air, how delicious!
   To speak, to walk, to seize something by the hand! . . .
   To be this incredible God I am! . . .
   O amazement of things, even the least particle!
   O spirituality of things!
   I too carol the Sun, usher'd or at noon, or as now, setting;
   I too throb to the brain and beauty of the earth and of all the
      growths of the earth. . . .

   I sing to the last the equalities, modern or old,
   I sing the endless finales of things,
   I say Nature continues — glory continues.
   I praise with electric voice,
   For I do not see one imperfection in the universe,
   And I do not see one cause or result lamentable at last."

So Rousseau, writing of the nine years he spent at Annecy, with nothing but his happiness to tell: —

" How tell what was neither said nor done nor even thought, but tasted only and felt, with no object of my felicity but the emotion of felicity itself! I rose with the sun, and I was happy; I went to walk, and I was happy; I saw 'Maman,' and I was happy; I left her, and I was happy. I rambled through the woods and over the vine-slopes, I wandered in the valleys, I read, I lounged, I

3

worked in the garden, I gathered the fruits, I helped at the indoor work, and happiness followed me everywhere. It was in no one assignable thing; it was all within myself; it could not leave me for a single instant."

If moods like this could be made permanent, and constitutions like these universal, there would never be any occasion for such discourses as the present one. No philosopher would seek to prove articulately that life is worth living, for the fact that it absolutely is so would vouch for itself, and the problem disappear in the vanishing of the question rather than in the coming of anything like a reply. But we are not magicians to make the optimistic temperament universal; and alongside of the deliverances of temperamental optimism concerning life, those of temperamental pessimism always exist, and oppose to them a standing refutation. In what is called 'circular insanity,' phases of melancholy succeed phases of mania, with no outward cause that we can discover; and often enough to one and the same well person life will present incarnate radiance to-day and incarnate dreariness to-morrow, according to the fluctuations of what the older medical books used to call "the concoction of the humors." In the words of the newspaper joke, "it depends on the liver." Rousseau's ill-balanced constitution undergoes a change, and behold him in his latter evil days a prey to melancholy and black delusions of suspicion and fear. Some men seem launched upon the world even from their birth with souls as incapable of happiness as Walt Whitman's was of gloom, and they have left us their messages in even more lasting verse than his, — the exquisite Leopardi, for example; or our own contemporary,

James Thomson, in that pathetic book, The City of
Dreadful Night, which I think is less well-known
than it should be for its literary beauty, simply because men are afraid to quote its words, — they are
so gloomy, and at the same time so sincere. In one
place the poet describes a congregation gathered to
listen to a preacher in a great unillumined cathedral
at night. The sermon is too long to quote, but it
ends thus : —

> " ' O Brothers of sad lives ! they are so brief ;
> A few short years must bring us all relief :
>   Can we not bear these years of laboring breath ?
> But if you would not this poor life fulfil,
> Lo, you are free to end it when you will,
>   Without the fear of waking after death.' —

> " The organ-like vibrations of his voice
>   Thrilled through the vaulted aisles and died away ;
> The yearning of the tones which bade rejoice
>   Was sad and tender as a requiem lay :
> Our shadowy congregation rested still,
> As brooding on that ' End it when you will.'

> .   .   .   .   .   .

> " Our shadowy congregation rested still,
>   As musing on that message we had heard,
> And brooding on that ' End it when you will,'
>   Perchance awaiting yet some other word ;
> When keen as lightning through a muffled sky
> Sprang forth a shrill and lamentable cry : —

> " ' The man speaks sooth, alas ! the man speaks sooth ;
>   We have no personal life beyond the grave ;
> There is no God ; Fate knows nor wrath nor ruth :
>   Can I find here the comfort which I crave ?

> " ' In all eternity I had one chance,
>   One few years' term of gracious human life, —
> The splendors of the intellect's advance,
>   The sweetness of the home with babes and wife ;

" ' The social pleasures with their genial wit;
    The fascination of the worlds of art;
The glories of the worlds of Nature lit
    By large imagination's glowing heart;

" 'The rapture of mere being, full of health;
    The careless childhood and the ardent youth;
The strenuous manhood winning various wealth,
    The reverend age serene with life's long truth:

" ' All the sublime prerogatives of Man;
    The storied memories of the times of old,
The patient tracking of the world's great plan
    Through sequences and changes myriadfold.

" 'This chance was never offered me before;
    For me the infinite past is blank and dumb;
This chance recurreth never, nevermore;
    Blank, blank for me the infinite To-come.

" ' And this sole chance was frustrate from my birth,
    A mockery, a delusion; and my breath
Of noble human life upon this earth
    So racks me that I sigh for senseless death.

" ' My wine of life is poison mixed with gall,
    My noonday passes in a nightmare dream,
I worse than lose the years which are my all:
    What can console me for the loss supreme?

" ' Speak not of comfort where no comfort is,
    Speak not at all: can words make foul things fair?
Our life 's a cheat, our death a black abyss:
    Hush, and be mute, envisaging despair.'

" This vehement voice came from the northern aisle,
    Rapid and shrill to its abrupt harsh close;
And none gave answer for a certain while,
    For words must shrink from these most wordless woes;
At last the pulpit speaker simply said,
With humid eyes and thoughtful, drooping head, —

> " ' My Brother, my poor Brothers, it is thus:
>   This life holds nothing good for us,
>   But it ends soon and nevermore can be;
>   And we knew nothing of it ere our birth,
>   And shall know nothing when consigned to earth:
>   I ponder these thoughts, and they comfort me.' "

"It ends soon, and never more can be," "Lo, you are free to end it when you will," — these verses flow truthfully from the melancholy Thomson's pen, and are in truth a consolation for all to whom, as to him, the world is far more like a steady den of fear than a continual fountain of delight. That life is *not* worth living the whole army of suicides declare, — an army whose roll-call, like the famous evening gun of the British army, follows the sun round the world and never terminates. We, too, as we sit here in our comfort, must ' ponder these things ' also, for we are of one substance with these suicides, and their life is the life we share. The plainest intellectual integrity, — nay, more, the simplest manliness and honor, forbid us to forget their case.

"If suddenly," says Mr. Ruskin, "in the midst of the enjoyments of the palate and lightnesses of heart of a London dinner-party, the walls of the chamber were parted, and through their gap the nearest human beings who were famishing and in misery were borne into the midst of the company feasting and fancy free ; if, pale from death, horrible in destitution, broken by despair, body by body they were laid upon the soft carpet, one beside the chair of every guest, — would only the crumbs of the dainties be cast to them ; would only a passing glance, a passing thought, be vouchsafed to them ? Yet the actual facts, the real relation of each Dives and Lazarus, are not altered by the interven-

tion of the house-wall between the table and the sick-bed, —
by the few feet of ground (how few !) which are, indeed, all
that separate the merriment from the misery."

II.

To come immediately to the heart of my theme,
then, what I propose is to imagine ourselves reasoning with a fellow-mortal who is on such terms with
life that the only comfort left him is to brood on the
assurance, "You may end it when you will." What
reasons can we plead that may render such a brother
(or sister) willing to take up the burden again?
Ordinary Christians, reasoning with would-be suicides, have little to offer them beyond the usual
negative, "Thou shalt not." God alone is master of
life and death, they say, and it is a blasphemous act
to anticipate his absolving hand. But can *we* find
nothing richer or more positive than this, no reflections to urge whereby the suicide may actually see,
and in all sad seriousness feel, that in spite of adverse
appearances even for him life is still worth living?
There are suicides and suicides (in the United States
about three thousand of them every year), and I
must frankly confess that with perhaps the majority
of these my suggestions are impotent to deal. Where
suicide is the result of insanity or sudden frenzied
impulse, reflection is impotent to arrest its headway;
and cases like these belong to the ultimate mystery
of evil, concerning which I can only offer considerations tending toward religious patience at the end of
this hour. My task, let me say now, is practically
narrow, and my words are to deal only with that
metaphysical *tedium vitæ* which is peculiar to reflect-

ing men. Most of you are devoted, for good or ill, to the reflective life. Many of you are students of philosophy, and have already felt in your own persons the scepticism and unreality that too much grubbing in the abstract roots of things will breed. This is, indeed, one of the regular fruits of the over-studious career. Too much questioning and too little active responsibility lead, almost as often as too much sensualism does, to the edge of the slope, at the bottom of which lie pessimism and the night-mare or suicidal view of life. But to the diseases which reflection breeds, still further reflection can oppose effective remedies; and it is of the melan-choly and *Weltschmerz* bred of reflection that I now proceed to speak.

Let me say, immediately, that my final appeal is to nothing more recondite than religious faith. So far as my argument is to be destructive, it will consist in nothing more than the sweeping away of certain views that often keep the springs of religious faith com-pressed; and so far as it is to be constructive, it will consist in holding up to the light of day certain con-siderations calculated to let loose these springs in a normal, natural way. Pessimism is essentially a re-ligious disease. In the form of it to which you are most liable, it consists in nothing but a religious demand to which there comes no normal religious reply.

Now, there are two stages of recovery from this disease, two different levels upon which one may emerge from the midnight view to the daylight view of things, and I must treat of them in turn. The second stage is the more complete and joyous, and it corresponds to the freer exercise of religious trust and fancy. There are, as is well known, persons who are naturally very free in this regard, others who are not at all so. There are persons, for instance, whom we find indulging to their heart's content in prospects of immortality; and there are others who experience the greatest difficulty in making such a notion seem real to themselves at all. These latter persons are tied to their senses, restricted to their natural experience; and many of them, moreover, feel a sort of intellectual loyalty to what they call ' hard facts,' which is positively shocked by the easy excursions into the unseen that other people make at the bare call of sentiment. Minds of either class may, however, be intensely religious. They may equally desire atonement and reconciliation, and crave acquiescence and communion with the total soul of things. But the craving, when the mind is pent in to the hard facts, especially as science now reveals them, can breed pessimism, quite as easily as it breeds optimism when it inspires religious trust and fancy to wing their way to another and a better world.

That is why I call pessimism an essentially religious disease. The nightmare view of life has plenty of organic sources; but its great reflective source has at all times been the contradiction between the phenomena of nature and the craving of the heart to believe that behind nature there is a spirit whose expression nature is. What philosophers call ' natural theology' has been one way of appeasing this craving; that poetry of nature in which our English literature is so rich has been another way. Now, suppose a mind of the latter of our two classes, whose imagination is pent in consequently, and who takes its facts ' hard; ' suppose it, moreover, to feel strongly the craving for communion, and yet to realize how desperately difficult it is to construe the scientific order of nature either theologically or poetically, — and what result *can* there be but inner discord and contradiction? Now, this inner discord (merely as discord) can be relieved in either of two ways: The longing to read the facts religiously may cease, and leave the bare facts by themselves; or, supplementary facts may be discovered or believed-in, which permit the religious reading to go on. These two ways of relief are the two stages of recovery, the two levels of escape from pessimism, to which I made allusion a moment ago, and which the sequel will, I trust, make more clear.

III.

Starting then with nature, we naturally tend, if we have the religious craving, to say with Marcus Aurelius, " O Universe! what thou wishest I wish." Our sacred books and traditions tell us of one God who made heaven and earth, and, looking on them, saw that they were good. Yet, on more intimate acquaintance, the visible surfaces of heaven and earth refuse to be brought by us into any intelligible unity at all. Every phenomenon that we would praise there exists cheek by jowl with some contrary phenomenon that cancels all its religious effect upon the mind. Beauty and hideousness, love and cruelty, life and death keep house together in indissoluble partnership; and there gradually steals over us, instead of the old warm notion of a man-loving Deity, that of an awful power that neither hates nor loves, but rolls all things to-

gether meaninglessly to a common doom. **This is**
an uncanny, a sinister, a nightmare view of life, and
its peculiar *unheimlichkeit*, or poisonousness, lies expressly in our holding two things together which cannot possibly agree, — in our clinging, on the one
hand, to the demand that there shall be a living spirit
of the whole; and, on the other, to the belief that
the course of nature must be such a spirit's adequate
manifestation and expression. It is in the contradiction between the supposed being of a spirit that
encompasses and owns us, and with which we ought
to have some communion, and the character of such
a spirit as revealed by the visible world's course, that
this particular death-in-life paradox and this melan-
choly-breeding puzzle reside. Carlyle expresses the
result in that chapter of his immortal ' Sartor Resartus ' entitled ' The Everlasting No.' " I lived," writes
poor Teufelsdröckh, " in a continual, indefinite, pining
fear; tremulous, pusillanimous, apprehensive of I
knew not what: it seemed as if all things in the heavens above and the earth beneath would hurt me; as
if the heavens and the earth were but boundless jaws
of a devouring monster, wherein I, palpitating, lay
waiting to be devoured."

This is the first stage of speculative melancholy.
No brute can have this sort of melancholy; no man
who is irreligious can become its prey. It is the sick
shudder of the frustrated religious demand, and not
the mere necessary outcome of animal experience.
Teufelsdröckh himself could have made shift to face
the general chaos and bedevilment of this world's
experiences very well, were he not the victim of an
originally unlimited trust and affection towards them.
If he might meet them piecemeal, with no suspicion

of any whole expressing itself in them, shunning the
bitter parts and husbanding the sweet ones, as the
occasion served, and as the day was foul or fair, he
could have zigzagged toward an easy end, and felt
no obligation to make the air vocal with his lamen-
tations. The mood of levity, of ' I don't care,' is for
this world's ills a sovereign and practical anæsthetic.
But, no ! something deep down in Teufelsdröckh and
in the rest of us tells us that there *is* a Spirit in things
to which we owe allegiance, and for whose sake we
must keep up the serious mood. And so the inner
fever and discord also are kept up; for nature taken
on her visible surface reveals no such Spirit, and beyond the facts of nature we are at the present stage
of our inquiry not supposing ourselves to look.

Now, I do not hesitate frankly and sincerely to confess to you that this real and genuine discord seems
to me to carry with it the inevitable bankruptcy of
natural religion naïvely and simply taken. There
were times when Leibnitzes with their heads buried
in monstrous wigs could compose Theodicies, and
when stall-fed officials of an established church could
prove by the valves in the heart and the round liga-
ment of the hip-joint the existence of a " Moral and
Intelligent Contriver of the World." But those times
are past; and we of the nineteenth century, with our
evolutionary theories and our mechanical philosophies, already know nature too impartially and too
well to worship unreservedly any God of whose character she can be an adequate expression. Truly, all
we know of good and duty proceeds from nature;
but none the less so all we know of evil. Visible
nature is all plasticity and indifference, — a moral
multiverse, as one might call it, and not a moral uni-

verse. To such a harlot we owe no allegiance; with her as a whole we can establish no moral communion; and we are free in our dealings with her several parts to obey or destroy, and to follow no law but that of prudence in coming to terms with such of her particular features as will help us to our private ends. If there be a divine Spirit of the universe, nature, such as we know her, cannot possibly be its *ultimate word* to man. Either there is no Spirit revealed in nature, or else it is inadequately revealed there; and (as all the higher religions have assumed) what we call visible nature, or *this* world, must be but a veil and surface-show whose full meaning resides in a supplementary unseen or *other* world.

I cannot help, therefore, accounting it on the whole a gain (though it may seem for certain poetic constitutions a very sad loss) that the naturalistic superstition, the worship of the God of nature, simply taken as such, should have begun to loosen its hold upon the educated mind. In fact, if I am to express my personal opinion unreservedly, I should say (in spite of its sounding blasphemous at first to certain ears) that the initial step towards getting into healthy ultimate relations with the universe is the act of rebellion against the idea that such a God exists. Such rebellion essentially is that which in the chapter I have quoted from Carlyle goes on to describe: —

"'Wherefore, like a coward, dost thou forever pip and whimper, and go cowering and trembling? Despicable biped! . . . Hast thou not a heart; canst thou not suffer whatsoever it be; and, as a Child of Freedom, though outcast, trample Tophet itself under thy feet, while it consumes thee? Let it come, then; I will meet it and defy it!' And as I so thought, there rushed like a stream of fire over my whole soul; and I shook base Fear away from me forever. . . .

"Thus had the Everlasting No pealed authoritatively through all the recesses of my being, of my Me; and then was it that my whole Me stood up, in native God-created majesty, and recorded its Protest. Such a Protest, the most important transaction in life, may that same Indignation and Defiance, in a psychological point of view, be fitly called. The Everlasting No had said: ' Behold, thou art fatherless, outcast, and the Universe is mine; ' to which my whole Me now made answer: ' I am not thine, but Free, and forever hate thee ! ' From that hour," Teufelsdröckh-Carlyle adds, " I began to be a man."

And our poor friend, James Thomson, similarly writes: —

> "Who is most wretched in this dolorous place?
> I think myself; yet I would rather be
> My miserable self than He, than He
> Who formed such creatures to his own disgrace.
>
> The vilest thing must be less vile than Thou
> From whom it had its being, God and Lord!
> Creator of all woe and sin ! abhorred,
> Malignant and implacable ! I vow
>
> That not for all Thy power furled and unfurled,
> For all the temples to Thy glory built,
> Would I assume the ignominious guilt
> Of having made such men in such a world."

We are familiar enough in this community with the spectacle of persons exulting in their emancipation from belief in the God of their ancestral Calvinism, — him who made the garden and the serpent, and preappointed the eternal fires of hell. Some of them have found humaner gods to worship, others are simply converts from all theology; but, both alike, they

assure us that to have got rid of the sophistication ot
thinking they could feel any reverence or duty toward
that impossible idol gave a tremendous happiness to
their souls. Now, to make an idol of the spirit of
nature, and worship it, also leads to sophistication;
and in souls that are religious and would also be
scientific the sophistication breeds a philosophical
melancholy, from which the first natural step of escape is the denial of the idol; and with the downfall
of the idol, whatever lack of positive joyousness may
remain, there comes also the downfall of the whimpering and cowering mood. With evil simply taken
as such, men can make short work, for their relations
with it then are only practical. It looms up no longer
so spectrally, it loses all its haunting and perplexing
significance, as soon as the mind attacks the instances
of it singly, and ceases to worry about their derivation
from the ' one and only Power.'

Here, then, on this stage of mere emancipation
from monistic superstition, the would-be suicide may
already get encouraging answers to his question about
the worth of life. There are in most men instinctive
springs of vitality that respond healthily when the
burden of metaphysical and infinite responsibility
rolls off. The certainty that you now *may* step out
of life whenever you please, and that to do so is not
blasphemous or monstrous, is itself an immense relief.
The thought of suicide is now no longer a guilty
challenge and obsession.

> " This little life is all we must endure;
>   The grave's most holy peace is ever sure," —

says Thomson; adding, " I ponder these thoughts,
and they comfort me." Meanwhile we can always

stand it for twenty-four hours longer, if only to see what to-morrow's newspaper will contain, or what the next postman will bring.

But far deeper forces than this mere vital curiosity are arousable, even in the pessimistically-tending mind; for where the loving and admiring impulses are dead, the hating and fighting impulses will still respond to fit appeals. This evil which we feel so deeply is something that we can also help to overthrow; for its sources, now that no 'Substance' or 'Spirit' is behind them, are finite, and we can deal with each of them in turn. It is, indeed, a remarkable fact that sufferings and hardships do not, as a rule, abate the love of life; they seem, on the contrary, usually to give it a keener zest. The sovereign source of melancholy is repletion. Need and struggle are what excite and inspire us; our hour of triumph is what brings the void. Not the Jews of the captivity, but those of the days of Solomon's glory are those from whom the pessimistic utterances in our Bible come. Germany, when she lay trampled beneath the hoofs of Bonaparte's troopers, produced perhaps the most optimistic and idealistic literature that the world has seen; and not till the French 'milliards' were distributed after 1871 did pessimism overrun the country in the shape in which we see it there to-day. The history of our own race is one long commentary on the cheerfulness that comes with fighting ills. Or take the Waldenses, of whom I lately have been reading, as examples of what strong men will endure. In 1485 a papal bull of Innocent VIII. enjoined their extermination. It absolved those who should take up the crusade against them from all ecclesiastical pains and penalties, released them from any oath, legitimized their title to all property which they might have illegally acquired, and promised remission of sins to all who should kill the heretics.

"There is no town in Piedmont," says a Vaudois writer, "where some of our brethren have not been put to death. Jordan Terbano was burnt alive at Susa; Hippolite Rossiero at Turin; Michael Goneto, an octogenarian, at Sarcena; Vilermin Ambrosio hanged on the Col di Meano; Hugo Chiambs, of Fenestrelle, had his entrails torn from his living body at Turin; Peter Geymarali of Bobbio in like manner had his entrails taken out in Lucerna, and a fierce cat thrust in their place to torture him further; Maria Romano was buried alive at Rocca Patia; Magdalena Fauno underwent the same fate at San Giovanni; Susanna Michelini was bound hand and foot, and left to perish of cold and hunger on the snow at Sarcena: Bartolomeo Fache, gashed with sabres, had the wounds filled up with quicklime, and perished thus in agony at Fenile; Daniel Michelini had his tongue torn out at Bobbo for having praised God; James Baridari perished covered with sulphurous matches which had been forced into his flesh under the nails, between the fingers, in the nostrils, in the lips, and all over the body, and then lighted; Daniel Rovelli had his mouth filled with gunpowder, which, being lighted, blew his head to pieces; . . . Sara Rostignol was slit open from the legs to the bosom, and left so to perish on the road between Eyral and Lucerna; Anna Charbonnier was impaled, and carried thus on a pike from San Giovanni to La Torre." [1]

Und dergleichen mehr! In 1630 the plague swept away one-half of the Vaudois population, including fifteen of their seventeen pastors. The places of these were supplied from Geneva and Dauphiny, and

---

[1] Quoted by George E. Waring in his book on Tyrol. Compare A. Bérard: Les Vaudois, Lyon, Storck, 1892.

the whole Vaudois people learned French in order to follow their services. More than once their number fell, by unremitting persecution, from the normal standard of twenty-five thousand to about four thousand. In 1686 the Duke of Savoy ordered the three thousand that remained to give up their faith or leave the country. Refusing, they fought the French and Piedmontese armies till only eighty of their fighting men remained alive or uncaptured, when they gave up, and were sent in a body to Switzerland. But in 1689, encouraged by William of Orange and led by one of their pastor-captains, between eight hundred and nine hundred of them returned to conquer their old homes again. They fought their way to Bobi, reduced to four hundred men in the first half year, and met every force sent against them; until at last the Duke of Savoy, giving up his alliance with that abomination of desolation, Louis XIV., restored them to comparative freedom, — since which time they have increased and multiplied in their barren Alpine valleys to this day.

What are our woes and sufferance compared with these? Does not the recital of such a fight so obstinately waged against such odds fill us with resolution against *our* petty powers of darkness, — machine politicians, spoilsmen, and the rest? Life is worth living, no matter what it bring, if only such combats may be carried to successful terminations and one's heel set on the tyrant's throat. To the suicide, then, in his supposed world of multifarious and immoral nature, you can appeal — and appeal in the name of the very evils that make his heart sick there — to wait and see *his* part of the battle out. And the consent to live on, which you ask of him under these circumstances, is not the sophistical ' resignation ' which devotees of cowering religions preach: it is not resignation in the sense of licking a despotic Deity's hand. It is, on the contrary, a resignation based on manliness and pride. So long as your would-be suicide leaves an evil of his own unremedied, so long he has strictly no concern with evil in the abstract and at large. The submission which you demand of yourself to the general fact of evil in the world, your apparent acquiescence in it, is here nothing but the conviction that evil at large is *none of your business* until your business with your private particular evils is liquidated and settled up. A challenge of this sort, with proper designation of detail, is one that need only be made to be accepted by men whose normal instincts are not decayed; and your reflective would-be suicide may easily be moved by it to face life with a certain interest again. The sentiment of honor is a very penetrating thing. When you and I, for instance, realize how many innocent beasts have had to suffer in cattle-cars and slaughter-pens and lay down their lives that we might grow up, all fattened and clad, to sit together here in comfort and carry on this discourse, it does, indeed, put our relation to the universe in a more solemn light. "Does not," as a young Amherst philosopher (Xenos Clark, now dead) once wrote, "the acceptance of a happy life upon such terms involve a point of honor?" Are we not bound to take some suffering upon ourselves, to do some self-denying service with our lives, in return for all those lives upon which ours are built? To hear this question is to answer it in but one possible way, if one have a normally constituted heart.

Thus, then, we see that mere instinctive curiosity, pugnacity, and honor may make life on a purely naturalistic basis seem worth living from day to day to men who have cast away all metaphysics in order to get rid of hypochondria, but who are resolved to owe nothing as yet to religion and its more positive gifts. A poor half-way stage, some of you may be inclined to say; but at least you must grant it to be an honest stage; and no man should dare to speak meanly of these instincts which are our nature's best equipment, and to which religion herself must in the last resort address her own peculiar appeals.

IV.

And now, in turning to what religion may have to say to the question, I come to what is the soul of my discourse. Religion has meant many things in human history; but when from now onward I use the word I mean to use it in the supernaturalist sense, as declaring that the so-called order of nature, which constitutes this world's experience, is only one portion of the total universe, and that there stretches beyond this visible world an unseen world of which we now know nothing positive, but in its relation to which the true significance of our present mundane life consists. A man's religious faith (whatever more special items of doctrine it may involve) means for me essentially his faith in the existence of an unseen order of some kind in which the riddles of the natural order may be found explained. In the more developed religions the natural world has always been regarded as the mere scaffolding or vestibule of a truer, more eternal world, and affirmed to be a sphere of education, trial, or redemption.   In these religions, one must in some fashion die to the natural life before one can enter into life eternal.   The notion that this physical world of wind and water, where the sun rises and the moon sets, is absolutely and ultimately the divinely aimed-at and established thing, is one which we find only in very early religions, such as that of the most primitive Jews.   It is this natural religion (primitive still, in spite of the fact that poets and men of science whose good-will exceeds their per-spicacity keep publishing it in new editions tuned to our contemporary ears) that, as I said a while ago, has suffered definitive bankruptcy in the opinion of a circle of persons, among whom I must count myself, and who are growing more numerous every day.   For such persons the physical order of nature, taken sim-ply as science knows it, cannot be held to reveal any one harmonious spiritual intent.   It is mere *weather*, as Chauncey Wright called it, doing and undoing without end.

Now, I wish to make you feel, if I can in the short remainder of this hour, that we have a right to believe the physical order to be only a partial order; that we have a right to supplement it by an unseen spiritual order which we assume on trust, if only thereby life may seem to us better worth living again. But as such a trust will seem to some of you sadly mystical and execrably unscientific, I must first say a word or two to weaken the veto which you may con-sider that science opposes to our act.

There is included in human nature an ingrained naturalism and materialism of mind which can only admit facts that are actually tangible.   Of this sort of mind the entity called 'science' is the idol.

Fondness for the word 'scientist' is one of the notes by which you may know its votaries; and its short way of killing any opinion that it disbelieves in is to call it 'unscientific.' It must be granted that there is no slight excuse for this. Science has made such glorious leaps in the last three hundred years, and extended our knowledge of nature so enormously both in general and in detail; men of science, more-over, have as a class displayed such admirable vir-tues, — that it is no wonder if the worshippers of science lose their head. In this very University, accordingly, I have heard more than one teacher say that all the fundamental conceptions of truth have already been found by science, and that the future has only the details of the picture to fill in. But the slightest reflection on the real conditions will suffice to show how barbaric such notions are. They show such a lack of scientific imagination, that it is hard to see how one who is actively advancing any part of science can make a mistake so crude. Think how many absolutely new scientific conceptions have arisen in our own generation, how many new prob-lems have been formulated that were never thought of before, and then cast an eye upon the brevity of science's career. It began with Galileo, not three hundred years ago. Four thinkers since Galileo, each informing his successor of what discoveries his own lifetime had seen achieved, might have passed the torch of science into our hands as we sit here in this room. Indeed, for the matter of that, an audi-ence much smaller than the present one, an audience of some five or six score people, if each person in it could speak for his own generation, would carry us away to the black unknown of the human species,

to days without a document or monument to tell
their tale. Is it credible that such a mushroom
knowledge, such a growth overnight as this, *can*
represent more than the minutest glimpse of what
the universe will really prove to be when adequately
understood? No! our science is a drop, our ignorance a sea. Whatever else be certain, this at least
is certain, — that the world of our present natural
knowledge *is* enveloped in a larger world of *some*
sort of whose residual properties we at present can
frame no positive idea.

Agnostic positivism, of course, admits this principle theoretically in the most cordial terms, but
insists that we must not turn it to any practical use.
We have no right, this doctrine tells us, to dream
dreams, or suppose anything about the unseen part
of the universe, merely because to do so may be for
what we are pleased to call our highest interests.
We must always wait for sensible evidence for our
beliefs; and where such evidence is inaccessible we
must frame no hypotheses whatever. Of course this
is a safe enough position *in abstracto*. If a thinker
had no stake in the unknown, no vital needs, to live
or languish according to what the unseen world contained, a philosophic neutrality and refusal to believe
either one way or the other would be his wisest cue.
But, unfortunately, neutrality is not only inwardly
difficult, it is also outwardly unrealizable, where our
relations to an alternative are practical and vital.
This is because, as the psychologists tell us, belief
and doubt are living attitudes, and involve conduct
on our part. Our only way, for example, of doubting, or refusing to believe, that a certain thing *is*, is
continuing to act as if it were *not*. If, for instance,

I refuse to believe that the room is getting cold, I leave the windows open and light no fire just as if it still were warm. If I doubt that you are worthy of my confidence, I keep you uninformed of all my secrets just as if you were *un*worthy of the same. If I doubt the need of insuring my house, I leave it uninsured as much as if I believed there were no need. And so if I must not believe that the world is divine, I can only express that refusal by declining ever to act distinctively as if it were so, which can only mean acting on certain critical occasions as if it were *not* so, or in an irreligious way. There are, you see, inevitable occasions in life when inaction is a kind of action, and must count as action, and when not to be for is to be practically against; and in all such cases strict and consistent neutrality is an unattainable thing.

And, after all, is not this duty of neutrality where only our inner interests would lead us to believe, the most ridiculous of commands? Is it not sheer dogmatic folly to say that our inner interests can have no real connection with the forces that the hidden world may contain? In other cases divinations based on inner interests have proved prophetic enough. Take science itself! Without an imperious inner demand on our part for ideal logical and mathematical harmonies, we should never have attained to proving that such harmonies lie hidden between all the chinks and interstices of the crude natural world. Hardly a law has been established in science, hardly a fact ascertained, which was not first sought after, often with sweat and blood, to gratify an inner need. Whence such needs come from we do not know: we find them in us, and biological psychology so far only classes them with Darwin's 'accidental variations.'

But the inner need of believing that this world of nature is a sign of something more spiritual and eternal than itself is just as strong and authoritative in those who feel it, as the inner need of uniform laws of causation ever can be in a professionally scientific head. The toil of many generations has proved the latter need prophetic. Why *may* not the former one be prophetic, too? And if needs of ours outrun the visible universe, why *may* not that be a sign that an invisible universe is there? What, in short, has authority to debar us from trusting our religious demands? Science as such assuredly has no authority, for she can only say what is, not what is not; and the agnostic "thou shalt not believe without coercive sensible evidence" is simply an expression (free to any one to make) of private personal appetite for evidence of a certain peculiar kind.

Now, when I speak of trusting our religious demands, just what do I mean by 'trusting'? Is the word to carry with it license to define in detail an invisible world, and to anathematize and excommunicate those whose trust is different? Certainly not! Our faculties of belief were not primarily given us to make orthodoxies and heresies withal; they were given us to live by. And to trust our religious demands means first of all to live in the light of them, and to act as if the invisible world which they suggest were real. It is a fact of human nature, that men can live and die by the help of a sort of faith that goes without a single dogma or definition. The bare assurance that this natural order is not ultimate but a mere sign or vision, the external staging of a many-storied universe, in which spiritual forces have the last word and are eternal, — this bare assurance is to such men enough to make life seem worth living in spite of every contrary presumption suggested by its circumstances on the natural plane. Destroy this inner assurance, however, vague as it is, and all the light and radiance of existence is extinguished for these persons at a stroke. Often enough the wild-eyed look at life — the suicidal mood — will then set in.

And now the application comes directly home to you and me. Probably to almost every one of us here the most adverse life would seem well worth living, if we only could be *certain* that our bravery and patience with it were terminating and eventuating and bearing fruit somewhere in an unseen spiritual world. But granting we are not certain, does it then follow that a bare trust in such a world is a fool's paradise and lubberland, or rather that it is a living attitude in which we are free to indulge? Well, we are free to trust at our own risks anything that is not impossible, and that can bring analogies to bear in its behalf. That the world of physics is probably not absolute, all the converging multitude of arguments that make in favor of idealism tend to prove; and that our whole physical life may lie soaking in a spiritual atmosphere, a dimension of being that we at present have no organ for apprehending, is vividly suggested to us by the analogy of the life of our domestic animals. Our dogs, for example, are in our human life but not of it. They witness hourly the outward body of events whose inner meaning cannot, by any possible operation, be revealed to their intelligence, — events in which they themselves often play the cardinal part. My terrier bites a teasing boy, for example, and the father demands damages. The dog may be present at every step of the negotiations, and see the money paid, without an inkling of what it all means, without a suspicion that it has anything to do with *him ;* and he never *can* know in his natural dog's life. Or take another case which used greatly to impress me in my medical-student days. Consider a poor dog whom they are vivisecting in a laboratory. He lies strapped on a board and shrieking at his executioners, and to his own dark consciousness is literally in a sort of hell. He cannot see a single redeeming ray in the whole business; and yet all these diabolical-seeming events are often controlled by human intentions with which, if his poor benighted mind could only be made to catch a glimpse of them, all that is heroic in him would religiously acquiesce. Healing truth, relief to future sufferings of beast and man, are to be bought by them. It may be genuinely a process of redemption. Lying on his back on the board there he may be performing a function incalculably higher than any that prosperous canine life admits of; and yet, of the whole performance, this function is the one portion that must remain absolutely beyond his ken.

Now turn from this to the life of man. In the dog's life we see the world invisible to him because we live in both worlds. In human life, although we only see our world, and his within it, yet encompassing both these worlds a still wider world may be there, as unseen by us as our world is by him; and to believe in that world *may* be the most essential function that our lives in this world have to perform. But " *may* be! *may* be!" one now hears the positivist contemptuously exclaim; "what use can a scientific life have for maybes?" Well, I reply, the 'scien-

tific' life itself has much to do with maybes, and human
life at large has everything to do with them. So far
as man stands for anything, and is productive or
originative at all, his entire vital function may be said
to have to deal with maybes. Not a victory is gained,
not a deed of faithfulness or courage is done, except
upon a maybe; not a service, not a sally of generos-
ity, not a scientific exploration or experiment or text-
book, that may not be a mistake. It is only by risk-
ing our persons from one hour to another that we
live at all. And often enough our faith beforehand
in an uncertified result *is the only thing that makes
the result come true.* Suppose, for instance, that you
are climbing a mountain, and have worked yourself
into a position from which the only escape is by a
terrible leap. Have faith that you can successfully
make it, and your feet are nerved to its accomplish-
ment. But mistrust yourself, and think of all the
sweet things you have heard the scientists say of
maybes, and you will hesitate so long that, at last, all
unstrung and trembling, and launching yourself in a
moment of despair, you roll in the abyss. In such a
case (and it belongs to an enormous class), the part
of wisdom as well as of courage is to *believe what is
in the line of your needs*, for only by such belief is the
need fulfilled. Refuse to believe, and you shall indeed be right, for you shall irretrievably perish. But
believe, and again you shall be right, for you shall
save yourself. You make one or the other of two
possible universes true by your trust or mistrust, —
both universes having been only *maybes*, in this particular, before you contributed your act.

Now, it appears to me that the question whether
life is worth living is subject to conditions logically

much like these. It does, indeed, depend on you *the
liver.* If you surrender to the nightmare view and
crown the evil edifice by your own suicide, you have
indeed made a picture totally black. Pessimism,
completed by your act, is true beyond a doubt, so
far as your world goes. Your mistrust of life has removed whatever worth your own enduring existence
might have given to it; and now, throughout the
whole sphere of possible influence of that existence,
the mistrust has proved itself to have had divining
power. But suppose, on the other hand, that instead
of giving way to the nightmare view you cling to it
that this world is not the *ultimatum.* Suppose you find
yourself a very well-spring, as Wordsworth says, of —

> " Zeal, and the virtue to exist by faith
> As soldiers live by courage ; as, by strength
> Of heart, the sailor fights with roaring seas."

Suppose, however thickly evils crowd upon you, that
your unconquerable subjectivity proves to be their
match, and that you find a more wonderful joy than
any passive pleasure can bring in trusting ever in the
larger whole. Have you not now made life worth
living on these terms? What sort of a thing would
life really be, with your qualities ready for a tussle
with it, if it only brought fair weather and gave these
higher faculties of yours no scope? Please remember
that optimism and pessimism are definitions of the
world, and that our own reactions on the world, small
as they are in bulk, are integral parts of the whole
thing, and necessarily help to determine the definition. They may even be the decisive elements in
determining the definition. A large mass can have
its unstable equilibrium overturned by the addition

of a feather's weight; a long phrase may have its sense reversed by the addition of the three letters *n-o-t.* This life *is* worth living, we can say, *since it is what we make it, from the moral point of view;* and we are determined to make it from that point of view, so far as we have anything to do with it, a success.

Now, in this description of faiths that verify themselves I have assumed that our faith in an invisible order is what inspires those efforts and that patience which make this visible order good for moral men. Our faith in the seen world's goodness (goodness now meaning fitness for successful moral and religious life) has verified itself by leaning on our faith in the unseen world. But will our faith in the unseen world similarly verify itself? Who knows?

Once more it is a case of *maybe;* and once more *maybes* are the essence of the situation. I confess that I do not see why the very existence of an invisible world may not in part depend on the personal response which any one of us may make to the religious appeal. God himself, in short, may draw vital strength and increase of very being from our fidelity. For my own part, I do not know what the sweat and blood and tragedy of this life mean, if they mean anything short of this. If this life be not a real fight, in which something is eternally gained for the universe by success, it is no better than a game of private theatricals from which one may withdraw at will. But it *feels* like a real fight, — as if there were something really wild in the universe which we, with all our idealities and faithfulnesses, are needed to redeem; and first of all to redeem our own hearts from atheisms and fears. For such a half-wild, half-saved universe our nature is adapted. The deepest thing in our nature is this *Binnenleben* (as a German doctor lately has called it), this dumb region of the heart in which we dwell alone with our willingnesses and unwillingnesses, our faiths and fears. As through the cracks and crannies of caverns those waters exude from the earth's bosom which then form the fountain-heads of springs, so in these crepuscular depths of personality the sources of all our outer deeds and decisions take their rise. Here is our deepest organ of communication with the nature of things; and compared with these concrete movements of our soul all abstract statements and scientific arguments — the veto, for example, which the strict positivist pronounces upon our faith — sound to us like mere chatterings of the teeth. For here possibilities, not finished facts, are the realities with which we have actively to deal; and to quote my friend William Salter, of the Philadelphia Ethical Society, " as the essence of courage is to stake one's life on a possibility, so the essence of faith is to believe that the possibility exists."

These, then, are my last words to you: Be not afraid of life. Believe that life *is* worth living, and your belief will help create the fact. The ' scientific proof' that you are right may not be clear before the day of judgment (or some stage of being which that expression may serve to symbolize) is reached. But the faithful fighters of this hour, or the beings that then and there will represent them, may then turn to the faint-hearted, who here decline to go on, with words like those with which Henry IV. greeted the tardy Crillon after a great victory had been gained: " Hang yourself, brave Crillon! we fought at Arques, and you were not there."

THE SENTIMENT OF RATIONALITY.[1]

I.

WHAT is the task which philosophers set themselves to perform; and why do they philos-
ophize at all? Almost every one will immediately
reply: They desire to attain a conception of the
frame of things which shall on the whole be more rational than that somewhat chaotic view which every
one by nature carries about with him under his hat.
But suppose this rational conception attained, how is
the philosopher to recognize it for what it is, and not
let it slip through ignorance? The only answer can
be that he will recognize its rationality as he recognizes everything else, by certain subjective marks
with which it affects him. When he gets the marks,
he may know that he has got the rationality.

What, then, are the marks? A strong feeling of
ease, peace, rest, is one of them. The transition
from a state of puzzle and perplexity to rational com-
prehension is full of lively relief and pleasure.

But this relief seems to be a negative rather than
a positive character. Shall we then say that the feeling of rationality is constituted merely by the absence

[1] This essay as far as page 75 consists of extracts from an article
printed in Mind for July, 1879. Thereafter it is a reprint of an
address to the Harvard Philosophical Club, delivered in 1880, and
published in the Princeton Review, July, 1882.

of any feeling of irrationality? I think there are very good grounds for upholding such a view. All feeling whatever, in the light of certain recent psychological speculations, seems to depend for its physical condition not on simple discharge of nerve-currents, but on their discharge under arrest, impediment, or resistance. Just as we feel no particular pleasure when we breathe freely, but a very intense feeling of distress when the respiratory motions are prevented, — so any unobstructed tendency to action discharges itself without the production of much cogitative accompaniment, and any perfectly fluent course of thought awakens but little feeling; but when the movement is inhibited, or when the thought meets with difficulties, we experience distress. It is only when the distress is upon us that we can be said to strive, to crave, or to aspire. When enjoying plenary freedom either in the way of motion or of thought, we are in a sort of anæsthetic state in which we might say with Walt Whitman, if we cared to say anything about ourselves at such times, "I am sufficient as I am." This feeling of the sufficiency of the present moment, of its absoluteness, — this absence of all need to explain it, account for it, or justify it, — is what I call the Sentiment of Rationality. As soon, in short, as we are enabled from any cause whatever to think with perfect fluency, the thing we think of seems to us *pro tanto* rational.

Whatever modes of conceiving the cosmos facilitate this fluency, produce the sentiment of rationality. Conceived in such modes, being vouches for itself and needs no further philosophic formulation. But this fluency may be obtained in various ways; and first I will take up the theoretic way.

The facts of the world in their sensible diversity are always before us, but our theoretic need is that they should be conceived in a way that reduces their manifoldness to simplicity. Our pleasure at finding that a chaos of facts is the expression of a single underlying fact is like the relief of the musician at resolving a confused mass of sound into melodic or harmonic order. The simplified result is handled with far less mental effort than the original data; and a philosophic conception of nature is thus in no metaphorical sense a labor-saving contrivance. The passion for parsimony, for economy of means in thought, is the philosophic passion *par excellence;* and any character or aspect of the world's phenomena which gathers up their diversity into monotony will gratify that passion, and in the philosopher's mind stand for that essence of things compared with which all their other determinations may by him be overlooked.

More universality or extensiveness is, then, one mark which the philosopher's conceptions must possess. Unless they apply to an enormous number of cases they will not bring him relief. The knowledge of things by their causes, which is often given as a definition of rational knowledge, is useless to him unless the causes converge to a minimum number, while still producing the maximum number of effects. The more multiple then are the instances, the more flowingly does his mind rove from fact to fact. The phenomenal transitions are no real transitions; each item is the same old friend with a slightly altered dress.

Who does not feel the charm of thinking that the moon and the apple are, as far as their relation to the earth goes, identical; of knowing respiration and combustion to be one; of understanding that the balloon rises by the same law whereby the stone sinks; of feeling that the warmth in one's palm when one rubs one's sleeve is identical with the motion which the friction checks; of recognizing the difference between beast and fish to be only a higher degree of that between human father and son; of believing our strength when we climb the mountain or fell the tree to be no other than the strength of the sun's rays which made the corn grow out of which we got our morning meal?

But alongside of this passion for simplification there exists a sister passion, which in some minds — though they perhaps form the minority — is its rival. This is the passion for distinguishing; it is the impulse to be *acquainted* with the parts rather than to comprehend the whole. Loyalty to clearness and integrity of perception, dislike of blurred outlines, of vague identifications, are its characteristics. It loves to recognize particulars in their full completeness, and the more of these it can carry the happier it is. It prefers any amount of incoherence, abruptness, and fragmentariness (so long as the literal details of the separate facts are saved) to an abstract way of conceiving things that, while it simplifies them, dissolves away at the same time their concrete fulness. Clearness and simplicity thus set up rival claims, and make a real dilemma for the thinker.

A man's philosophic attitude is determined by the balance in him of these two cravings. No system of philosophy can hope to be universally accepted among men which grossly violates either need, or entirely subordinates the one to the other. The fate of Spinoza, with his barren union of all things in one substance, on the one hand; that of Hume, with his equally barren 'looseness and separateness' of everything, on the other, — neither philosopher owning any strict and systematic disciples to-day, each being to posterity a warning as well as a stimulus, — show us that the only possible philosophy must be a compromise between an abstract monotony and a concrete heterogeneity. But the only way to mediate between diversity and unity is to class the diverse items as cases of a common essence which you discover in them. Classification of things into extensive 'kinds' is thus the first step; and classification of their relations and conduct into extensive 'laws' is the last step, in their philosophic unification. A completed theoretic philosophy can thus never be anything more than a completed classification of the world's ingredients; and its results must always be abstract, since the basis of every classification is the abstract essence embedded in the living fact, — the rest of the living fact being for the time ignored by the classifier. This means that none of our explanations are complete. They subsume things under heads wider or more familiar; but the last heads, whether of things or of their connections, are mere abstract genera, data which we just find in things and write down.

When, for example, we think that we have rationally explained the connection of the facts A and B by classing both under their common attribute x, it is obvious that we have really explained only so much of these items as *is* x. To explain the connection of choke-damp and suffocation by the lack of oxygen is to leave untouched all the other peculiarities both of choke-damp and of suffocation, — such as convulsions and agony on the one hand, density and explosibility on the other. In a word, so far as A and B contain l, m, n, and o, p, q, respectively, in addition to x, they are not explained by x. Each additional particularity makes its distinct appeal. A single explanation of a fact only explains it from a single point of view. The entire fact is not accounted for until each and all of its characters have been classed with their likes elsewhere. To apply this now to the case of the universe, we see that the explanation of the world by molecular movements explains it only so far as it actually *is* such movements. To invoke the 'Unknowable' explains only so much as is unknowable, 'Thought' only so much as is thought, 'God' only so much as is God. *Which* thought? *Which* God? — are questions that have to be answered by bringing in again the residual data from which the general term was abstracted. All those data that cannot be analytically identified with the attribute invoked as universal principle, remain as independent kinds or natures, associated empirically with the said attribute but devoid of rational kinship with it.

Hence the unsatisfactoriness of all our speculations. On the one hand, so far as they retain any multiplicity in their terms, they fail to get us out of the empirical sand-heap world; on the other, so far as they eliminate multiplicity the practical man despises their empty barrenness. The most they can say is that the elements of the world are such and such, and that each is identical with itself wherever found; but the question Where is it found? the practical man is left to answer by his own wit. Which, of all the essences, shall here and now be held the essence of this concrete thing, the fundamental philosophy never attempts to decide. We are thus led to the conclusion that the simple classification of things is, on the one hand, the best possible theoretic philosophy, but is, on the other, a most miserable and inadequate substitute for the fulness of the truth. It is a monstrous abridgment of life, which, like all abridgments is got by the absolute loss and casting out of real matter. This is why so few human beings truly care for philosophy. The particular determinations which she ignores are the real matter exciting needs, quite as potent and authoritative as hers. What does the moral enthusiast care for philosophical ethics? Why does the *Æsthetik* of every German philosopher appear to the artist an abomination of desolation?

> Grau, theurer Freund, ist alle Theorie
> Und grün des Lebens goldner Baum.

The entire man, who feels all needs by turns, will take nothing as an equivalent for life but the fulness of living itself. Since the essences of things are as a matter of fact disseminated through the whole extent of time and space, it is in their spread-outness and alternation that he will enjoy them. When weary of the concrete clash and dust and pettiness, he will refresh himself by a bath in the eternal springs, or fortify himself by a look at the immutable natures. But he will only be a visitor, not a dweller in the region; he will never carry the philosophic yoke upon his shoulders, and when tired of the gray monotony of her problems and insipid spaciousness of her results, will always escape gleefully into the teeming and dramatic richness of the concrete world.

So our study turns back here to its beginning. Every way of classifying a thing is but a way of handling it for some particular purpose. Conceptions, 'kinds,' are teleological instruments. No abstract concept can be a valid substitute for a concrete reality except with reference to a particular interest in the conceiver. The interest of theoretic rationality, the relief of identification, is but one of a thousand human purposes. When others rear their heads, it must pack up its little bundle and retire till its turn recurs. The exaggerated dignity and value that philosophers have claimed for their solutions is thus greatly reduced. The only virtue their theoretic conception need have is simplicity, and a simple conception is an equivalent for the world only so far as the world is simple, — the world meanwhile, whatever simplicity it may harbor, being also a mightily complex affair. Enough simplicity remains, however, and enough urgency in our craving to reach it, to make the theoretic function one of the most invincible of human impulses. The quest of the fewest elements of things is an ideal that some will follow, as long as there are men to think at all.

But suppose the goal attained. Suppose that at last we have a system unified in the sense that has been explained. Our world can now be conceived simply, and our mind enjoys the relief. Our universal concept has made the concrete chaos rational. But now I ask, Can that which is the ground of rationality in all else be itself properly called rational? It would seem at first sight that it might. One is tempted at any rate to say that, since the craving for rationality is appeased by the identification of one thing with another, a datum which left nothing else outstanding might quench that craving definitively, or be rational *in se*. No otherness being left to annoy us, we should sit down at peace. In other words, as the theoretic tranquillity of the boor results from his spinning no further considerations about his chaotic universe, so any datum whatever (provided it were simple, clear, and ultimate) ought to banish puzzle from the universe of the philosopher and confer peace, inasmuch as there would then be for him absolutely no further considerations to spin.

This in fact is what some persons think. Professor Bain says, —

"A difficulty is solved, a mystery unriddled, when it can be shown to resemble something else ; to be an example of a fact already known. Mystery is isolation, exception, or it may be apparent contradiction : the resolution of the mystery is found in assimilation, identity, fraternity. When all things are assimilated, so far as assimilation can go, so far as likeness holds, there is an end to explanation ; there is an end to what the mind can do, or can intelligently desire. . . . The path of science as exhibited in modern ages is toward generality, wider and wider, until we reach the highest, the widest laws of every department of things ; there explanation is finished, mystery ends, perfect vision is gained."

But, unfortunately, this first answer will not hold. Our mind is so wedded to the process of seeing an *other* beside every item of its experience, that when the notion of an absolute datum is presented to it, it goes through its usual procedure and remains pointing at the void beyond, as if in that lay further matter for contemplation. In short, it spins for itself the further positive consideration of a nonentity envel-

oping the being of its datum; and as that leads nowhere, back recoils the thought toward its datum
again. But there is no natural bridge between nonentity and this particular datum, and the thought stands
oscillating to and fro, wondering "Why was there anything but nonentity; why just this universal datum
and not another?" and finds no end, in wandering
mazes lost. Indeed, Bain's words are so untrue that
in reflecting men it is just when the attempt to fuse
the manifold into a single totality has been most
successful, when the conception of the universe as a
unique fact is nearest its perfection, that the craving
for further explanation, the ontological wonder-sickness, arises in its extremest form. As Schopenhauer
says, "The uneasiness which keeps the never-resting
clock of metaphysics in motion, is the consciousness
that the non-existence of this world is just as possible
as its existence."

The notion of nonentity may thus be called the
parent of the philosophic craving in its subtilest and
profoundest sense. Absolute existence is absolute
mystery, for its relations with the nothing remain
unmediated to our understanding. One philosopher
only has pretended to throw a logical bridge over
this chasm. Hegel, by trying to show that nonentity and concrete being are linked together by a
series of identities of a synthetic kind, binds everything conceivable into a unity, with no outlying notion to disturb the free rotary circulation of the mind
within its bounds. Since such unchecked movement
gives the feeling of rationality, he must be held, if
he has succeeded, to have eternally and absolutely
quenched all rational demands.

But for those who deem Hegel's heroic effort to

have failed, nought remains but to confess that when all things have been unified to the supreme degree, the notion of a possible other than the actual may still haunt our imagination and prey upon our system. The bottom of being is left logically opaque to us, as something which we simply come upon and find, and about which (if we wish to act) we should pause and wonder as little as possible. The philosopher's logical tranquillity is thus in essence no other than the boor's. They differ only as to the point at which each refuses to let further considerations upset the absoluteness of the data he assumes. The boor does so immediately, and is liable at any moment to the ravages of many kinds of doubt. The philosopher does not do so till unity has been reached, and is warranted against the inroads of those considerations, but only practically, not essentially, secure from the blighting breath of the ultimate Why? If he cannot exorcise this question, he must ignore or blink it, and, assuming the data of his system as something given, and the gift as ultimate, simply proceed to a life of contemplation or of action based on it. There is no doubt that this acting on an opaque necessity is accompanied by a certain pleasure. See the reverence of Carlyle for brute fact: "There is an infinite significance in fact." "Necessity," says Dühring, and he means not rational but given necessity, "is the last and highest point that we can reach. . . . It is not only the interest of ultimate and definitive knowledge, but also that of the feelings, to find a last repose and an ideal equilibrium in an uttermost datum which can simply not be other than it is."

Such is the attitude of ordinary men in their theism, God's fiat being in physics and morals such an uttermost datum. Such also is the attitude of all hard-minded analysts and *Verstandesmenschen.* Lotze, Renouvier, and Hodgson promptly say that of experience as a whole no account can be given, but neither seek to soften the abruptness of the confession nor to reconcile us with our impotence.

But mediating attempts may be made by more mystical minds. The peace of rationality may be sought through ecstasy when logic fails. To religious persons of every shade of doctrine moments come when the world, as it is, seems so divinely orderly, and the acceptance of it by the heart so rapturously complete, that intellectual questions vanish; nay, the intellect itself is hushed to sleep, — as Wordsworth says, "thought is not; in enjoyment it expires." Ontological emotion so fills the soul that ontological speculation can no longer overlap it and put her girdle of interrogation-marks round existence. Even the least religious of men must have felt with Walt Whitman, when loafing on the grass on some transparent summer morning, that " swiftly arose and spread round him the peace and knowledge that pass all the argument of the earth." At such moments of energetic living we feel as if there were something diseased and contemptible, yea vile, in theoretic grubbing and brooding. In the eye of healthy sense the philosopher is at best a learned fool.

Since the heart can thus wall out the ultimate irrationality which the head ascertains, the erection of its procedure into a systematized method would be a philosophic achievement of first-rate importance. But as used by mystics hitherto it has lacked universality, being available for few persons and at few times, and even in these being apt to be followed by fits of reaction and dryness; and if men should agree that the mystical method is a subterfuge without logical pertinency, a plaster but no cure, and that the idea of nonentity can never be exorcised, empiricism will be the ultimate philosophy. Existence then will be a brute fact to which as a whole the emotion of ontologic wonder shall rightfully cleave, but remain eternally unsatisfied. Then wonderfulness or mysteriousness will be an essential attribute of the nature of things, and the exhibition and emphasizing of it will continue to be an ingredient in the philosophic industry of the race. Every generation will produce its Job, its Hamlet, its Faust, or its Sartor Resartus.

With this we seem to have considered the possibilities of purely theoretic rationality. But we saw at the outset that rationality meant only unimpeded mental function. Impediments that arise in the theoretic sphere might perhaps be avoided if the stream of mental action should leave that sphere betimes and pass into the practical. Let us therefore inquire what constitutes the feeling of rationality in its *practical* aspect. If thought is not to stand forever pointing at the universe in wonder, if its movement is to be diverted from the issueless channel of purely theoretic contemplation, let us ask what conception of the universe will awaken active impulses capable of effecting this diversion. A definition of the world which will give back to the mind the free motion which has been blocked in the purely contemplative path may so far make the world seem rational again.

Well, of two conceptions equally fit to satisfy the logical demand, that one which awakens the active impulses, or satisfies other æsthetic demands better than the other, will be accounted the more rational conception, and will deservedly prevail.

There is nothing improbable in the supposition that an analysis of the world may yield a number of formulæ, all consistent with the facts. In physical science different formulæ may explain the phenomena equally well, — the one-fluid and the two-fluid theories of electricity, for example. Why may it not be so with the world? Why may there not be different points of view for surveying it, within each of which all data harmonize, and which the observer may therefore either choose between, or simply cumulate one upon another? A Beethoven string-quartet is truly, as some one has said, a scraping of horses' tails on cats' bowels, and may be exhaustively described in such terms; but the application of this description in no way precludes the simultaneous applicability of an entirely different description. Just so a thoroughgoing interpretation of the world in terms of mechanical sequence is compatible with its being interpreted teleologically, for the mechanism itself may be designed.

If, then, there were several systems excogitated, equally satisfying to our purely logical needs, they would still have to be passed in review, and approved or rejected by our æsthetic and practical nature. Can we define the tests of rationality which these parts of our nature would use?

Philosophers long ago observed the remarkable fact that mere familiarity with things is able to produce a feeling of their rationality. The empiricist school has been so much struck by this circumstance as to have laid it down that the feeling of rationality and the feeling of familiarity are one and the same thing, and that no other kind of rationality than this exists. The daily contemplation of phenomena juxtaposed in a certain order begets an acceptance of their connection, as absolute as the repose engendered by theoretic insight into their coherence. To explain a thing is to pass easily back to its antecedents; to know it is easily to foresee its consequents. Custom, which lets us do both, is thus the source of whatever rationality the thing may gain in our thought.

In the broad sense in which rationality was defined at the outset of this essay, it is perfectly apparent that custom must be one of its factors. We said that any perfectly fluent and easy thought was devoid of the sentiment of irrationality. Inasmuch then as custom acquaints us with all the relations of a thing, it teaches us to pass fluently from that thing to others, and *pro tanto* tinges it with the rational character.

Now, there is one particular relation of greater practical importance than all the rest, — I mean the relation of a thing to its future consequences. So long as an object is unusual, our expectations are baffled; they are fully determined as soon as it becomes familiar. I therefore propose this as the first practical requisite which a philosophic conception must satisfy: *It must, in a general way at least, banish uncertainty from the future.* The permanent presence of the sense of futurity in the mind has been strangely ignored by most writers, but the fact is that our consciousness at a given moment is never free from the ingredient of expectancy. Every one knows how when a painful thing has to be undergone in the near future, the vague feeling that it is impending penetrates all our thought with uneasiness and subtly vitiates our mood even when it does not control our attention; it keeps us from being at rest, at home in the given present. The same is true when a great happiness awaits us. But when the future is neutral and perfectly certain, 'we do not mind it,' as we say, but give an undisturbed attention to the actual. Let now this haunting sense of futurity be thrown off its bearings or left without an object, and immediately uneasiness takes possession of the mind. But in every novel or unclassified experience this is just what occurs; we do not know what will come next; and novelty *per se* becomes a mental irritant, while custom *per se* is a mental sedative, merely because the one baffles while the other settles our expectations.

Every reader must feel the truth of this. What is meant by coming 'to feel at home' in a new place, or with new people? It is simply that, at first, when we take up our quarters in a new room, we do not know what draughts may blow in upon our back, what doors may open, what forms may enter, what interesting objects may be found in cupboards and corners. When after a few days we have learned the range of all these possibilities, the feeling of strangeness disappears. And so it does with people, when we have got past the point of expecting any essentially new manifestations from their character.

The utility of this emotional effect of expectation is perfectly obvious; 'natural selection,' in fact, was bound to bring it about sooner or later. It is of the utmost practical importance to an animal that he should have prevision of the qualities of the objects

that surround him, and especially that he should not
come to rest in presence of circumstances that might
be fraught either with peril or advantage, — go to
sleep, for example, on the brink of precipices, in the
dens of enemies, or view with indifference some new-
appearing object that might, if chased, prove an
important addition to the larder. Novelty *ought* to
irritate him. All curiosity has thus a practical genesis. We need only look at the physiognomy of a
dog or a horse when a new object comes into his
view, his mingled fascination and fear, to see that the
element of conscious insecurity or perplexed expectation lies at the root of his emotion. A dog's curiosity about the movements of his master or a strange
object only extends as far as the point of deciding
what is going to happen next. That settled, curiosity is quenched. The dog quoted by Darwin,
whose behavior in presence of a newspaper moved
by the wind seemed to testify to a sense 'of the
supernatural,' was merely exhibiting the irritation of
an uncertain future. A newspaper which could move
spontaneously was in itself so unexpected that the
poor brute could not tell what new wonders the next
moment might bring forth.

To turn back now to philosophy. An ultimate
datum, even though it be logically unrationalized,
will, if its quality is such as to define expectancy, be
peacefully accepted by the mind; while if it leave
the least opportunity for ambiguity in the future, it
will to that extent cause mental uneasiness if not
distress. Now, in the ultimate explanations of the
universe which the craving for rationality has elicited
from the human mind, the demands of expectancy to
be satisfied have always played a fundamental part.

The term set up by philosophers as primordial has been one which banishes the incalculable. 'Substance,' for example, means, as Kant says, *das Beharrliche*, which will be as it has been, because its being is essential and eternal. And although we may not be able to prophesy in detail the future phenomena to which the substance shall give rise, we may set our minds at rest in a general way, when we have called the substance God, Perfection, Love, or Reason, by the reflection that whatever is in store for us can never at bottom be inconsistent with the character of this term; so that our attitude even toward the unexpected is in a general sense defined. Take again the notion of immortality, which for common people seems to be the touchstone of every philosophic or religious creed: what is this but a way of saying that the determination of expectancy is the essential factor of rationality? The wrath of science against miracles, of certain philosophers against the doctrine of free-will, has precisely the same root, — dislike to admit any ultimate factor in things which may rout our prevision or upset the stability of our outlook.

Anti-substantialist writers strangely overlook this function in the doctrine of substance: "If there be such a *substratum*," says Mill, "suppose it at this instant miraculously annihilated, and let the sensations continue to occur in the same order, and how would the *substratum* be missed? By what signs should we be able to discover that its existence had terminated? Should we not have as much reason to believe that it still existed as we now have? And if we should not then be warranted in believing it, how can we be so now?" Truly enough, if we have already securely bagged our facts in a certain order, we can dispense with any further warrant for that order. But with regard to the facts yet to come the case is far different. It does not follow that if substance may be dropped from our conception of the irrecoverably past, it need be an equally empty complication to our notions of the future. Even if it were true that, for aught we know to the contrary, the substance might develop at any moment a wholly new set of attributes, the mere logical form of referring things to a substance would still (whether rightly or wrongly) remain accompanied by a feeling of rest and future confidence. In spite of the acutest nihilistic criticism, men will therefore always have a liking for any philosophy which explains things *per substantiam*.

A very natural reaction against the theosophizing conceit and hide-bound confidence in the upshot of things, which vulgarly optimistic minds display, has formed one factor of the scepticism of empiricists, who never cease to remind us of the reservoir of possibilities alien to our habitual experience which the cosmos may contain, and which, for any warrant we have to the contrary, may turn it inside out to-morrow. Agnostic substantialism like that of Mr. Spencer, whose Unknowable is not merely the unfathomable but the absolute-irrational, on which, if consistently represented in thought, it is of course impossible to count, performs the same function of rebuking a certain stagnancy and smugness in the manner in which the ordinary philistine feels his security. But considered as anything else than as reactions against an opposite excess, these philosophies of uncertainty cannot be acceptable; the general mind will fail to come to rest in their presence, and will seek for solutions of a more reassuring kind.

We may then, I think, with perfect confidence lay down as a first point gained in our inquiry, that a prime factor in the philosophic craving is the desire to have expectancy defined; and that no philosophy will definitively triumph which in an emphatic manner denies the possibility of gratifying this need.

We pass with this to the next great division of our topic. It is not sufficient for our satisfaction merely to know the future as determined, for it may be determined in either of many ways, agreeable or disagreeable. For a philosophy to succeed on a universal scale it must define the future *congruously with our spontaneous powers.* A philosophy may be unimpeachable in other respects, but either of two defects will be fatal to its universal acceptance. First, its ultimate principle must not be one that essentially baffles and disappoints our dearest desires and most cherished powers. A pessimistic principle like Schopenhauer's incurably vicious Will-substance, or Hartmann's wicked jack-of-all-trades the Unconscious, will perpetually call forth essays at other philosophies. Incompatibility of the future with their desires and active tendencies is, in fact, to most men a source of more fixed disquietude than uncertainty itself. Witness the attempts to overcome the 'problem of evil,' the 'mystery of pain.' There is no 'problem of good.'

But a second and worse defect in a philosophy than that of contradicting our active propensities is to give them no object whatever to press against. A philosophy whose principle is so incommensurate with our most intimate powers as to deny them all

relevancy in universal affairs, as to annihilate their
motives at one blow, will be even more unpopular
than pessimism. Better face the enemy than the
eternal Void! This is why materialism will always
fail of universal adoption, however well it may fuse
things into an atomistic unity, however clearly it may
prophesy the future eternity. For materialism denies
reality to the objects of almost all the impulses which
we most cherish. The real *meaning* of the impulses,
it says, is something which has no emotional interest
for us whatever. Now, what is called ' extradition '
is quite as characteristic of our emotions as of our
senses: both point to an object as the cause of the
present feeling. What an intensely objective reference lies in fear! In like manner an enraptured man
and a dreary-feeling man are not simply aware of
their subjective states; if they were, the force of their
feelings would all evaporate. Both believe there is
outward cause why they should feel as they do:
either, "It is a glad world! how good life is!" or,
"What a loathsome tedium is existence!" Any
philosophy which annihilates the validity of the reference by explaining away its objects or translating
them into terms of no emotional pertinency, leaves the
mind with little to care or act for. This is the opposite condition from that of nightmare, but when
acutely brought home to consciousness it produces
a kindred horror. In nightmare we have motives
to act, but no power; here we have powers, but no
motives. A nameless *unheimlichkeit* comes over us
at the thought of there being nothing eternal in our
final purposes, in the objects of those loves and aspi-
rations which are our deepest energies. The mon-
strously lopsided equation of the universe and its

knower, which we postulate as the ideal of cognition, is perfectly paralleled by the no less lopsided equation of the universe and the *doer*. We demand in it a character for which our emotions and active propensities shall be a match. Small as we are, minute as is the point by which the cosmos impinges upon each one of us, each one desires to feel that his reaction at that point is congruous with the demands of the vast whole, — that he balances the latter, so to speak, and is able to do what it expects of him. But as his abilities to do lie wholly in the line of his natural propensities; as he enjoys reacting with such emotions as fortitude, hope, rapture, admiration, earnestness, and the like; and as he very unwillingly reacts with fear, disgust, despair, or doubt, — a philosophy which should only legitimate emotions of the latter sort would be sure to leave the mind a prey to discontent and craving.

It is far too little recognized how entirely the intellect is built up of practical interests. The theory of evolution is beginning to do very good service by its reduction of all mentality to the type of reflex action. Cognition, in this view, is but a fleeting moment, a cross-section at a certain point, of what in its totality is a motor phenomenon. In the lower forms of life no one will pretend that cognition is anything more than a guide to appropriate action. The germinal question concerning things brought for the first time before consciousness is not the theoretic 'What is that?' but the practical 'Who goes there?' or rather, as Horwicz has admirably put it, 'What is to be done?' — 'Was fang' ich an?' In all our discussions about the intelligence of lower animals, the only test we use is that of their *acting* as if for a purpose.

Cognition, in short, is incomplete until discharged in act; and although it is true that the later mental development, which attains its maximum through the hypertrophied cerebrum of man, gives birth to a vast amount of theoretic activity over and above that which is immediately ministerial to practice, yet the earlier claim is only postponed, not effaced, and the active nature asserts its rights to the end.

When the cosmos in its totality is the object offered to consciousness, the relation is in no whit altered. React on it we must in some congenial way. It was a deep instinct in Schopenhauer which led him to reinforce his pessimistic argumentation by a running volley of invective against the practical man and his requirements. No hope for pessimism unless he is slain !

Helmholtz's immortal works on the eye and ear are to a great extent little more than a commentary on the law that practical utility wholly determines which parts of our sensations we shall be aware of, and which parts we shall ignore. We notice or discriminate an ingredient of sense only so far as we depend upon it to modify our actions. We *comprehend* a thing when we synthetize it by identity with another thing. But the other great department of our understanding, *acquaintance* (the two departments being recognized in all languages by the antithesis of such words as *wissen* and *kennen ; scire* and *noscere*, etc.), what is that also but a synthesis, — a synthesis of a passive perception with a certain tendency to reaction? We are acquainted with a thing as soon as we have learned how to behave towards it, or how to meet the behavior which we expect from it. Up to that point it is still ' strange ' to us.

If there be anything at all in this view, it follows
that however vaguely a philosopher may define the
ultimate universal datum, he cannot be said to leave
it unknown to us so long as he in the slightest degree
pretends that our emotional or active attitude toward
it should be of one sort rather than another. He
who says " life is real, life is earnest," however much
he may speak of the fundamental mysteriousness of
things, gives a distinct definition to that mysteriousness by ascribing to it the right to claim from us the
particular mood called seriousness, — which means the
willingness to live with energy, though energy bring
pain. The same is true of him who says that all is
vanity. For indefinable as the predicate ' vanity ' may
be *in se*, it is clearly something that permits anæsthesia, mere escape from suffering, to be our rule of life.
There can be no greater incongruity than for a disciple
of Spencer to proclaim with one breath that the substance of things is unknowable, and with the next that
the thought of it should inspire us with awe, reverence,
and a willingness to add our co-operative push in the
direction toward which its manifestations seem to be
drifting. The unknowable may be unfathomed, but
if it make such distinct demands upon our activity we
surely are not ignorant of its essential quality.

If we survey the field of history and ask what
feature all great periods of revival, of expansion of
the human mind, display in common, we shall find, I
think, simply this: that each and all of them have
said to the human being, " The inmost nature of the
reality is congenial to *powers* which you possess."
In what did the emancipating message of primitive
Christianity consist but in the announcement that

God recognizes those weak and tender impulses which paganism had so rudely overlooked ? Take repentance : the man who can do nothing rightly can at least repent of his failures. But for paganism this faculty of repentance was a pure supernumerary, a straggler too late for the fair. Christianity took it, and made it the one power within us which appealed straight to the heart of God. And after the night of the middle ages had so long branded with obloquy even the generous impulses of the flesh, and defined the reality to be such that only slavish natures could commune with it, in what did the *sursum corda* of the platonizing renaissance lie but in the proclamation that the archetype of verity in things laid claim on the widest activity of our whole æsthetic being ? What were Luther's mission and Wesley's but appeals to powers which even the meanest of men might carry with them, — faith and self-despair, — but which were personal, requiring no priestly intermediation, and which brought their owner face to face with God ? What caused the wildfire influence of Rousseau but the assurance he gave that man's nature was in harmony with the nature of things, if only the paralyzing corruptions of custom would stand from between? How did Kant and Fichte, Goethe and Schiller, inspire their time with cheer, except by saying, " Use all your powers ; that is the only obedience the universe exacts " ? And Carlyle with his gospel of work, of fact, of veracity, how does he move us except by saying that the universe imposes no tasks upon us but such as the most humble can perform ? Emerson's creed that everything that ever was or will be is here in the enveloping now ; that man has but to obey himself, — " He who will rest in what he *is*, is a part of destiny," — is in like manner nothing but an exorcism of all scepticism as to the pertinency of one's natural faculties.

In a word, " Son of Man, *stand upon thy feet* and I will speak unto thee!" is the only revelation of truth to which the solving epochs have helped the disciple. But that has been enough to satisfy the greater part of his rational need. *In se* and *per se* the universal essence has hardly been more defined by any of these formulas than by the agnostic x; but the mere assurance that my powers, such as they are, are not irrelevant to it, but pertinent; that it speaks to them and will in some way recognize their reply; that I can be a match for it if I will, and not a footless waif, — suffices to make it rational to my feeling in the sense given above. Nothing could be more absurd than to hope for the definitive triumph of any philosophy which should refuse to legitimate, and to legitimate in an emphatic manner, the more powerful of our emotional and practical tendencies. Fatalism, whose solving word in all crises of behavior is "all striving is vain," will never reign supreme, for the impulse to take life strivingly is indestructible in the race. Moral creeds which speak to that impulse will be widely successful in spite of inconsistency, vagueness, and shadowy determination of expectancy. Man needs a rule for his will, and will invent one if one be not given him.

But now observe a most important consequence. Men's active impulses are so differently mixed that a philosophy fit in this respect for Bismarck will almost certainly be unfit for a valetudinarian poet. In other words, although one can lay down in advance the

rule that a philosophy which utterly denies all fundamental ground for seriousness, for effort, for hope,
which says the nature of things is radically alien to
human nature, can never succeed, — one cannot in
advance say what particular dose of hope, or of gnosticism of the nature of things, the definitely successful
philosophy shall contain.   In short, it is almost certain
that personal temperament will here make itself felt,
and that although all men will insist on being spoken
to by the universe in some way, few will insist on being
spoken to in just the same way.   We have here, in
short, the sphere of what Matthew Arnold likes to
call *Aberglaube*, legitimate, inexpugnable, yet doomed
to eternal variations and disputes.

   Take idealism and materialism as examples of what
I mean, and suppose for a moment that both give a
conception of equal theoretic clearness and consistency, and that both determine our expectations equally
well.   Idealism will be chosen by a man of one emotional constitution, materialism by another.   At this
very day all sentimental natures, fond of conciliation
and intimacy, tend to an idealistic faith.   Why?   Because idealism gives to the nature of things such kinship with our personal selves.   Our own thoughts are
what we are most at home with, what we are least
afraid of.   To say then that the universe essentially is
thought, is to say that I myself, potentially at least,
am all.   There is no radically alien corner, but an all-
pervading *intimacy*.   Now, in certain sensitively ego-
tistic minds this conception of reality is sure to put
on a narrow, close, sick-room air.   Everything sentimental and priggish will be consecrated by it.   That
element in reality which every strong man of common-sense willingly feels there because it calls forth

powers that he owns — the rough, harsh, sea-wave, north-wind element, the denier of persons, the democratizer — is banished because it jars too much on the desire for communion. Now, it is the very enjoyment of this element that throws many men upon the materialistic or agnostic hypothesis, as a polemic reaction against the contrary extreme. They sicken at a life wholly constituted of intimacy. There is an overpowering desire at moments to escape personality, to revel in the action of forces that have no respect for our ego, to let the tides flow, even though they flow over us. The strife of these two kinds of mental temper will, I think, always be seen in philosophy. Some men will keep insisting on the reason, the atonement, that lies in the heart of things, and that we can act *with ;* others, on the opacity of brute fact that we must react *against.*

Now, there is one element of our active nature which the Christian religion has emphatically recognized, but which philosophers as a rule have with great insincerity tried to huddle out of sight in their pretension to found systems of absolute certainty. I mean the element of faith. Faith means belief in something concerning which doubt is still theoretically possible ; and as the test of belief is willingness to act, one may say that faith is the readiness to act in a cause the prosperous issue of which is not certified to us in advance. It is in fact the same moral quality which we call courage in practical affairs ; and there will be a very widespread tendency in men of vigorous nature to enjoy a certain amount of uncertainty in their philosophic creed, just as risk lends a zest to worldly activity. Absolutely certified philosophies seeking the *inconcussum* are fruits of mental natures in which the passion for identity (which we saw to be but one factor of the rational appetite) plays an abnormally exclusive part. In the average man, on the contrary, the power to trust, to risk a little beyond the literal evidence, is an essential function. Any mode of conceiving the universe which makes an appeal to this generous power, and makes the man seem as if he were individually helping to create the actuality of the truth whose metaphysical reality he is willing to assume, will be sure to be responded to by large numbers.

The necessity of faith as an ingredient in our mental attitude is strongly insisted on by the scientific philosophers of the present day; but by a singularly arbitrary caprice they say that it is only legitimate when used in the interests of one particular proposition, — the proposition, namely, that the course of nature is uniform. That nature will follow to-morrow the same laws that she follows to-day is, they all admit, a truth which no man can *know;* but in the interests of cognition as well as of action we must postulate or assume it. As Helmholtz says: "Hier gilt nur der eine Rath: vertraue und handle!" And Professor Bain urges: "Our only error is in proposing to give any reason or justification of the postulate, or to treat it as otherwise than begged at the very outset."

With regard to all other possible truths, however, a number of our most influential contemporaries think that an attitude of faith is not only illogical but shameful. Faith in a religious dogma for which there is no outward proof, but which we are tempted to postulate for our emotional interests, just as we pos-

tulate the uniformity of nature for our intellectual
interests, is branded by Professor Huxley as "the
lowest depth of immorality." Citations of this kind
from leaders of the modern *Aufklärung* might be
multiplied almost indefinitely. Take Professor Clifford's article on the 'Ethics of Belief.' He calls it
'guilt' and 'sin' to believe even the truth without
'scientific evidence.' But what is the use of being a
genius, unless *with the same scientific evidence* as
other men, one can reach more truth than they?
Why does Clifford fearlessly proclaim his belief in the
conscious-automaton theory, although the 'proofs' before him are the same which make Mr. Lewes reject
it? Why does he believe in primordial units of 'mind-
stuff' on evidence which would seem quite worthless
to Professor Bain? Simply because, like every human
being of the slightest mental originality, he is peculiarly sensitive to evidence that bears in some one direction. It is utterly hopeless to try to exorcise such
sensitiveness by calling it the disturbing subjective
factor, and branding it as the root of all evil. 'Subjective' be it called! and 'disturbing' to those whom
it foils! But if it helps those who, as Cicero says,
"vim naturæ magis sentiunt," it is good and not evil.
Pretend what we may, the whole man within us is at
work when we form our philosophical opinions. Intellect, will, taste, and passion co-operate just as they
do in practical affairs; and lucky it is if the passion
be not something as petty as a love of personal conquest over the philosopher across the way. The absurd abstraction of an intellect verbally formulating
all its evidence and carefully estimating the probability thereof by a vulgar fraction by the size of whose
denominator and numerator alone it is swayed, is

ideally as inept as it is actually impossible. It is almost incredible that men who are themselves working philosophers should pretend that any philosophy can be, or ever has been, constructed without the help of personal preference, belief, or divination. How have they succeeded in so stultifying their sense for the living facts of human nature as not to perceive that every philosopher, or man of science either, whose initiative counts for anything in the evolution of thought, has taken his stand on a sort of dumb conviction that the truth must lie in one direction rather than another, and a sort of preliminary assurance that his notion can be made to work; and has borne his best fruit in trying to make it work? These mental instincts in different men are the spontaneous variations upon which the intellectual struggle for existence is based. The fittest conceptions survive, and with them the names of their champions shining to all futurity.

The coil is about us, struggle as we may. The only escape from faith is mental nullity. What we enjoy most in a Huxley or a Clifford is not the professor with his learning, but the human personality ready to go in for what it feels to be right, in spite of all appearances. The concrete man has but one interest, — to be right. That for him is the art of all arts, and all means are fair which help him to it. Naked he is flung into the world, and between him and nature there are no rules of civilized warfare. The rules of the scientific game, burdens of proof, presumptions, *experimenta crucis*, complete inductions, and the like, are only binding on those who enter that game. As a matter of fact we all more or less do enter it, because it helps us to our end. But if the means presume to frustrate the end and call us cheats for being right in

advance of their slow aid, by guesswork or by hook
or crook, what shall we say of them? Were all of
Clifford's works, except the Ethics of Belief, forgotten, he might well figure in future treatises on psychology in place of the somewhat threadbare instance
of the miser who has been led by the association of
ideas to prefer his gold to all the goods he might buy
therewith.

In short, if I am born with such a superior general
reaction to evidence that I can guess right and act
accordingly, and gain all that comes of right action,
while my less gifted neighbor (paralyzed by his scruples and waiting for more evidence which he dares
not anticipate, much as he longs to) still stands
shivering on the brink, by what law shall I be for-
bidden to reap the advantages of my superior native
sensitiveness? Of course I yield to my belief in such
a case as this or distrust it, alike at my peril, just as
I do in any of the great practical decisions of life.
If my inborn faculties are good, I am a prophet; if
poor, I am a failure: nature spews me out of her
mouth, and there is an end of me. In the total game
of life we stake our persons all the while; and if in its
theoretic part our persons will help us to a conclusion, surely we should also stake them there, however inarticulate they may be.[1]

---

[1] At most, the command laid upon us by science to believe nothing
not yet verified by the senses is a prudential rule intended to maxim-
ize our right thinking and minimize our errors *in the long run*. In the
particular instance we must frequently lose truth by obeying it; but
on the whole we are safer if we follow it consistently, for we are sure to
cover our losses with our gains. It is like those gambling and insur-
ance rules based on probability, in which we secure ourselves against
losses in detail by hedging on the total run. But this hedging philosophy requires that long run should be there; and this makes it inap-

But in being myself so very articulate in proving what to all readers with a sense for reality will seem a platitude, am I not wasting words? We cannot live or think at all without some degree of faith. Faith is synonymous with working hypothesis. The only difference is that while some hypotheses can be refuted in five minutes, others may defy ages. A chemist who conjectures that a certain wall-paper contains arsenic, and has faith enough to lead him to take the trouble to put some of it into a hydrogen bottle, finds out by the results of his action whether he was right or wrong. But theories like that of Darwin, or that of the kinetic constitution of matter, may exhaust the labors of generations in their corroboration, each tester of their truth proceeding in this simple way, — that he acts as if it were true, and expects the result to disappoint him if his assumption is false. The longer disappointment is delayed, the stronger grows his faith in his theory.

Now, in such questions as God, immortality, absolute morality, and free-will, no non-papal believer at the present day pretends his faith to be of an essentially different complexion; he can always doubt his creed. But his intimate persuasion is that the odds in its favor are strong enough to warrant him in acting all along on the assumption of its truth. His corroboration or repudiation by the nature of things may be deferred until the day of judgment. The

plicable to the question of religious faith as the latter comes home to the individual man. He plays the game of life not to escape losses, for he brings nothing with him to lose; he plays it for gains; and it is now or never with him, for the long run which exists indeed for humanity, is not there for him. Let him doubt, believe, or deny, he runs his risk, and has the natural right to choose which one it shall be.

uttermost he now means is something like this: "I *expect* then to triumph with tenfold glory; but if it should turn out, as indeed it may, that I have spent my days in a fool's paradise, why, better have been the dupe of *such* a dreamland than the cunning reader of a world like that which then beyond all doubt unmasks itself to view." In short, we *go in* against materialism very much as we should *go in*, had we a chance, against the second French empire or the Church of Rome, or any other system of things toward which our repugnance is vast enough to determine energetic action, but too vague to issue in distinct argumentation. Our reasons are ludicrously incommensurate with the volume of our feeling, yet on the latter we unhesitatingly act.

Now, I wish to show what to my knowledge has never been clearly pointed out, that belief (as measured by action) not only does and must continually outstrip scientific evidence, but that there is a certain class of truths of whose reality belief is a factor as well as a confessor; and that as regards this class of truths faith is not only licit and pertinent, but essential and indispensable. The truths cannot become true till our faith has made them so.

Suppose, for example, that I am climbing in the Alps, and have had the ill-luck to work myself into a position from which the only escape is by a terrible leap. Being without similar experience, I have no evidence of my ability to perform it successfully; but hope and confidence in myself make me sure I shall not miss my aim, and nerve my feet to execute what without those subjective emotions would perhaps have been impossible. But suppose that, on the contrary, the emotions of fear and mistrust preponderate; or suppose that, having just read the Ethics of Belief, I feel it would be sinful to act upon an assumption un-verified by previous experience, — why, then I shall hesitate so long that at last, exhausted and trembling, and launching myself in a moment of despair, I miss my foothold and roll into the abyss. In this case (and it is one of an immense class) the part of wisdom clearly is to believe what one desires; for the belief is one of the indispensable preliminary conditions of the realization of its object. *There are then cases where faith creates its own verification.* Believe, and you shall be right, for you shall save yourself; doubt, and you shall again be right, for you shall perish. The only difference is that to believe is greatly to your advantage.

The future movements of the stars or the facts of past history are determined now once for all, whether I like them or not. They are given irrespective of my wishes, and in all that concerns truths like these subjective preference should have no part; it can only obscure the judgment. But in every fact into which there enters an element of personal contribution on my part, as soon as this personal contribution demands a certain degree of subjective energy which, in its turn, calls for a certain amount of faith in the result, — so that, after all, the future fact is conditioned by my present faith in it, — how trebly asinine would it be for me to deny myself the use of the subjective method, the method of belief based on desire!

In every proposition whose bearing is universal (and such are all the propositions of philosophy), the acts of the subject and their consequences throughout eternity should be included in the formula. If M

represent the entire world *minus* the reaction of the
thinker upon it, and if $M + x$ represent the absolutely
total matter of philosophic propositions (x standing for
the thinker's reaction and its results), — what would be
a universal truth if the term x were of one complexion,
might become egregious error if x altered its character.   Let it not be said that x is too infinitesimal a
component to change the character of the immense
whole in which it lies imbedded.   Everything depends
on the point of view of the philosophic proposition
in question.   If we have to define the universe from
the point of view of sensibility, the critical material
for our judgment lies in the animal kingdom, insignificant as that is, quantitatively considered.   The moral
definition of the world may depend on phenomena
more restricted still in range.   In short, many a long
phrase may have its sense reversed by the addition of
three letters, *n-o-t;* many a monstrous mass have its
unstable equilibrium discharged one way or the other
by a feather weight that falls.

Let us make this clear by a few examples.   The philosophy of evolution offers us to-day a new criterion
to serve as an ethical test between right and wrong.
Previous criteria, it says, being subjective, have left
us still floundering in variations of opinion and the
status belli.   Here is a criterion which is objective
and fixed : *That is to be called good which is destined
to prevail or survive.*   But we immediately see that this
standard can only remain objective by leaving myself
and my conduct out.   If what prevails and survives
does so by my help, and cannot do so without that
help ; if something else will prevail in case I alter my
conduct, — how can I possibly now, conscious of alternative courses of action open before me, either of which

I may suppose capable of altering the path of events, decide which course to take by asking what path events will follow? If they follow my direction, evidently my direction cannot wait on them. The only possible manner in which an evolutionist can use his standard is the obsequious method of forecasting the course society would take *but for him*, and then putting an extinguisher on all personal idiosyncrasies of desire and interest, and with bated breath and tiptoe tread following as straight as may be at the tail, and bringing up the rear of everything. Some pious creatures may find a pleasure in this; but not only does it violate our general wish to lead and not to follow (a wish which is surely not immoral if we but lead aright), but if it be treated as every ethical principle must be treated, — namely, as a rule good for all men alike, — its general observance would lead to its practical refutation by bringing about a general deadlock. Each good man hanging back and waiting for orders from the rest, absolute stagnation would ensue. Happy, then, if a few unrighteous ones contribute an initiative which sets things moving again!

All this is no caricature. That the course of destiny may be altered by individuals no wise evolutionist ought to doubt. Everything for him has small beginnings, has a bud which may be 'nipped,' and nipped by a feeble force. Human races and tendencies follow the law, and have also small beginnings. The best, according to evolution, is that which has the biggest endings. Now, if a present race of men, enlightened in the evolutionary philosophy, and able to forecast the future, were able to discern in a tribe arising near them the potentiality of future supremacy; were able to see that their own race would eventually be wiped out of existence by the new-comers if the expansion of these were left unmolested, — these present sages would have two courses open to them, either perfectly in harmony with the evolutionary test: Strangle the new race *now*, and ours survives; help the new race, and *it* survives. In both cases the action is right as measured by the evolutionary standard, — it is action for the winning side.

Thus the evolutionist foundation of ethics is purely objective only to the herd of nullities whose votes count for zero in the march of events. But for others, leaders of opinion or potentates, and in general those to whose actions position or genius gives a far-reaching import, and to the rest of us, each in his measure, — whenever we espouse a cause we contribute to the determination of the evolutionary standard of right. The truly wise disciple of this school will then admit faith as an ultimate ethical factor. Any philosophy which makes such questions as, What is the ideal type of humanity? What shall be reckoned virtues? What conduct is good? depend on the question, What is going to succeed? — must needs fall back on personal belief as one of the ultimate conditions of the truth. For again and again success depends on energy of act; energy again depends on faith that we shall not fail; and that faith in turn on the faith that we are right, — which faith thus verifies itself.

Take as an example the question of optimism or pessimism, which makes so much noise just now in Germany. Every human being must sometime decide for himself whether life is worth living. Suppose that in looking at the world and seeing how full it is of misery, of old age, of wickedness and pain, and how unsafe is his own future, he yields to the pessimistic conclusion, cultivates disgust and dread, ceases striving, and finally commits suicide. He thus adds to the mass M of mundane phenomena, independent of his subjectivity, the subjective complement x, which makes of the whole an utterly black picture illumined by no gleam of good. Pessimism completed, verified by his moral reaction and the deed in which this ends, is true beyond a doubt. $M + x$ expresses a state of things totally bad. The man's belief supplied all that was lacking to make it so, and now that it is made so the belief was right.

But now suppose that with the same evil facts M, the man's reaction x is exactly reversed; suppose that instead of giving way to the evil he braves it, and finds a sterner, more wonderful joy than any passive pleasure can yield in triumphing over pain and defying fear; suppose he does this successfully, and however thickly evils crowd upon him proves his dauntless subjectivity to be more than their match, — will not every one confess that the bad character of the M is here the *conditio sine qua non* of the good character of the x? Will not every one instantly declare a world fitted only for fair-weather human beings susceptible of every passive enjoyment, but without independence, courage, or fortitude, to be from a moral point of view incommensurably inferior to a world framed to elicit from the man every form of triumphant endurance and conquering moral energy? As James Hinton says, —

" Little inconveniences, exertions, pains, — these are the only things in which we rightly feel our life at all. If these be not there, existence becomes worthless, or worse; suc-

cess in putting them all away is fatal. So it is men engage
in athletic sports, spend their holidays in climbing up mountains, find nothing so enjoyable as that which taxes their
endurance and their energy. This is the way we are made,
I say. It may or may not be a mystery or a paradox; it is
a fact. Now, this enjoyment in endurance is just according
to the intensity of life: the more physical vigor and balance,
the more endurance can be made an element of satisfaction.
A sick man cannot stand it. The line of enjoyable suffering
is not a fixed one; it fluctuates with the perfectness of the
life. That our pains are, as they are, unendurable, awful,
overwhelming, crushing, not to be borne save in 'misery
and dumb impatience, which utter exhaustion alone makes
patient, — that our pains are thus unendurable, means not
that they are too great, but that *we are sick.* We have not
got our proper life. So you perceive pain is no more
necessarily an evil, but an essential element of the highest
good." [1]

But the highest good can be achieved only by our
getting our proper life; and that can come about
only by help of a moral energy born of the faith
that in some way or other we shall succeed in getting
it if we try pertinaciously enough. This world *is*
good, we must say, since it is what we make it, — and
we shall make it good. How can we exclude from
the cognition of a truth a faith which is involved in
the creation of the truth? *M* has its character indeterminate, susceptible of forming part of a thorough-
going pessimism on the one hand, or of a meliorism,
a moral (as distinguished from a sensual) optimism
on the other. All depends on the character of the

---

[1] Life of James Hinton, pp. 172, 173. See also the excellent chapter on Faith and Sight in the Mystery of Matter, by J. Allanson
Picton. Hinton's Mystery of Pain will undoubtedly always remain
the classical utterance on this subject.

personal contribution *x.* Wherever the facts to be formulated contain such a contribution, we may logically, legitimately, and inexpugnably believe what we desire. The belief creates its verification. The thought becomes literally father to the fact, as the wish was father to the thought.[1]

Let us now turn to the radical question of life, — the question whether this be at bottom a moral or an unmoral universe, — and see whether the method of faith may legitimately have a place there. It is really the question of materialism. Is the world a simple brute actuality, an existence *de facto* about which the deepest thing that can be said is that it happens so to be; or is the judgment of *better* or *worse,* of *ought,* as intimately pertinent to phenomena as the simple judgment *is* or *is not ?* The materialistic theorists say that judgments of worth are themselves mere matters of fact; that the words 'good' and 'bad' have no sense apart from subjective passions and interests which we may, if we please, play fast and loose with at will, so far as any duty of ours to the non-human universe is concerned. Thus, when a materialist says it is better for him to suffer great inconvenience than to break a promise, he only means that his social interests have become so knit up with

---

[1] Observe that in all this not a word has been said of free-will. It all applies as well to a predetermined as to an indeterminate universe. If $M + x$ is fixed in advance, the belief which leads to x and the desire which prompts the belief are also fixed. But fixed or not, these subjective states form a phenomenal condition necessarily preceding the facts; necessarily constitutive, therefore, of the truth $M + x$ which we seek. If, however, free acts be possible, a faith in their possibility, by augmenting the moral energy which gives them birth, will increase their frequency in a given individual.

keeping faith that, those interests once being granted, it *is* better for him to keep the promise in spite of everything. But the interests themselves are neither right nor wrong, except possibly with reference to some ulterior order of interests which themselves again are mere subjective data without character, either good or bad.

For the absolute moralists, on the contrary, the interests are not there merely to be felt, — they are to be believed in and obeyed. Not only is it best for my social interests to keep my promise, but best for me to have those interests, and best for the cosmos to have this me. Like the old woman in the story who described the world as resting on a rock, and then explained that rock to be supported by another rock, and finally when pushed with questions said it was rocks all the way down, — he who believes this to be a radically moral universe must hold the moral order to rest either on an absolute and ultimate *should*, or on a series of *shoulds* all the way down.[1]

The practical difference between this objective sort of moralist and the other one is enormous. The subjectivist in morals, when his moral feelings are at war with the facts about him, is always free to seek harmony by toning down the sensitiveness of the feelings. Being mere data, neither good nor evil in themselves, he may pervert them or lull them to sleep by any means at his command. Truckling, compromise, time-serving, capitulations of conscience, are conventionally opprobrious names for what, if successfully carried out,

---

[1] In either case, as a later essay explains (see p. 193), the *should* which the moralist regards as binding upon *him* must be rooted in the feeling of some other thinker, or collection of thinkers, to whose demands he individually bows.

would be on his principles by far the easiest and most praiseworthy mode of bringing about that harmony between inner and outer relations which is all that he means by good. The absolute moralist, on the other hand, when his interests clash with the world, is not free to gain harmony by sacrificing the ideal interests. According to him, these latter should be as they are and not otherwise. Resistance then, poverty, martyrdom if need be, tragedy in a word, — such are the solemn feasts of his inward faith. Not that the contradiction between the two men occurs every day; in commonplace matters all moral schools agree. It is only in the lonely emergencies of life that our creed is tested: then routine maxims fail, and we fall back on our gods. It cannot then be said that the question, Is this a moral world? is a meaningless and unverifiable question because it deals with something non-phenomenal. Any question is full of meaning to which, as here, contrary answers lead to contrary behavior. And it seems as if in answering such a question as this we might proceed exactly as does the physical philosopher in testing an hypothesis. He deduces from the hypothesis an experimental action, x; this he adds to the facts M already existing. It fits them if the hypothesis be true; if not, there is discord. The results of the action corroborate or refute the idea from which it flowed. So here: the verification of the theory which you may hold as to the objectively moral character of the world can consist only in this, — that if you proceed to act upon your theory it will be reversed by nothing that later turns up as your action's fruit; it will harmonize so well with the entire drift of experience that the latter will, as it were, adopt it. or at most give it an ampler interpretation, without obliging you in any way to change the essence of its formulation. If this be an objectively moral universe, all acts that I make on that assumption, all expectations that I ground on it, will tend more and more completely to interdigitate with the phenomena already existing. $M + x$ will be in accord; and the more I live, and the more the fruits of my activity come to light, the more satisfactory the consensus will grow. While if it be not such a moral universe, and I mistakenly assume that it is, the course of experience will throw ever new impediments in the way of my belief, and become more and more difficult to express in its language. Epicycle upon epicycle of subsidiary hypothesis will have to be invoked to give to the discrepant terms a temporary appearance of squaring with each other; but at last even this resource will fail.

If, on the other hand, I rightly assume the universe to be not moral, in what does my verification consist? It is that by letting moral interests sit lightly, by disbelieving that there is any duty about *them* (since duty obtains only as *between* them and other phenomena), and so throwing them over if I find it hard to get them satisfied, — it is that by refusing to take up a tragic attitude, I deal in the long-run most satisfactorily with the facts of life. "All is vanity" is here the last word of wisdom. Even though in certain limited series there may be a great appearance of seriousness, he who in the main treats things with a degree of good-natured scepticism and radical levity will find that the practical fruits of his epicurean hypothesis verify it more and more, and not only save him from pain but do honor to his sagacity. While, on the other hand, he who contrary to reality stiffens himself in the notion that certain things absolutely should be, and rejects the truth that at bottom it makes no difference what is, will find himself evermore thwarted and perplexed and be-muddled by the facts of the world, and his tragic dis-appointment will, as experience accumulates, seem to drift farther and farther away from that final atone-ment or reconciliation which certain partial tragedies often get.

Anæsthesia is the watchword of the moral sceptic brought to bay and put to his trumps. *Energy* is that of the moralist. Act on my creed, cries the latter, and the results of your action will prove the creed true, and that the nature of things is earnest infinitely. Act on mine, says the epicurean, and the results will prove that seriousness is but a superficial glaze upon a world of fundamentally trivial import. You and your acts and the nature of things will be alike enveloped in a single formula, a universal *vanitas vanitatum.*

For the sake of simplicity I have written as if the verification might occur in the life of a single philoso-pher, — which is manifestly untrue, since the theories still face each other, and the facts of the world give countenance to both. Rather should we expect, that, in a question of this scope, the experience of the en-tire human race must make the verification, and that all the evidence will not be 'in' till the final integra-tion of things, when the last man has had his say and contributed his share to the still unfinished x. Then the proof will be complete; then it will appear with-out doubt whether the moralistic x has filled up the gap which alone kept the M of the world from form-ing an even and harmonious unity, or whether the non-moralistic x has given the finishing touches which were alone needed to make the M appear outwardly as vain as it inwardly was.

But if this be so, is it not clear that the facts M, taken *per se*, are inadequate to justify a conclusion either way in advance of my action? My action is the complement which, by proving congruous or not, reveals the latent nature of the mass to which it is applied. The world may in fact be likened unto a lock, whose inward nature, moral or unmoral, will never reveal itself to our simply expectant gaze. The positivists, forbidding us to make any assumptions regarding it, condemn us to eternal ignorance, for the 'evidence' which they wait for can never come so long as we are passive. But nature has put into our hands two keys, by which we may test the lock. If we try the moral key *and it fits*, it is a moral lock. If we try the unmoral key and *it* fits, it is an unmoral lock. I cannot possibly conceive of any other sort of 'evidence' or 'proof' than this. It is quite true that the co-operation of generations is needed to educe it. But in these matters the solidarity (so called) of the human race is a patent fact. The essential thing to notice is that our active preference is a legitimate part of the game, — that it is our plain business as men to try one of the keys, and the one in which we most confide. If then the proof exist not till I have acted, and I must needs in acting run the risk of being wrong, how can the popular science professors be right in objurgating in me as infamous a 'credulity' which the strict logic of the situation requires? If this really be a moral universe; if by my acts I be a factor of its destinies; if to believe where I may doubt be itself a moral act

analogous to voting for a side not yet sure to win, —
by what right shall they close in upon me and
steadily negate the deepest conceivable function of
my being by their preposterous command that I
shall stir neither hand nor foot, but remain balancing
myself in eternal and insoluble doubt? Why, doubt
itself is a decision of the widest practical reach, if
only because we may miss by doubting what goods
we might be gaining by espousing the winning side.
But more than that! it is often practically impossible
to distinguish doubt from dogmatic negation. If I
refuse to stop a murder because I am in doubt
whether it be not justifiable homicide, I am virtually
abetting the crime. If I refuse to bale out a boat
because I am in doubt whether my efforts will keep
her afloat, I am really helping to sink her. If in the
mountain precipice I doubt my right to risk a leap, I
actively connive at my destruction. He who commands himself not to be credulous of God, of duty, of
freedom, of immortality, may again and again be
indistinguishable from him who dogmatically denies
them. Scepticism in moral matters is an active ally
of immorality. Who is not for is against. The
universe will have no neutrals in these questions.
In theory as in practice, dodge or hedge, or talk as
we like about a wise scepticism, we are really doing
volunteer military service for one side or the other.

Yet obvious as this necessity practically is, thousands of innocent magazine readers lie paralyzed and
terrified in the network of shallow negations which
the leaders of opinion have thrown over their souls.
All they need to be free and hearty again in the
exercise of their birthright is that these fastidious
vetoes should be swept away. All that the human

heart wants is its chance. It will willingly forego certainty in universal matters if only it can be allowed to feel that in them it has that same inalienable right to run risks, which no one dreams of refusing to it in the pettiest practical affairs. And if I, in these last pages, like the mouse in the fable, have gnawed a few of the strings of the sophistical net that has been binding down its lion-strength, I shall be more than rewarded for my pains.

To sum up: No philosophy will permanently be deemed rational by all men which (in addition to meeting logical demands) does not to some degree pretend to determine expectancy, and in a still greater degree make a direct appeal to all those powers of our nature which we hold in highest esteem. Faith, being one of these powers, will always remain a factor not to be banished from philosophic constructions, the more so since in many ways it brings forth its own verification. In these points, then, it is hopeless to look for literal agreement among mankind.

The ultimate philosophy, we may therefore conclude, must not be too strait-laced in form, must not in all its parts divide heresy from orthodoxy by too sharp a line. There must be left over and above the propositions to be subscribed, *ubique, semper, et ab omnibus*, another realm into which the stifled soul may escape from pedantic scruples and indulge its own faith at its own risks; and all that can here be done will be to mark out distinctly the questions which fall within faith's sphere.

REFLEX ACTION AND THEISM.[1]

MEMBERS OF THE MINISTERS' INSTITUTE:

LET me confess to the diffidence with which I find myself standing here to-day. When the invitation of your committee reached me last fall, the simple truth is that I accepted it as most men accept a challenge, — not because they wish to fight, but because they are ashamed to say no. Pretending in my small sphere to be a teacher, I felt it would be cowardly to shrink from the keenest ordeal to which a teacher can be exposed, — the ordeal of teaching other teachers. Fortunately, the trial will last but one short hour; and I have the consolation of remembering Goethe's verses, —

> " Vor den Wissenden sich stellen,
> Sicher ist 's in allen Fällen," —

for if experts are the hardest people to satisfy, they have at any rate the liveliest sense of the difficulties of one's task, and they know quickest when one hits the mark.

Since it was as a teacher of physiology that I was most unworthily officiating when your committee's invi-

[1] Address delivered to the Unitarian Ministers' Institute at Princeton, Mass., 1881, and printed in the Unitarian Review for October of that year.

tation reached me, I must suppose it to be for the sake of bringing a puff of the latest winds of doctrine which blow over that somewhat restless sea that my presence is desired. Among all the healthy symptoms that characterize this age, I know no sounder one than the eagerness which theologians show to assimilate results of science, and to hearken to the conclusions of men of science about universal matters. One runs a better chance of being listened to to-day if one can quote Darwin and Helmholtz than if one can only quote Schleiermacher or Coleridge. I almost feel myself this moment that were I to produce a frog and put him through his physiological performances in a masterly manner before your eyes, I should gain more reverential ears for what I have to say during the remainder of the hour. I will not ask whether there be not something of mere fashion in this prestige which the words of the physiologists enjoy just now. If it be a fashion, it is certainly a beneficial one upon the whole; and to challenge it would come with a poor grace from one who at the moment he speaks is so conspicuously profiting by its favors.

I will therefore only say this: that the *latest* breeze from the physiological horizon need not necessarily be the most important one. Of the immense amount of work which the laboratories of Europe and America, and one may add of Asia and Australia, are producing every year, much is destined to speedy refutation; and of more it may be said that its interest is purely technical, and not in any degree philosophi‑cal or universal.

This being the case, I know you will justify me if I fall back on a doctrine which is fundamental and well established rather than novel, and ask you whether

by taking counsel together we may not trace some
new consequences from it which shall interest us all
alike as men.   I refer to the doctrine of reflex action,
especially as extended to the brain.   This is, of course,
so familiar to you that I hardly need define it.   In a
general way, all educated people know what reflex
action means.

It means that the acts we perform are always the
result of outward discharges from the nervous centres,
and that these outward discharges are themselves
the result of impressions from the external world, carried in along one or another of our sensory nerves.
Applied at first to only a portion of our acts, this
conception has ended by being generalized more
and more, so that now most physiologists tell us
that every action whatever, even the most deliberately weighed and calculated, does, so far as its organic
conditions go, follow the reflex type.   There is not
one which cannot be remotely, if not immediately,
traced to an origin in some incoming impression of
sense.   There is no impression of sense which, unless
inhibited by some other stronger one, does not immediately or remotely express itself in action of some
kind.   There is no one of those complicated performances in the convolutions of the brain to which our
trains of thought correspond, which is not a mere
middle term interposed between an incoming sensation that arouses it and an outgoing discharge of some
sort, inhibitory if not exciting, to which itself gives
rise.   The structural unit of the nervous system is in
fact a triad, neither of whose elements has any independent existence.   The sensory impression exists
only for the sake of awaking the central process of
reflection, and the central process of reflection exists

only for the sake of calling forth the final act. All action is thus *re*-action upon the outer world; and the middle stage of consideration or contemplation or thinking is only a place of transit, the bottom of a loop, both whose ends have their point of application in the outer world. If it should ever have no roots in the outer world, if it should ever happen that it led to no active measures, it would fail of its essential function, and would have to be considered either pathological or abortive. The current of life which runs in at our eyes or ears is meant to run out at our hands, feet, or lips. The only use of the thoughts it occasions while inside is to determine its direction to whichever of these organs shall, on the whole, under the circumstances actually present, act in the way most propitious to our welfare.

The willing department of our nature, in short, dominates both the conceiving department and the feeling department; or, in plainer English, perception and thinking are only there for behavior's sake.

I am sure I am not wrong in stating this result as one of the fundamental conclusions to which the entire drift of modern physiological investigation sweeps us. If asked what great contribution physiology has made to psychology of late years, I am sure every competent authority will reply that her influence has in no way been so weighty as in the copious illustration, verification, and consolidation of this broad, general point of view.

I invite you, then, to consider what may be the possible speculative consequences involved in this great achievement of our generation. Already, it dominates all the new work done in psychology; but what I wish to ask is whether its influence may not extend far beyond the limits of psychology, even into those of theology herself. The relations of the doctrine of reflex action with no less a matter than the doctrine of theism is, in fact, the topic to which I now invite your attention.

We are not the first in the field. There have not been wanting writers enough to say that reflex action and all that follows from it give the *coup de grâce* to the superstition of a God.

If you open, for instance, such a book on comparative psychology, as der Thierische Wille of G. H. Schneider, you will find, sandwiched in among the admirable dealings of the author with his proper subject, and popping out upon us in unexpected places, the most delightfully *naïf* German onslaughts on the degradation of theologians, and the utter incompatibility of so many reflex adaptations to the environment with the existence of a creative intelligence. There was a time, remembered by many of us here, when the existence of reflex action and all the other harmonies between the organism and the world were held to prove a God. Now, they are held to disprove him. The next turn of the whirligig may bring back proof of him again.

Into this debate about his existence, I will not pretend to enter. I must take up humbler ground, and limit my ambition to showing that a God, whether existent or not, is at all events the kind of being which, if he did exist, would form *the most adequate possible object* for minds framed like our own to conceive as lying at the root of the universe. My thesis, in other words, is this: that *some* outward reality of a nature defined as God's nature must be defined, is the only ultimate object that is at the same time rational and possible for the human mind's contemplation. *Anything short of God is not rational, anything more than God is not possible,* if the human mind be in truth the triadic structure of impression, reflection, and reaction which we at the outset allowed.

Theism, whatever its objective warrant, would thus be seen to have a subjective anchorage in its congruity with our nature as thinkers; and, however it may fare with its truth, to derive from this subjective adequacy the strongest possible guaranty of its permanence. It is and will be the classic mean of rational opinion, the centre of gravity of all attempts to solve the riddle of life, — some falling below it by defect, some flying above it by excess, itself alone satisfying every mental need in strictly normal measure. Our gain will thus in the first instance be psychological. We shall merely have investigated a chapter in the natural history of the mind, and found that, as a matter of such natural history, God may be called the normal object of the mind's belief. Whether over and above this he be really the living truth is another question. If he is, it will show the structure of our mind to be in accordance with the nature of reality. Whether it be or not in such accordance is, it seems to me, one of those questions that belong to the province of personal faith to decide. I will not touch upon the question here, for I prefer to keep to the strictly natural-history point of view. I will only remind you that each one of us is entitled either to doubt or to believe in the harmony between his faculties and the truth; and that, whether he doubt or be

lieve, he does it alike on his personal responsibility
and risk.

> " Du musst glauben, du musst wagen,
> Denn die Götter leihn kein Pfand,
> Nur ein Wunder kann dich tragen
> In das schöne Wunderland."

I will presently define exactly what I mean by God
and by Theism, and explain what theories I referred
to when I spoke just now of attempts to fly beyond
the one and to outbid the other.

But, first of all, let me ask you to linger a moment
longer over what I have called the reflex theory of
mind, so as to be sure that we understand it absolutely before going on to consider those of its consequences of which I am more particularly to speak.
I am not quite sure that its full scope is grasped even
by those who have most zealously promulgated it.   I
am not sure, for example, that all physiologists see that
it commits them to regarding the mind as an essentially teleological mechanism.   I mean by this that the
conceiving or theorizing faculty — the mind's middle
department — functions *exclusively for the sake of
ends* that do not exist at all in the world of impressions we receive by way of our senses, but are set by
our emotional and practical subjectivity altogether.[1]
It is a transformer of the world of our impressions
into a totally different world, — the world of our conception; and the transformation is effected in the
interests of our volitional nature, and for no other
purpose whatsoever.   Destroy the volitional nature,
the definite subjective purposes, preferences, fond-

---

[1] See some Remarks on Spencer's Definition of Mind, in the
Journal of Speculative Philosophy for January, 1878.

nesses for certain effects, forms, orders, and not the slightest motive would remain for the brute order of our experience to be remodelled at all. But, as we have the elaborate volitional constitution we do have, the remodelling must be effected; there is no escape. The world's contents are *given* to each of us in an order so foreign to our subjective interests that we can hardly by an effort of the imagination picture to ourselves what it is like. We have to break that order altogether, — and by picking out from it the items which concern us, and connecting them with others far away, which we say 'belong' with them, we are able to make out definite threads of sequence and tendency; to foresee particular liabilities and get ready for them; and to enjoy simplicity and harmony in place of what was chaos. Is not the sum of your actual experience taken at this moment and impartially added together an utter chaos? The strains of my voice, the lights and shades inside the room and out, the murmur of the wind, the ticking of the clock, the various organic feelings you may happen individually to possess, do these make a whole at all? Is it not the only condition of your mental sanity in the midst of them that most of them should become non-existent for you, and that a few others — the sounds, I hope, which I am uttering — should evoke from places in your memory that have nothing to do with this scene associates fitted to combine with them in what we call a rational train of thought, — rational, because it leads to a conclusion which we have some organ to appreciate? We have no organ or faculty to appreciate the simply given order. The real world as it is given objectively at this moment is the sum total of all its beings and

events now. But can we think of such a sum? Can
we realize for an instant what a cross-section of all
existence at a definite point of time would be? While
I talk and the flies buzz, a sea-gull catches a fish at
the mouth of the Amazon, a tree falls in the Adiron-
dack wilderness, a man sneezes in Germany, a horse
dies in Tartary, and twins are born in France. What
does that mean? Does the contemporaneity of these
events with one another and with a million others as
disjointed, form a rational bond between them, and
unite them into anything that means for us a world?
Yet just such a collateral contemporaneity, and nothing else, is the real order of the world. It is an order
with which we have nothing to do but to get away
from it as fast as possible. As I said, we break it:
we break it into histories, and we break it into arts,
and we break it into sciences; and then we begin to
feel at home. We make ten thousand separate serial
orders of it, and on any one of these we react as
though the others did not exist. We discover among
its various parts relations that were never given to
sense at all (mathematical relations, tangents, squares,
and roots and logarithmic functions), and out of an
infinite number of these we call certain ones essential
and lawgiving, and ignore the rest. Essential these
relations are, but only *for our purpose,* the other relations being just as real and present as they; and our
purpose is to *conceive simply* and to *foresee.* Are not
simple conception and prevision subjective ends pure
and simple? They are the ends of what we call
science; and the miracle of miracles, a miracle not
yet exhaustively cleared up by any philosophy, is
that the given order lends itself to the remodelling.
It shows itself plastic to many of our scientific, to

many of our æsthetic, to many of our practical purposes and ends.

When the man of affairs, the artist, or the man of science fails, he is not rebutted. He tries again. He says the impressions of sense *must* give way, *must* be reduced to the desiderated form.[1] They all postulate in the interests of their volitional nature a harmony between the latter and the nature of things. The theologian does no more. And the reflex doctrine of the mind's structure, though all theology should as yet have failed of its endeavor, could but confess that the endeavor itself at least obeyed in form the mind's most necessary law.[2]

Now for the question I asked above: What kind of a being would God be if he did exist ? The word ' God ' has come to mean many things in the history

[1] "No amount of failure in the attempt to subject the world of sensible experience to a thorough-going system of conceptions, and to bring all happenings back to cases of immutably valid law, is able to shake our faith in the rightness of our principles. We hold fast to our demand that even the greatest apparent confusion must sooner or later solve itself in transparent formulas. We begin the work ever afresh ; and, refusing to believe that nature will permanently withhold the reward of our exertions, think rather that we have hitherto only failed to push them in the right direction. And all this pertinacity flows from a conviction that we *have no right* to renounce the fulfilment of our task. What, in short sustains the courage of investigators is the force of obligation of an ethical idea." (Sigwart: Logik, bd. ii., p. 23.)

This is a true account of the spirit of science. Does it essentially differ from the spirit of religion ? And is any one entitled to say in advance, that, while the one form of faith shall be crowned with success, the other is certainly doomed to fail?

[2] Concerning the transformation of the given order into the order of conception, see S. H. Hodgson, The Philosophy of Reflection, chap. v. ; H. Lotze, Logik, sects. 342–351 ; C. Sigwart, Logik, sects. 60-63, 105.

of human thought, from Venus and Jupiter to the 'Idee' which figures in the pages of Hegel. Even the laws of physical nature have, in these positivistic times, been held worthy of divine honor and presented as the only fitting object of our reverence.[1] Of course, if our discussion is to bear any fruit, we must mean something more definite than this. We must not call any object of our loyalty a 'God' without more ado, simply because to awaken our loyalty happens to be one of God's functions. He must have some intrinsic characteristics of his own besides; and theism must mean the faith of that man who believes that the object of *his* loyalty has those other attributes, negative or positive, as the case may be.

Now, as regards a great many of the attributes of God, and their amounts and mutual relations, the world has been delivered over to disputes. All such may for our present purpose be considered as quite inessential. Not only such matters as his mode of revealing himself, the precise extent of his providence and power and their connection with our free-will, the proportion of his mercy to his justice, and the amount of his responsibility for evil; but also his metaphysical relation to the phenomenal world, whether causal, substantial, ideal, or what not, — are affairs of purely sectarian opinion that need not concern us at all. Whoso debates them presupposes the essential features of theism to be granted already; and it is with these essential features, the bare poles of the subject, that our business exclusively lies.

[1] Haeckel has recently (Der Monismus, 1893, p. 37) proposed the Cosmic Ether as a divinity fitted to reconcile science with theistic faith.

Now, what are these essential features ? First, it is essential that God be conceived as the deepest power in the universe; and, second, he must be conceived under the form of a mental personality. The personality need not be determined intrinsically any further than is involved in the holding of certain things dear, and in the recognition of our dispositions toward those things, the things themselves being all good and righteous things. But, extrinsically considered, so to speak, God's personality is to be regarded, like any other personality, as something lying outside of my own and other than me, and whose existence I simply come upon and find. A power not ourselves, then, which not only makes for righteousness, but means it, and which recognizes us, — such is the definition which I think nobody will be inclined to dispute. Various are the attempts to shadow forth the other lineaments of so supreme a personality to our human imagination; various the ways of conceiving in what mode the recognition, the hearkening to our cry, can come. Some are gross and idolatrous; some are the most sustained efforts man's intellect has ever made to keep still living on that subtle edge of things where speech and thought expire. But, with all these differences, the essence remains unchanged. In whatever other respects the divine personality may differ from ours or may resemble it, the two are consanguineous at least in this, — that both have purposes for which they care, and each can hear the other's call.

Meanwhile, we can already see one consequence and one point of connection with the reflex-action theory of mind. Any mind, constructed on the

triadic-reflex pattern, must first get its impression
from the object which it confronts; then define what
that object is, and decide what active measures its
presence demands; and finally react. The stage of
reaction depends on the stage of definition, and these,
of course, on the nature of the impressing object.
When the objects are concrete, particular, and familiar, our reactions are firm and certain enough,
— often instinctive. I see the desk, and lean on it;
I see your quiet faces, and I continue to talk. But
the objects will not stay concrete and particular:
they fuse themselves into general essences, and they
sum themselves into a whole,—the universe. And
then the object that confronts us, that knocks on
our mental door and asks to be let in, and fixed and
decided upon and actively met, is just this whole
universe itself and its essence.

What are *they*, and how shall I meet *them* ?

The whole flood of faiths and systems here rush in.
Philosophies and denials of philosophy, religions and
atheisms, scepticisms and mysticisms, confirmed
emotional moods and habitual practical biases, jos-
tle one another; for all are alike trials, hasty, prolix,
or of seemly length, to answer this momentous question. And the function of them all, long or short,
that which the moods and the systems alike subserve and pass into, is the third stage, — the stage
of action. For no one of them itself is final. They
form but the middle segment of the mental curve,
and not its termination. As the last theoretic pulse
dies away, it does not leave the mental process complete: it is but the forerunner of the practical moment, in which alone the cycle of mentality finds its
rhythmic pause.

We easily delude ourselves about this middle stage. Sometimes we think it final, and sometimes we fail to see, amid the monstrous diversity in the length and complication of the cogitations which may fill it, that it can have but one essential function, and that the one we have pointed out, — the function of defining the direction which our activity, immediate or remote, shall take.

If I simply say, "Vanitas vanitatum, omnia vanitas!" I am defining the total nature of things in a way that carries practical consequences with it as decidedly as if I write a treatise De Natura Rerum in twenty volumes. The treatise may trace its consequences more minutely than the saying; but the only worth of either treatise or saying is that the consequences are there. The long definition can do no more than draw them; the short definition does no less. Indeed, it may be said that if two apparently different definitions of the reality before us should have identical consequences, those two definitions would really be identical definitions, made delusively to appear different merely by the different verbiage in which they are expressed.[1]

My time is unfortunately too short to stay and give to this truth the development it deserves; but I will assume that you grant it without further parley, and pass to the next step in my argument. And here, too, I shall have to bespeak your close attention for a moment, while I pass over the subject far more rap-

[1] See the admirably original "Illustrations of the Logic of Science," by C. S. Peirce, especially the second paper, "How to make our Thoughts clear," in the Popular Science Monthly for January, 1878.

idly than it deserves. Whether true or false, any view of the universe which shall completely satisfy the mind must obey conditions of the mind's own imposing, must at least let the mind be the umpire to decide whether it be fit to be called a rational universe or not. Not any nature of things which may seem to *be* will also seem to be *ipso facto* rational; and if it do not seem rational, it will afflict the mind with a ceaseless uneasiness, till it be formulated or interpreted in some other and more congenial way. The study of what the mind's criteria of rationality are, the definition of its exactions in this respect, form an intensely interesting subject into which I cannot enter now with any detail.[1] But so much I think you will grant me without argument, — that all three departments of the mind alike have a vote in the matter, and that no conception will pass muster which violates any of their essential modes of activity, or which leaves them without a chance to work. By what title is it that every would-be universal formula, every system of philosophy which rears its head, receives the inevitable critical volley from one half of mankind, and falls to the rear, to become at the very best the creed of some partial sect? Either it has dropped out of its net some of our impressions of sense, — what we call the facts of nature, — or it has left the theoretic and defining department with a lot of inconsistencies and unmediated transitions on its hands; or else, finally, it has left some one or more of our fundamental active and emotional powers with no object outside of themselves to react-on or to live for. Any one of these defects is fatal to its complete success. Some one

---

[1] On this subject, see the preceding Essay.

will be sure to discover the flaw, to scout the system, and to seek another in its stead.

I need not go far to collect examples to illustrate to an audience of theologians what I mean. Nor will you in particular, as champions of the Unitarianism of New England, be slow to furnish, from the motives which led to your departure from our orthodox ancestral Calvinism, instances enough under the third or practical head. A God who gives so little scope to love, a predestination which takes from endeavor all its zest with all its fruit, are irrational conceptions, because they say to our most cherished powers, There is no object for you.

Well, just as within the limits of theism some kinds are surviving others by reason of their greater practical rationality, so theism itself, by reason of its practical rationality, is certain to survive all lower creeds. Materialism and agnosticism, even were they true, could never gain universal and popular acceptance; for they both, alike, give a solution of things which is irrational to the practical third of our nature, and in which we can never volitionally feel at home. Each comes out of the second or theoretic stage of mental functioning, with its definition of the essential nature of things, its formula of formulas prepared. The whole array of active forces of our nature stands waiting, impatient for the word which shall tell them how to discharge themselves most deeply and worthily upon life. "Well!" cry they, "what shall we do?" "Ignoramus, ignorabimus!" says agnosticism. "React upon atoms and their concussions!" says materialism. What a collapse! The mental train misses fire, the middle fails to ignite the end, the cycle breaks down half-way to its conclusion; and the active powers left alone, with no proper object on which to vent their energy, must either atrophy, sicken, and die, or else by their pent-up convulsions and excitement keep the whole machinery in a fever until some less incommensurable solution, some more practically rational formulá, shall provide a normal issue for the currents of the soul.

Now, theism always stands ready with the most practically rational solution it is possible to conceive. Not an energy of our active nature to which it does not authoritatively appeal, not an emotion of which it does not normally and naturally release the springs. At a single stroke, it changes the dead blank *it* of the world into a living *thou*, with whom the whole man may have dealings. To you, at any rate, I need waste no words in trying to prove its supreme commensurateness with all the demands that department Number Three of the mind has the power to impose on department Number Two.

Our volitional nature must then, until the end of time, exert a constant pressure upon the other departments of the mind to induce them to function to theistic conclusions. No contrary formulas can be more than provisionally held. Infra-theistic theories must be always in unstable equilibrium; for department Number Three ever lurks in ambush, ready to assert its rights; and on the slightest show of justification it makes its fatal spring, and converts them into the other form in which alone mental peace and order can permanently reign.

The question is, then, *Can* departments One and Two, *can* the facts of nature and the theoretic elaboration of them, always lead to theistic conclusions?

The future history of philosophy is the only authority capable of answering that question. I, at all events, must not enter into it to-day, as that would be to abandon the purely natural-history point of view I mean to keep.

This only is certain, that the theoretic faculty lives between two fires which never give her rest, and make her incessantly revise her formulations. If she sink into a premature, short-sighted, and idolatrous theism, in comes department Number One with its battery of facts of sense, and dislodges her from her dogmatic repose. If she lazily subside into equilibrium with the same facts of sense viewed in their simple mechanical outwardness, up starts the practical reason with its demands, and makes *that* couch a bed of thorns. From generation to generation thus it goes, — now a movement of reception from without, now one of expansion from within; department Number Two always worked to death, yet never excused from taking the most responsible part in the arrangements. To-day, a crop of new facts; to-morrow, a flowering of new motives, — the theoretic faculty always having to effect the transition, and life growing withal so complex and subtle and immense that her powers of conceiving are almost ruptured with the strain. See how, in France, the mummy-cloths of the academic and official theistic philosophy are rent by the facts of evolution, and how the young thinkers are at work! See, in Great Britain, how the dryness of the strict associationist school, which under the ministration of Mill, Bain, and Spencer dominated us but yesterday, gives way to more generous idealisms, born of more urgent emotional needs and wrapping the same facts in far more massive intellectual harmonies! These are but tackings to the common

port, to that ultimate *Weltanschauung* of maximum
subjective as well as objective richness, which, whatever its other properties may be, will at any rate wear
the theistic form.

Here let me say one word about a remark we often
hear coming from the anti-theistic wing: It is base,
it is vile, it is the lowest depth of immorality, to allow
department Number Three to interpose its demands,
and have any vote in the question of what is true and
what is false; the mind must be a passive, reactionless sheet of white paper, on which reality will simply
come and register its own philosophic definition, as
the pen registers the curve on the sheet of a chrono-
graph. " Of all the cants that are canted in this cant-
ing age" this has always seemed to me the most
wretched, especially when it comes from professed
psychologists. As if the mind could, consistently
with its definition, be a reactionless sheet at all! As
if conception could possibly occur except for a teleological purpose, except to show us the way from a
state of things our senses cognize to another state
of things our will desires! As if 'science' itself
were anything else than such an end of desire,
and a most peculiar one at that! And as if the
'truths' of bare physics in particular, which these
sticklers for intellectual purity contend to be the only
uncontaminated form, were not as great an alteration
and falsification of the simply 'given' order of the
world, into an order conceived solely for the mind's
convenience and delight, as any theistic doctrine possibly can be!

Physics is but one chapter in the great jugglery
which our conceiving faculty is forever playing with

the order of being as it presents itself to our reception. It transforms the unutterable dead level and
continuum of the 'given' world into an utterly unlike
world of sharp differences and hierarchic subordina-
tions for no other reason than to satisfy certain subjective passions we possess.[1]

And, so far as we can see, the given world is there
only for the sake of the operation. At any rate, to
operate upon it is our only chance of approaching it;
for never can we get a glimpse of it in the unimaginable insipidity of its virgin estate. To bid the man's
subjective interests be passive till truth express itself
from out the environment, is to bid the sculptor's
chisel be passive till the statue express itself from out
the stone. Operate we must! and the only choice
left us is that between operating to poor or to rich
results. The only possible duty there can be in the
matter is the duty of getting the richest results that
the material given will allow. The richness lies, of
course, in the energy of all three departments of the
mental cycle. Not a sensible 'fact' of department
One must be left in the cold, not a faculty of department Three be paralyzed; and department Two must
form an indestructible bridge. It is natural that the
habitual neglect of department One by theologians
should arouse indignation; but it is most *un*natural
that the indignation should take the form of a wholesale denunciation of department Three. It is the
story of Kant's dove over again, denouncing the pres-

---

[1] "As soon as it is recognized that our thought, as logic deals with
it, reposes on our *will to think*, the primacy of the will, even in
the theoretical sphere, must be conceded; and the last of presup-
positions is not merely [Kant's] that 'I think' must accompany all
my representations, but also that 'I will' must dominate all my
thinking." (Sigwart: Logik, ii. 25.)

sure of the air. Certain of our positivists keep chim-
ing to us, that, amid the wreck of every other god
and idol, one divinity still stands upright, — that his
name is Scientific Truth, and that he has but one
commandment, but that one supreme, saying, *Thou
shalt not be a theist,* for that would be to satisfy thy
subjective propensities, and the satisfaction of those
is intellectual damnation. These most conscientious
gentlemen think they have jumped off their own feet,
— emancipated their mental operations from the control of their subjective propensities at large and *in
toto.* But they are deluded. They have simply
chosen from among the entire set of propensities at
their command those that were certain to construct,
out of the materials given, the leanest, lowest, arid-
est result, — namely, the bare molecular world, — and
they have sacrificed all the rest.[1]

Man's chief difference from the brutes lies in the
exuberant excess of his subjective propensities, —
his pre-eminence over them simply and solely in the
number and in the fantastic and unnecessary character of his wants, physical, moral, æsthetic, and intellectual. Had his whole life not been a quest for the
superfluous, he would never have established himself
as inexpugnably as he has done in the necessary.
And from the consciousness of this he should draw
the lesson that his wants are to be trusted; that even

---

[1] As our ancestors said, *Fiat justitia, pereat mundus,* so we, who do
not believe in justice or any absolute good, must, according to these
prophets, be willing to see the world perish, in order that *scientia fiat.*
Was there ever a more exquisite idol of the den, or rather of the *shop*?
In the clean sweep to be made of superstitions, let the idol of stern
obligation to be scientific go with the rest, and people will have a
fair chance to understand one another. But this blowing of hot and
of cold makes nothing but confusion.

when their gratification seems farthest off, the uneasiness they occasion is still the best guide of his life, and will lead him to issues entirely beyond his present powers of reckoning. Prune down his extravagance, sober him, and you undo him. The appetite for immediate consistency at any cost, or what the logicians call the 'law of parsimony,' — which is nothing but the passion for conceiving the universe in the most labor-saving way, — will, if made the exclusive law of the mind, end by blighting the development of the intellect itself quite as much as that of the feelings or the will. The scientific conception· of the world as an army of molecules gratifies this appetite after its fashion most exquisitely. But if the religion of exclusive scientificism should ever succeed in suffocating all other appetites out of a nation's mind, and imbuing a whole race with the persuasion that simplicity and consistency demand a *tabula rasa* to be made of every notion that does not form part of the *soi-disant* scientific synthesis, that nation, that race, will just as surely go to ruin, and fall a prey to their more richly constituted neighbors, as the beasts of the field, as a whole, have fallen a prey to man.

I have myself little fear for our Anglo-Saxon race. Its moral, æsthetic, and practical wants form too dense a stubble to be mown by any scientific Occam's razor that has yet been forged. The knights of the razor will never form among us more than a sect; but when I see their fraternity increasing in numbers, and, what is worse, when I see their negations acquiring almost as much prestige and authority as their affirmations legitimately claim over the minds of the docile public, I feel as if the influences working in the direction of our mental barbarization were be-

ginning to be rather strong, and needed some positive counteraction. And when I ask myself from
what quarter the invasion may best be checked, I
can find no answer as good as the one suggested by
casting my eyes around this room. For this needful
task, no fitter body of men than the Unitarian clergy
exists. Who can uphold the rights of department
Three of the mind with better grace than those who
long since showed how they could fight and suffer for
department One ? As, then, you burst the bonds of
a narrow ecclesiastical tradition, by insisting that no
fact of sense or result of science must be left out of
account in the religious synthesis, so may you still be
the champions of mental completeness and all-sided-
ness. May you, with equal success, avert the forma-
tion of a narrow scientific tradition, and burst the
bonds of any synthesis which would pretend to leave
out of account those forms of being, those relations
of reality, to which at present our active and emotional tendencies are our only avenues of approach.
I hear it said that Unitarianism is not growing in
these days. I know nothing of the truth of the statement; but if it be true, it is surely because the great
ship of Orthodoxy is nearing the port and the pilot
is being taken on board. If you will only lead
in a theistic science, as successfully as you have led
in a scientific theology, your separate name as Uni-
tarians may perish from the mouths of men ; for your
task will have been done, and your function at an end.
Until that distant day, you have work enough in both
directions awaiting you.

Meanwhile, let me pass to the next division of our
subject. I said that we are forced to regard God as

the normal object of the mind's belief, inasmuch as any conception that falls short of God is irrational, if the word 'rational' be taken in its fullest sense; while any conception that goes beyond God is impossible, if the human mind be constructed after the triadic-reflex pattern we have discussed at such length. The first half of the thesis has been disposed of. Infra-theistic conceptions, materialisms and agnosticisms, are irrational because they are inadequate stimuli to man's practical nature. I have now to justify the latter half of the thesis.

I dare say it may for an instant have perplexed some of you that I should speak of conceptions that aimed at going beyond God, and of attempts to fly above him or outbid him; so I will now explain exactly what I mean. In defining the essential attributes of God, I said he was a personality lying outside our own and other than us, — a power not ourselves. Now, the attempts to fly beyond theism, of which I speak, are attempts to get over this ultimate duality of God and his believer, and to transform it into some sort or other of identity. If infra-theistic ways of looking on the world leave it in the third person, a mere *it;* and if theism turns the *it* into a *thou,* — so we may say that these other theories try to cover it with the mantle of the first person, and to make it a part of *me.*

I am well aware that I begin here to tread on ground in which trenchant distinctions may easily seem to mutilate the facts.

That sense of emotional reconciliation with God which characterizes the highest moments of the theistic consciousness may be described as 'oneness' with him, and so from the very bosom of theism a

monistic doctrine seem to arise. But this consciousness of self-surrender, of absolute practical union
between one's self and the divine object of one's contemplation, is a totally different thing from any sort
of substantial identity. Still the object God and the
subject I are two. Still I simply come upon him, and
find his existence given to me; and the climax of my
practical union with what is given, forms at the same
time the climax of my perception that as a numerical
fact of existence I am something radically other than
the Divinity with whose effulgence I am filled.

Now, it seems to me that the only sort of union of
creature with creator with which theism, properly so
called, comports, is of this emotional and practical
kind; and it is based unchangeably on the empirical
fact that the thinking subject and the object thought
are numerically two. How my mind and will, which
are not God, can yet cognize and leap to meet him,
how I ever came to be so separate from him, and how
God himself came to be at all, are problems that for
the theist can remain unsolved and insoluble forever.
It is sufficient for him to know that he himself simply
is, and needs God; and that behind this universe God
simply is and will be forever, and will in some way
hear his call. In the practical assurance of these
empirical facts, without 'Erkentnisstheorie' or philosophical ontology, without metaphysics of emanation
or creation to justify or make them more intelligible,
in the blessedness of their mere acknowledgment as
given, lie all the peace and power he craves. The
floodgates of the religious life are opened, and the full
currents can pour through.

It is this empirical and practical side of the theistic
position, its theoretic chastity and modesty, which I

wish to accentuate here. The highest flights of theistic mysticism, far from pretending to penetrate the
secrets of the *me* and the *thou* in worship, and to
transcend the dualism by an act of intelligence, simply turn their backs on such attempts. The problem
for them has simply vanished, — vanished from the
sight of an attitude which refuses to notice such futile
theoretic difficulties. Get but that "peace of God
which passeth understanding," and the questions of
the understanding will cease from puzzling and pedantic scruples be at rest. In other words, theistic mysticism, that form of theism which at first sight seems
most to have transcended the fundamental otherness
of God from man, has done it least of all in the theoretic way. The pattern of its procedure is precisely
that of the simplest man dealing with the simplest
fact of his environment. Both he and the theist tarry
in department Two of their minds only so long as is
necessary to define what is the presence that confronts them. The theist decides that its character is
such as to be fitly responded to on his part by a
religious reaction; and into that reaction he forthwith pours his soul. His insight into the *what* of life
leads to results so immediately and intimately rational
that the *why*, the *how*, and the *whence* of it are questions that lose all urgency. 'Gefühl ist Alles,' Faust
says. The channels of department Three have drained
those of department Two of their contents; and happiness over the fact that being has made itself what
it is, evacuates all speculation as to how it could make
itself at all.

But now, although to most human minds such a
position as this will be the position of rational equilibrium, it is not difficult to bring forward certain

considerations, in the light of which so simple and practical a mental movement begins to seem rather short-winded and second-rate and devoid of intellectual style. This easy acceptance of an opaque limit to our speculative insight; this satisfaction with a Being whose character we simply apprehend without comprehending anything more about him, and with whom after a certain point our dealings can be only of a volitional and emotional sort; above all, this sitting down contented with a blank unmediated dualism, — are they not the very picture of unfaithfulness to the rights and duties of our theoretic reason?

Surely, if the universe is reasonable (and we must believe that it is so), it must be susceptible, potentially at least, of being reasoned *out* to the last drop without residuum. Is it not rather an insult to the very word 'rational' to say that the rational character of the universe and its creator means no more than that we practically feel at home in their presence, and that our powers are a match for their demands? Do they not in fact demand to be *understood* by us still more than to be reacted on? Is not the unparalleled development of department Two of the mind in man his crowning glory and his very essence; and may not the *knowing of the truth* be his absolute vocation? And if it is, ought he flatly to acquiesce in a spiritual life of 'reflex type,' whose form is no higher than that of the life that animates his spinal cord, — nay, indeed, that animates the writhing segments of any mutilated worm?

It is easy to see how such arguments and queries may result in the erection of an ideal of our mental destiny, far different from the simple and practical religious one we have described. We may well begin

to ask whether such things as practical reactions can
be the final upshot and purpose of all our cognitive energy.   Mere outward acts, changes in the position of parts of matter (for they are nothing else),
can they possibly be the culmination and consummation of our relations with the nature of things?   Can
they possibly form a result to which our godlike
powers of insight shall be judged merely subservient?
Such an idea, if we scan it closely, soon begins to
seem rather absurd.   Whence this piece of matter
comes and whither that one goes, what difference
ought that to make to the nature of things, except
so far as with the comings and the goings our wonderful inward conscious harvest may be reaped?

And so, very naturally and gradually, one may be
led from the theistic and practical point of view to
what I shall call the *gnostical* one.   We may think
that department Three of the mind, with its doings of
right and its doings of wrong, must be there only to
serve department Two; and we may suspect that the
sphere of our activity exists for no other purpose than
to illumine our cognitive consciousness by the experience of its results.   Are not all sense and all emotion at bottom but turbid and perplexed modes of what
in its clarified shape is intelligent cognition?   Is not
all experience just the eating of the fruit of the tree
of *knowledge* of good and evil, and nothing more?

These questions fan the fire of an unassuageable
gnostic thirst, which is as far removed from theism in
one direction as agnosticism was removed from it in
the other; and which aspires to nothing less than an
absolute unity of knowledge with its object, and refuses
to be satisfied short of a fusion and solution and satu-
ration of both impression and action with reason, and

an absorption of all three departments of the mind
into one.   Time would fail us to-day (even had I the
learning, which I have not) to speak of gnostic systems in detail.   The aim of all of them is to shadow
forth a sort of process by which spirit, emerging from
its beginnings and exhausting the whole circle of finite
experience in its sweep, shall at last return and possess itself as its own object at the climax of its career.
This climax is the religious consciousness.   At the
giddy height of this conception, whose latest and
best known form is the Hegelian philosophy, definite
words fail to serve their purpose; and the ultimate
goal, — where object and subject, worshipped and wor-
shipper, facts and the knowledge of them, fall into
one, and where no other is left outstanding beyond this
one that alone is, and that we may call indifferently
act or fact, reality or idea, God or creation, — this
goal, I say, has to be adumbrated to our halting and
gasping intelligence by coarse physical metaphors,
'positings' and 'self-returnings' and 'removals' and
'settings free,' which hardly help to make the matter
clear.

But from the midst of the curdling and the circling
of it all we seem dimly to catch a glimpse of a state
in which the reality to be known and the power of
knowing shall have become so mutually adequate
that each exhaustively is absorbed by the other and
the twain become one flesh, and in which the light
shall somehow have soaked up all the outer darkness
into its own ubiquitous beams.   Like all headlong
ideals, this apotheosis of the bare conceiving faculty
has its depth and wildness, its pang and its charm.
To many it sings a truly siren strain; and so long
as it is held only as a postulate, as a mere vanishing

point to give perspective to our intellectual aim, it is hard to see any empirical title by which we may deny the legitimacy of gnosticism's claims. That we are not as yet near the goal it prefigures can never be a reason why we might not continue indefinitely to approach it; and to all sceptical arguments, drawn from our reason's actual finiteness, gnosticism can still oppose its indomitable faith in the infinite character of its potential destiny.

Now, here it is that the physiologist's generalization, as it seems to me, may fairly come in, and by ruling any such extravagant faith out of court help to legitimate our personal mistrust of its pretensions. I confess that I myself have always had a great mistrust of the pretensions of the gnostic faith. Not only do I utterly fail to understand what a cognitive faculty erected into the absolute of being, with itself as its object, can mean; but even if we grant it a being other than itself for object, I cannot reason myself out of the belief that however familiar and at home we might become with the character of that being, the bare being of it, the fact that it is there at all, must always be something blankly given and presupposed in order that conception may begin its work; must in short lie beyond speculation, and not be enveloped in its sphere.

Accordingly, it is with no small pleasure that as a student of physiology and psychology I find the only lesson I can learn from these sciences to be one that corroborates these convictions. From its first dawn to its highest actual attainment, we find that the cognitive faculty, where it appears to exist at all, appears but as one element in an organic mental whole, and as a minister to higher mental powers, — the powers

of will. Such a thing as its emancipation and abso-
lution from these organic relations receives no faintest color of plausibility from any fact we can discern.
Arising as a part, in a mental and objective world
which are both larger than itself, it must, whatever its
powers of growth may be (and I am far from wishing
to disparage them), remain a part to the end. This
is the character of the cognitive element in all the
mental life we know, and we have no reason to suppose that that character will ever change. On the
contrary, it is more than probable that to the end of
time our power of moral and volitional response to
the nature of things will be the deepest organ of communication therewith we shall ever possess. In every
being that is real there is something external to, and
sacred from, the grasp of every other. God's being
is sacred from ours. To co-operate with his creation
by the best and rightest response seems all he wants
of us. In such co-operation with his purposes, not in
any chimerical speculative conquest of him, not in
any theoretic drinking of him up, must lie the real
meaning of our destiny.

This is nothing new. All men know it at those rare
moments when the soul sobers herself, and leaves off
her chattering and protesting and insisting about this
formula or that. In the silence of our theories we
then seem to listen, and to hear something like the
pulse of Being beat; and it is borne in upon us that
the mere turning of the character, the dumb willingness to suffer and to serve this universe, is more than
all theories about it put together. The most any
theory about it can do is to bring us to that. Certain it is that the acutest theories, the greatest intellectual power, the most elaborate education, are a

sheer mockery when, as too often happens, they feed
mean motives and a nerveless will.   And it is equally
certain that a resolute moral energy, no matter how
inarticulate or unequipped with learning its owner
may be, extorts from us a respect we should never pay
were we not satisfied that the essential root of human
personality lay there.

I have sketched my subject in the briefest outlines;
but still I hope you will agree that I have established
my point, and that the physiological view of mentality, so far from invalidating, can but give aid and comfort to the theistic attitude of mind.   Between agnosticism and gnosticism, theism stands midway, and
holds to what is true in each.   With agnosticism, it
goes so far as to confess that we cannot know how
Being made itself or us.   With gnosticism, it goes
so far as to insist that we can know Being's character
when made, and how it asks us to behave.

If any one fear that in insisting so strongly that behavior is the aim and end of every sound philosophy
I have curtailed the dignity and scope of the speculative function in us, I can only reply that in this ascertainment of the *character* of Being lies an almost infinite speculative task.   Let the voluminous considerations by which all modern thought converges toward
idealistic or pan-psychic conclusions speak for me.
Let the pages of a Hodgson, of a Lotze, of a Renouvier, reply whether within the limits drawn by
purely empirical theism the speculative faculty finds
not, and shall not always find, enough to do.   But do
it little or much, its *place* in a philosophy is always
the same, and is set by the structural form of the
mind.   Philosophies, whether expressed in sonnets or

systems, all must wear this form. The thinker starts from some experience of the practical world, and asks its meaning. He launches himself upon the speculative sea, and makes a voyage long or short. He ascends into the empyrean, and communes with the eternal essences. But whatever his achievements and discoveries be while gone, the utmost result they can issue in is some new practical maxim or resolve, or the denial of some old one, with which inevitably he is sooner or later washed ashore on the *terra firma* of concrete life again.

Whatever thought takes this voyage is a philosophy. We have seen how theism takes it. And in the philosophy of a thinker who, though long neglected, is doing much to renovate the spiritual life of his native France to-day (I mean Charles Renouvier, whose writings ought to be better known among us than they are), we have an instructive example of the way in which this very empirical element in theism, its confession of an ultimate opacity in things, of a dimension of being which escapes our theoretic control, may suggest a most definite practical conclusion, — this one, namely, that ' our wills are free.' I will say nothing of Renouvier's line of reasoning; it is contained in many volumes which I earnestly recommend to your attention.[1] But to enforce my doctrine that the number of volumes is not what makes the philosophy, let me conclude by recalling to you the little poem of Tennyson, published last year, in which the speculative voyage is made, and the same conclusion reached in a few lines : —

[1] Especially the Essais de Critique Générale, 2me Edition, 6 vols., 12mo, Paris, 1875; and the Esquisse d'une Classification Systématique des Doctrines Philosophiques, 2 vols., 8vo, Paris, 1885.

" Out of the deep, my child, out of the deep,
　From that great deep before our world begins,
　Whereon the Spirit of God moves as he will, —
　Out of the deep, my child, out of the deep,
　From that true world within the world we see,
　Whereof our world is but the bounding shore, —
　Out of the deep, Spirit, out of the deep,
　With this ninth moon that sends the hidden sun
　Down yon dark sea, thou comest, darling boy.
　For in the world which is not ours, they said,
　' Let us make man,' and that which should be man,
　From that one light no man can look upon,
　Drew to this shore lit by the suns and moons
　And all the shadows.　O dear Spirit, half-lost
　In thine own shadow and this fleshly sign
　That thou art thou, — who wailest being born
　And banish'd into mystery, . . .
　　　　　　　　. . . our mortal veil
　And shattered phantom of that Infinite One,
　Who made thee unconceivably thyself
　Out of his whole world-self and all in all, —
　Live thou, and of the grain and husk, the grape
　And ivyberry, choose; and still depart
　From death to death through life and life, and find
　Nearer and ever nearer Him who wrought
　Not matter, nor the finite-infinite,
　But this main miracle, that thou art thou,
　With power on thine own act and on the world."

THE DILEMMA OF DETERMINISM.[1]

A COMMON opinion prevails that the juice has ages ago been pressed out of the free-will controversy, and that no new champion can do more than warm up stale arguments which every one has heard. This is a radical mistake. I know of no subject less worn out, or in which inventive genius has a better chance of breaking open new ground, — not, perhaps, of forcing a conclusion or of coercing assent, but of deepening our sense of what the issue between the two parties really is, of what the ideas of fate and of free-will imply. At our very side almost, in the past few years, we have seen falling in rapid succession from the press works that present the alternative in entirely novel lights. Not to speak of the English disciples of Hegel, such as Green and Bradley; not to speak of Hinton and Hodgson, nor of Hazard here, — we see in the writings of Renouvier, Fouillée, and Delbœuf[2] how completely changed and refreshed is the form of all the old disputes. I cannot pretend to vie in originality with any of the masters I have named, and my ambition limits itself to just one little point. If I can make two of the necessarily implied corollaries

---

[1] An Address to the Harvard Divinity Students, published in the Unitarian Review for September, 1884.

[2] And I may now say Charles S. Peirce, — see the Monist, for 1892–93.

of determinism clearer to you than they have been made before, I shall have made it possible for you to decide for or against that doctrine with a better understanding of what you are about. And if you prefer not to decide at all, but to remain doubters, you will at least see more plainly what the subject of your hesitation is. I thus disclaim openly on the threshold all pretension to prove to you that the freedom of the will is true. The most I hope is to induce some of you to follow my own example in assuming it true, and acting as if it were true. If it be true, it seems to me that this is involved in the strict logic of the case. Its truth ought not to be forced willy-nilly down our indifferent throats. It ought to be freely espoused by men who can equally well turn their backs upon it. In other words, our first act of freedom, if we are free, ought in all inward propriety to be to affirm that we are free. This should exclude, it seems to me, from the free-will side of the question all hope of a coercive demonstration, — a demonstration which I, for one, am perfectly contented to go without.

With thus much understood at the outset, we can advance. But not without one more point understood as well. The arguments I am about to urge all proceed on two suppositions: first, when we make theories about the world and discuss them with one another, we do so in order to attain a conception of things which shall give us subjective satisfaction; and, second, if there be two conceptions, and the one seems to us, on the whole, more rational than the other, we are entitled to suppose that the more rational one is the truer of the two. I hope that you are all willing to make these suppositions with me;

for I am afraid that if there be any of you here who are not, they will find little edification in the rest of what I have to say. I cannot stop to argue the point; but I myself believe that all the magnificent achievements of mathematical and physical science — our doctrines of evolution, of uniformity of law, and the rest — proceed from our indomitable desire to cast the world into a more rational shape in our minds than the shape into which it is thrown there by the crude order of our experience. The world has shown itself, to a great extent, plastic to this demand of ours for rationality. How much farther it will show itself plastic no one can say. Our only means of finding out is to try; and I, for one, feel as free to try conceptions of moral as of mechanical or of logical rationality. If a certain formula for expressing the nature of the world violates my moral demand, I shall feel as free to throw it overboard, or at least to doubt it, as if it disappointed my demand for uniformity of sequence, for example; the one demand being, so far as I can see, quite as subjective and emotional as the other is. The principle of causality, for example, — what is it but a postulate, an empty name covering simply a demand that the sequence of events shall some day manifest a deeper kind of belonging of one thing with another than the mere arbitrary juxtaposition which now phenomenally appears? It is as much an altar to an unknown god as the one that Saint Paul found at Athens. All our scientific and philosophic ideals are altars to unknown gods. Uniformity is as much so as is free-will. If this be admitted, we can debate on even terms. But if any one pretends that while freedom and variety are, in the first instance, subjective demands, necessity and uniformity are something altogether different, I do not see how we can debate at all.[1]

To begin, then, I must suppose you acquainted with all the usual arguments on the subject. I cannot stop to take up the old proofs from causation, from statistics, from the certainty with which we can foretell one another's conduct, from the fixity of character, and all the rest. But there are two *words* which usually encumber these classical arguments,

[1] "The whole history of popular beliefs about Nature refutes the notion that the thought of a universal physical order can possibly have arisen from the purely passive reception and association of particular perceptions. Indubitable as it is that men infer from known cases to unknown, it is equally certain that this procedure, if restricted to the phenomenal materials that spontaneously offer themselves, would never have led to the belief in a general uniformity, but only to the belief that law and lawlessness rule the world in motley alternation. From the point of view of strict experience, nothing exists but the sum of particular perceptions, with their coincidences on the one hand, their contradictions on the other.

"That there is more order in the world than appears at first sight is not discovered *till the order is looked for*. The first impulse to look for it proceeds from practical needs: where ends must be attained, we must know trustworthy means which infallibly possess a property, or produce a result. But the practical need is only the first occasion for our reflection on the conditions of true knowledge; and even were there no such need, motives would still be present for carrying us beyond the stage of mere association. For not with an equal interest, or rather with an equal lack of interest, does man contemplate those natural processes in which a thing is linked with its former mate, and those in which it is linked to something else. *The former processes harmonize with the conditions of his own thinking:* the latter do not. In the former, his *concepts, general judgments*, and *inferences* apply to reality: in the latter, they have no such application. And thus the intellectual satisfaction which at first comes to him without reflection, at last excites in him the conscious wish to find realized throughout the entire phenomenal world those rational continuities, uniformities, and necessities which are the fundamental element and guiding principle of his own thought." (Sigwart, Logik, bd. 2, s. 382.)

and which we must immediately dispose of if we
are to make any progress.   One is the eulogistic
word *freedom*, and the other is the opprobrious word
chance.   The word 'chance' I wish to keep, but I
wish to get rid of the word 'freedom.'   Its eulogistic
associations have so far overshadowed all the rest of
its meaning that both parties claim the sole right to
use it, and determinists to-day insist that they alone
are freedom's champions.   Old-fashioned determinism was what we may call *hard* determinism.   It did
not shrink from such words as fatality, bondage of
the will, necessitation, and the like.   Nowadays, we
have a *soft* determinism which abhors harsh words,
and, repudiating fatality, necessity, and even prede-
termination, says that its real name is freedom; for
freedom is only necessity understood, and bondage
to the highest is identical with true freedom.   Even
a writer as little used to making capital out of soft
words as Mr. Hodgson hesitates not to call himself a
'free-will determinist.'

Now, all this is a quagmire of evasion under which
the real issue of fact has been entirely smothered.
Freedom in all these senses presents simply no problem at all.   No matter what the soft determinist mean
by it, — whether he mean the acting without external
constraint; whether he mean the acting rightly, or
whether he mean the acquiescing in the law of the
whole, — who cannot answer him that sometimes we
are free and sometimes we are not?   But there *is* a
problem, an issue of fact and not of words, an issue
of the most momentous importance, which is often
decided without discussion in one sentence, — nay,
in one clause of a sentence, — by those very writers
who spin out whole chapters in their efforts to show

what ' true ' freedom is ; and that is the question of determinism, about which we are to talk to-night.

Fortunately, no ambiguities hang about this word or about its opposite, indeterminism. Both designate an outward way in which things may happen, and their cold and mathematical sound has no sentimental associations that can bribe our partiality either way in advance. Now, evidence of an external kind to decide between determinism and indeterminism is, as I intimated a while back, strictly impossible to find. Let us look at the difference between them and see for ourselves. What does determinism profess?

It professes that those parts of the universe already laid down absolutely appoint and decree what the other parts shall be. The future has no ambiguous possibilities hidden in its womb : the part we call the present is compatible with only one totality. Any other future complement than the one fixed from eternity is impossible. The whole is in each and every part, and welds it with the rest into an absolute unity, an iron block, in which there can be no equivocation or shadow of turning.

> " With earth's first clay they did the last man knead,
> And there of the last harvest sowed the seed.
> And the first morning of creation wrote
> What the last dawn of reckoning shall read."

Indeterminism, on the contrary, says that the parts have a certain amount of loose play on one another, so that the laying down of one of them does not necessarily determine what the others shall be. It admits that possibilities may be in excess of actualities, and that things not yet revealed to our knowledge may really in themselves be ambiguous. Of two alternative futures which we conceive, both may now be really possible; and the one become impossible only at the very moment when the other excludes it by becoming real itself. Indeterminism thus denies the world to be one unbending unit of fact. It says there is a certain ultimate pluralism in it; and, so saying, it corroborates our ordinary unsophisticated view of things. To that view, actualities seem to float in a wider sea of possibilities from out of which they are chosen; and, *somewhere*, indeterminism says, such possibilities exist, and form a part of truth.

Determinism, on the contrary, says they exist *nowhere*, and that necessity on the one hand and impossibility on the other are the sole categories of the real. Possibilities that fail to get realized are, for determinism, pure illusions: they never were possibilities at all. There is nothing inchoate, it says, about this universe of ours, all that was or is or shall be actual in it having been from eternity virtually there. The cloud of alternatives our minds escort this mass of actuality withal is a cloud of sheer deceptions, to which ' impossibilities ' is the only name that rightfully belongs.

The issue, it will be seen, is a perfectly sharp one, which no eulogistic terminology can smear over or wipe out. The truth *must* lie with one side or the other, and its lying with one side makes the other false.

The question relates solely to the existence of possibilities, in the strict sense of the term, as things that may, but need not, be. Both sides admit that a volition, for instance, has occurred. The indeterminists say another volition might have occurred in its place : the determinists swear that nothing could possibly have occurred in its place. Now, can science be called in to tell us which of these two point-blank contradicters of each other is right? Science professes to draw no conclusions but such as are based on matters of fact, things that have actually happened; but how can any amount of assurance that something actually happened give us the least grain of information as to whether another thing might or might not have happened in its place? Only facts can be proved by other facts. With things that are possibilities and not facts, facts have no concern. If we have no other evidence than the evidence of existing facts, the possibility-question must remain a mystery never to be cleared up.

And the truth is that facts practically have hardly anything to do with making us either determinists or indeterminists. Sure enough, we make a flourish of quoting facts this way or that; and if we are determinists, we talk about the infallibility with which we can predict one another's conduct; while if we are indeterminists, we lay great stress on the fact that it is just because we cannot foretell one another's conduct, either in war or statecraft or in any of the great and small intrigues and businesses of men, that life is so intensely anxious and hazardous a game. But who does not see the wretched insufficiency of this so-called objective testimony on both sides? What fills up the gaps in our minds is something not objective, not external. What divides us into possibility men and anti-possibility men is different faiths or postulates, — postulates of rationality. To this man the world seems more rational with possibilities in it, — to that man more rational with possibilities excluded; and talk as we will about having to yield to evidence, what makes us monists or pluralists, determinists or indeterminists, is at bottom always some sentiment like this.

The stronghold of the deterministic sentiment is the antipathy to the idea of chance. As soon as we begin to talk indeterminism to our friends, we find a number of them shaking their heads. This notion of alternative possibility, they say, this admission that any one of several things may come to pass, is, after all, only a roundabout name for chance; and chance is something the notion of which no sane mind can for an instant tolerate in the world. What is it, they ask, but barefaced crazy unreason, the negation of intelligibility and law? And if the slightest particle of it exist anywhere, what is to prevent the whole fabric from falling together, the stars from going out, and chaos from recommencing her topsy-turvy reign?

Remarks of this sort about chance will put an end to discussion as quickly as anything one can find. I have already told you that 'chance' was a word I wished to keep and use. Let us then examine exactly what it means, and see whether it ought to be such a terrible bugbear to us. I fancy that squeezing the thistle boldly will rob it of its sting.

The sting of the word 'chance' seems to lie in the assumption that it means something positive, and that if anything happens by chance, it must needs be something of an intrinsically irrational and preposterous sort. Now, chance means nothing of the kind. It is a purely negative and relative term,[1] giving us

[1] Speaking technically, it is a word with a positive denotation, but a connotation that is negative. Other things must be silent about *what* it is: it alone can decide that point at the moment in which it reveals itself.

no information about that of which it is predicated, except that it happens to be disconnected with something else, — not controlled, secured, or necessitated by other things in advance of its own actual presence. As this point is the most subtile one of the whole lecture, and at the same time the point on which all the rest hinges, I beg you to pay particular attention to it. What I say is that it tells us nothing about what a thing may be in itself to call it 'chance.' It may be a bad thing, it may be a good thing. It may be lucidity, transparency, fitness incarnate, matching the whole system of other things, when it has once befallen, in an unimaginably perfect way. All you mean by calling it 'chance' is that this is not guaranteed, that it may also fall out otherwise. For the system of other things has no positive hold on the chance-thing. Its origin is in a certain fashion negative: it escapes, and says, Hands off! coming, when it comes, as a free gift, or not at all.

This negativeness, however, and this opacity of the chance-thing when thus considered *ab extra*, or from the point of view of previous things or distant things, do not preclude its having any amount of positiveness and luminosity from within, and at its own place and moment. All that its chance-character asserts about it is that there is something in it really of its own, something that is not the unconditional property of the whole. If the whole wants this property, the whole must wait till it can get it, if it be a matter of chance. That the universe may actually be a sort of joint-stock society of this sort, in which the sharers have both limited liabilities and limited powers, is of course a simple and conceivable notion.

Nevertheless, many persons talk as if the minutest

dose of disconnectedness of one part with another, the smallest modicum of independence, the faintest tremor of ambiguity about the future, for example, would ruin everything, and turn this goodly universe into a sort of insane sand-heap or nulliverse, no universe at all. Since future human volitions are as a matter of fact the only ambiguous things we are tempted to believe in, let us stop for a moment to make ourselves sure whether their independent and accidental character need be fraught with such direful consequences to the universe as these.

What is meant by saying that my choice of which way to walk home after the lecture is ambiguous and matter of chance as far as the present moment is concerned? It means that both Divinity Avenue and Oxford Street are called; but that only one, and that one *either* one, shall be chosen. Now, I ask you seriously to suppose that this ambiguity of my choice is real; and then to make the impossible hypothesis that the choice is made twice over, and each time falls on a different street. In other words, imagine that I first walk through Divinity Avenue, and then imagine that the powers governing the universe annihilate ten minutes of time with all that it contained, and set me back at the door of this hall just as I was before the choice was made. Imagine then that, everything else being the same, I now make a different choice and traverse Oxford Street. You, as passive spectators, look on and see the two alternative universes, — one of them with me walking through Divinity Avenue in it, the other with the same me walking through Oxford Street. Now, if you are determinists you believe one of these universes to have been from eternity impossible: you believe it to have been impossible because of the intrinsic irrationality or accidentality somewhere involved in it.   But looking outwardly at these universes, can you say which is the impossible and accidental one, and which the rational and necessary one?   I doubt if the most iron-clad determinist among you could have the slightest glimmer of light on this point.   In other words, either universe *after the fact* and once there would, to our means of observation and understanding, appear just as rational as the other.   There would be absolutely no criterion by which we might judge one necessary and the other matter of chance.   Suppose now we relieve the gods of their hypothetical task and assume my choice, once made, to be made forever.   I go through Divinity Avenue for good and all.   If, as good determinists, you now begin to affirm, what all good determinists punctually do affirm, that in the nature of things I *could n't* have gone through Oxford Street, — had I done so it would have been chance, irrationality, insanity, a horrid gap in nature, — I simply call your attention to this, that your affirmation is what the Germans call a *Machtspruch*, a mere conception fulminated as a dogma and based on no insight into details.   Before my choice, either street seemed as natural to you as to me.   Had I happened to take Oxford Street, Divinity Avenue would have figured in your philosophy as the gap in nature; and you would have so proclaimed it with the best deterministic conscience in the world.

But what a hollow outcry, then, is this against a chance which, if it were present to us, we could by no character whatever distinguish from a rational necessity!   I have taken the most trivial of examples, but no possible example could lead to any different result. For what are the alternatives which, in point of fact, offer themselves to human volition? What are those futures that now seem matters of chance? Are they not one and all like the Divinity Avenue and Oxford Street of our example? Are they not all of them *kinds* of things already here and based in the existing frame of nature? Is any one ever tempted to produce an *absolute* accident, something utterly irrelevant to the rest of the world? Do not all the motives that assail us, all the futures that offer themselves to our choice, spring equally from the soil of the past; and would not either one of them, whether realized through chance or through necessity, the moment it was realized, seem to us to fit that past, and in the completest and most continuous manner to interdigitate with the phenomena already there? [1]

The more one thinks of the matter, the more one wonders that so empty and gratuitous a hubbub as this outcry against chance should have found so great an echo in the hearts of men. It is a word which tells us absolutely nothing about what chances, or about the *modus operandi* of the chancing; and the use of it as a war-cry shows only a temper of intel-

---

[1] A favorite argument against free-will is that if it be true, a man's murderer may as probably be his best friend as his worst enemy, a mother be as likely to strangle as to suckle her first-born, and all of us be as ready to jump from fourth-story windows as to go out of front doors, etc. Users of this argument should properly be excluded from debate till they learn what the real question is. 'Free-will' does not say that everything that is physically conceivable is also morally possible. It merely says that of alternatives that really *tempt* our will more than one is really possible. Of course, the alternatives that do thus tempt our will are vastly fewer than the physical possibilities we can coldly fancy. Persons really tempted often do murder their best friends, mothers do strangle their first-born, people do jump out of fourth-story windows, etc.

lectual absolutism, a demand that the world shall be
a solid block, subject to one control, — which temper,
which demand, the world may not be bound to gratify
at all.   In every outwardly verifiable and practical
respect, a world in which the alternatives that now
actually distract *your* choice were decided by pure
chance would be by *me* absolutely undistinguished
from the world in which I now live.   I am, therefore,
entirely willing to call it, so far as your choices go,
a world of chance for me.   To *yourselves*, it is true,
those very acts of choice, which to me are so blind,
opaque, and external, are the opposites of this, for
you are within them and effect them.   To you they
appear as decisions; and decisions, for him who
makes them, are altogether peculiar psychic facts.
Self-luminous and self-justifying at the living moment at which they occur, they appeal to no outside
moment to put its stamp upon them or make them
continuous with the rest of nature.   Themselves it
is rather who seem to make nature continuous; and
in their strange and intense function of granting consent to one possibility and withholding it from another,
to transform an equivocal and double future into an
inalterable and simple past.

But with the psychology of the matter we have no
concern this evening.   The quarrel which determinism
has with chance fortunately has nothing to do with
this or that psychological detail.   It is a quarrel
altogether metaphysical.   Determinism denies the
ambiguity of future volitions, because it affirms that
nothing future can be ambiguous.   But we have said
enough to meet the issue.   Indeterminate future volitions *do* mean chance.   Let us not fear to shout it
from the house-tops if need be; for we now know that

the idea of chance is, at bottom, exactly the same thing as the idea of gift,—the one simply being a disparaging, and the other a eulogistic, name for anything on which we have no effective *claim*. And whether the world be the better or the worse for having either chances or gifts in it will depend altogether on *what* these uncertain and unclaimable things turn out to be.

And this at last brings us within sight of our subject. We have seen what determinism means: we have seen that indeterminism is rightly described as meaning chance; and we have seen that chance, the very name of which we are urged to shrink from as from a metaphysical pestilence, means only the negative fact that no part of the world, however big, can claim to control absolutely the destinies of the whole. But although, in discussing the word 'chance,' I may at moments have seemed to be arguing for its real existence, I have not meant to do so yet. We have not yet ascertained whether this be a world of chance or no; at most, we have agreed that it seems so. And I now repeat what I said at the outset, that, from any strict theoretical point of view, the question is insoluble. To deepen our theoretic sense of the *difference* between a world with chances in it and a deterministic world is the most I can hope to do; and this I may now at last begin upon, after all our tedious clearing of the way.

I wish first of all to show you just what the notion that this is a deterministic world implies. The implications I call your attention to are all bound up with the fact that it is a world in which we constantly have to make what I shall, with your permission, call judgments of regret. Hardly an hour passes in which we do not wish that something might be otherwise; and happy indeed are those of us whose hearts have never echoed the wish of Omar Khayam —

> " That we might clasp, ere closed, the book of fate,
> And make the writer on a fairer leaf
> Inscribe our names, or quite obliterate.
>
> " Ah! Love, could you and I with fate conspire
> To mend this sorry scheme of things entire,
> Would we not shatter it to bits, and then
> Remould it nearer to the heart's desire ? "

Now, it is undeniable that most of these regrets are foolish, and quite on a par in point of philosophic value with the criticisms on the universe of that friend of our infancy, the hero of the fable The Atheist and the Acorn, —

> " Fool ! had that bough a pumpkin bore,
> Thy whimsies would have worked no more," etc.

Even from the point of view of our own ends, we should probably make a botch of remodelling the universe. How much more then from the point of view of ends we cannot see! Wise men therefore regret as little as they can. But still some regrets are pretty obstinate and hard to stifle, — regrets for acts of wanton cruelty or treachery, for example, whether performed by others or by ourselves. Hardly any one can remain *entirely* optimistic after reading the confession of the murderer at Brockton the other day: how, to get rid of the wife whose continued existence bored him, he inveigled her into a desert spot, shot her four times, and then, as she lay on the ground and said to him, " You did n't do it on purpose, did you, dear?" replied, " No, I did n't do it on purpose," as he raised a rock and smashed her skull.   Such an occurrence, with the mild sentence and self-satisfaction of the prisoner, is a field for a crop of regrets, which one need not take up in detail.   We feel that, although a perfect mechanical fit to the rest of the universe, it is a bad moral fit, and that something else would really have been better in its place.

But for the deterministic philosophy the murder, the sentence, and the prisoner's optimism were all necessary from eternity; and nothing else for a moment had a ghost of a chance of being put into their place.   To admit such a chance, the determinists tell us, would be to make a suicide of reason; so we must steel our hearts against the thought. And here our plot thickens, for we see the first of those difficult implications of determinism and monism which it is my purpose to make you feel.   If this Brockton murder was called for by the rest of the universe, if it had to come at its preappointed hour, and if nothing else would have been consistent with the sense of the whole, what are we to think of the universe?   Are we stubbornly to stick to our judgment of regret, and say, though it *couldn't* be, yet it *would* have been a better universe with something different from this Brockton murder in it?   That, of course, seems the natural and spontaneous thing for us to do; and yet it is nothing short of deliberately espousing a kind of pessimism.   The judgment of regret calls the murder bad.   Calling a thing bad means, if it mean anything at all, that the thing ought not to be, that something else ought to be in its stead.   Determinism, in denying that anything else can be in its stead, virtually defines the universe

as a place in which what ought to be is impossible,—
in other words, as an organism whose constitution
is afflicted with an incurable taint, an irremediable
flaw. The pessimism of a Schopenhauer says no
more than this, — that the murder is a symptom;
and that it is a vicious symptom because it belongs
to a vicious whole, which can express its nature no
otherwise than by bringing forth just such a symptom as that at this particular spot. Regret for the
murder must transform itself, if we are determinists
and wise, into a larger regret. It is absurd to regret
the murder alone. Other things being what they are,
it could not be different. What we should regret is
that whole frame of things of which the murder is one
member. I see no escape whatever from this pessimistic conclusion, if, being determinists, our judgment
of regret is to be allowed to stand at all.

The only deterministic escape from pessimism is
everywhere to abandon the judgment of regret. That
this can be done, history shows to be not impossible.
The devil, *quoad existentiam*, may be good. That is,
although he be a *principle* of evil, yet the universe,
with such a principle in it, may practically be a
better universe than it could have been without. On
every hand, in a small way, we find that a certain
amount of evil is a condition by which a higher form
of good is bought. There is nothing to prevent
anybody from generalizing this view, and trusting
that if we could but see things in the largest of all
ways, even such matters as this Brockton murder
would appear to be paid for by the uses that follow
in their train. An optimism *quand même*, a systematic and infatuated optimism like that ridiculed
by Voltaire in his Candide, is one of the possible

ideal ways in which a man may train himself to look on life. Bereft of dogmatic hardness and lit up with the expression of a tender and pathetic hope, such an optimism has been the grace of some of the most religious characters that ever lived.

> " Throb thine with Nature's throbbing breast,
> And all is clear from east to west."

Even cruelty and treachery may be among the absolutely blessed fruits of time, and to quarrel with any of their details may be blasphemy. The only real blasphemy, in short, may be that pessimistic temper of the soul which lets it give way to such things as regrets, remorse, and grief.

Thus, our deterministic pessimism may become a deterministic optimism at the price of extinguishing our judgments of regret.

But does not this immediately bring us into a curious logical predicament? Our determinism leads us to call our judgments of regret wrong, because they are pessimistic in implying that what is impossible yet ought to be. But how then about the judgments of regret themselves? If they are wrong, other judgments, judgments of approval presumably, ought to be in their place. But as they are necessitated, nothing else *can* be in their place; and the universe is just what it was before, — namely, a place in which what ought to be appears impossible. We have got one foot out of the pessimistic bog, but the other one sinks all the deeper. We have rescued our actions from the bonds of evil, but our judgments are now held fast. When murders and treacheries cease to be sins, regrets are theoretic absurdities and errors. The theoretic and the active life thus play a kind of see-

saw with each other on the ground of evil. The rise
of either sends the other down. Murder and treachery cannot be good without regret being bad : regret
cannot be good without treachery and murder being
bad. Both, however, are supposed to have been
foredoomed ; so something must be fatally unreason-
able, absurd, and wrong in the world. It must be a
place of which either sin or error forms a necessary
part. From this dilemma there seems at first sight
no escape. Are we then so soon to fall back into the
pessimism from which we thought we had emerged?
And is there no possible way by which we may, with
good intellectual consciences, call the cruelties and
the treacheries, the reluctances and the regrets, *all*
good together?

Certainly there is such a way, and you are probably
most of you ready to formulate it yourselves. But,
before doing so, remark how inevitably the question
of determinism and indeterminism slides us into the
question of optimism and pessimism, or, as our fathers
called it, ' the question of evil.' The theological form
of all these disputes is the simplest and the deepest,
the form from which there is the least escape, — not
because, as some have sarcastically said, remorse and
regret are clung to with a morbid fondness by the
theologians as spiritual luxuries, but because they are
existing facts of the world, and as such must be taken
into account in the deterministic interpretation of all
that is fated to be. If they are fated to be error, does
not the bat's wing of irrationality still cast its shadow
over the world?

The refuge from the quandary lies, as I said, not
far off. The necessary acts we erroneously regret

may be good, and yet our error in so regretting them may be also good, on one simple condition; and that condition is this: The world must not be regarded as a machine whose final purpose is the making real of any outward good, but rather as a contrivance for deepening the theoretic consciousness of what goodness and evil in their intrinsic natures are. Not the doing either of good or of evil is what nature cares for, but the knowing of them. Life is one long eating of the fruit of the tree of *knowledge*. I am in the habit, in thinking to myself, of calling this point of view the *gnostical* point of view. According to it, the world is neither an optimism nor a pessimism, but a *gnosticism*. But as this term may perhaps lead to some misunderstandings, I will use it as little as possible here, and speak rather of *subjectivism*, and the *subjectivistic* point of view.

Subjectivism has three great branches, — we may call them scientificism, sentimentalism, and sensualism, respectively. They all agree essentially about the universe, in deeming that what happens there is subsidiary to what we think or feel about it. Crime justifies its criminality by awakening our intelligence of that criminality, and eventually our remorses and regrets; and the error included in remorses and regrets, the error of supposing that the past could have been different, justifies itself by its use. Its use is to quicken our sense of *what* the irretrievably lost is. When we think of it as that which might have been ('the saddest words of tongue or pen'), the quality of its worth speaks to us with a wilder sweetness; and, conversely, the dissatisfaction wherewith we think of what seems to have driven it from its natural place gives us the severer pang. Admirable artifice of

nature ! we might be tempted to exclaim, — deceiv-
ing us in order the better to enlighten us, and leaving
nothing undone to accentuate to our consciousness
the yawning distance of those opposite poles of good
and evil between which creation swings.

We have thus clearly revealed to our view what
may be called the dilemma of determinism, so far as
determinism pretends to think things out at all. A
merely mechanical determinism, it is true, rather
rejoices in not thinking them out. It is very sure
that the universe must satisfy its postulate of a physical continuity and coherence, but it smiles at any
one who comes forward with a postulate of moral coherence as well. I may suppose, however, that the
number of purely mechanical or hard determinists
among you this evening is small. The determinism
to whose seductions you are most exposed is what
I have called soft determinism, — the determinism
which allows considerations of good and bad to
mingle with those of cause and effect in deciding
what sort of a universe this may rationally be held
to be. The dilemma of this determinism is one
whose left horn is pessimism and whose right horn is
subjectivism. In other words, if determinism is to
escape pessimism, it must leave off looking at the
goods and ills of life in a simple objective way, and
regard them as materials, indifferent in themselves,
for the production of consciousness, scientific and
ethical, in us.

To escape pessimism is, as we all know, no easy
task. Your own studies have sufficiently shown you
the almost desperate difficulty of making the notion
that there is a single principle of things, and that
principle absolute perfection, rhyme together with

our daily vision of the facts of life.   If perfection be
the principle, how comes there any imperfection
here?   If God be good, how came he to create —
or, if he did not create, how comes he to permit — the
devil?   The evil facts must be explained as seeming:
the devil must be whitewashed, the universe must be
disinfected, if neither God's goodness nor his unity
and power are to remain impugned.   And of all
the various ways of operating the disinfection, and
making bad seem less bad, the way of subjectivism
appears by far the best.[1]

For, after all, is there not something rather absurd
in our ordinary notion of external things being good
or bad in themselves?   Can murders and treacheries,
considered as mere outward happenings, or motions
of matter, be bad without any one to feel their badness?   And could paradise properly be good in the
absence of a sentient principle by which the goodness
was perceived?   Outward goods and evils seem practically indistinguishable except in so far as they
result in getting moral judgments made about them.
But then the moral judgments seem the main thing,
and the outward facts mere perishing instruments for
their production.   This is subjectivism.   Every one
must at some time have wondered at that strange
paradox of our moral nature, that, though the pur-

---

[1] To a reader who says he is satisfied with a pessimism, and has
no objection to thinking the whole bad, I have no more to say: he
makes fewer demands on the world than I, who, making them, wish
to look a little further before I give up all hope of having them satisfied.   If, however, all he means is that the badness of some parts
does not prevent his acceptance of a universe whose *other* parts give
him satisfaction, I welcome him as an ally.   He has abandoned the
notion of the *Whole*, which is the essence of deterministic monism,
and views things as a pluralism, just as I do in this paper.

suit of outward good is the breath of its nostrils, the attainment of outward good would seem to be its suffocation and death. Why does the painting of any paradise or utopia, in heaven or on earth, awaken such yawnings for nirvana and escape? The white-robed harp-playing heaven of our sabbath-schools, and the ladylike tea-table elysium represented in Mr. Spencer's Data of Ethics, as the final consummation of progress, are exactly on a par in this respect, — lubberlands, pure and simple, one and all.[1] We look upon them from this delicious mess of insanities and realities, strivings and deadnesses, hopes and fears, agonies and exultations, which forms our present state, and *tedium vitæ* is the only sentiment they awaken in our breasts. To our crepuscular natures, born for the conflict, the Rembrandtesque moral chiaroscuro, the shifting struggle of the sunbeam in the gloom, such pictures of light upon light are vacuous and expressionless, and neither to be enjoyed nor understood. If *this* be the whole fruit of the victory, we say; if the generations of mankind suffered and laid down their lives; if prophets confessed and martyrs sang in the fire, and all the sacred tears were shed for no other end than that a race of creatures of such unexampled insipidity should succeed, and protract *in saecula saeculorum* their contented and inoffensive lives, — why, at such a rate, better lose than win the battle, or at all events better ring down the curtain before the last act of the play, so that a business that began so importantly may be saved from so singularly flat a winding-up.

---

[1] Compare Sir James Stephen's Essays by a Barrister, London, 1862, pp. 138, 318.

All this is what I should instantly say, were I called on to plead for gnosticism; and its real friends, of whom you will presently perceive I am not one, would say without difficulty a great deal more. Regarded as a stable finality, every outward good becomes a mere weariness to the flesh. It must be menaced, be occasionally lost, for its goodness to be fully felt as such. Nay, more than occasionally lost. No one knows the worth of innocence till he knows it is gone forever, and that money cannot buy it back. Not the saint, but the sinner that repenteth, is he to whom the full length and breadth, and height and depth, of life's meaning is revealed. Not the absence of vice, but vice there, and virtue holding her by the throat, seems the ideal human state. And there seems no reason to suppose it not a permanent human state. There is a deep truth in what the school of Schopenhauer insists on, — the illusoriness of the notion of moral progress. The more brutal forms of evil that go are replaced by others more subtle and more poisonous. Our moral horizon moves with us as we move, and never do we draw nearer to the far-off line where the black waves and the azure meet. The final purpose of our creation seems most plausibly to be the greatest possible enrichment of our ethical consciousness, through the intensest play of contrasts and the widest diversity of characters. This of course obliges some of us to be vessels of wrath, while it calls others to be vessels of honor. But the subjectivist point of view reduces all these outward distinctions to a common denominator. The wretch languishing in the felon's cell may be drinking draughts of the wine of truth that will never pass the lips of the so-called favorite of fortune. And the peculiar consciousness of

each of them is an indispensable note in the great
ethical concert which the centuries as they roll are
grinding out of the living heart of man.

So much for subjectivism! If the dilemma of determinism be to choose between it and pessimism, I
see little room for hesitation from the strictly theoretical point of view. Subjectivism seems the more
rational scheme. And the world may, possibly, for
aught I know, be nothing else. When the healthy
love of life is on one, and all its forms and its appetites seem so unutterably real; when the most brutal
and the most spiritual things are lit by the same sun,
and each is an integral part of the total richness, —
why, then it seems a grudging and sickly way of meeting so robust a universe to shrink from any of its facts
and wish them not to be. Rather take the strictly
dramatic point of view, and treat the whole thing as a
great unending romance which the spirit of the universe, striving to realize its own content, is eternally
thinking out and representing to itself.[1]

No one, I hope, will accuse me, after I have said
all this, of underrating the reasons in favor of subjectivism. And now that I proceed to say why those
reasons, strong as they are, fail to convince my own
mind, I trust the presumption may be that my objections are stronger still.

I frankly confess that they are of a practical order.
If we practically take up subjectivism in a sincere and
radical manner and follow its consequences, we meet
with some that make us pause. Let a subjectivism

[1] Cet univers est un spectacle que Dieu se donne à lui-même.
Servons les intentions du grand chorège en contribuant à rendre le
spectacle aussi brillant, aussi varié que possible. — RENAN.

begin in never so severe and intellectual a way, it is forced by the law of its nature to develop another side of itself and end with the corruptest curiosity. Once dismiss the notion that certain duties are good in themselves, and that we are here to do them, no matter how we feel about them; once consecrate the opposite notion that our performances and our violations of duty are for a common purpose, the attainment of subjective knowledge and feeling, and that the deepening of these is the chief end of our lives, — and at what point on the downward slope are we to stop? In theology, subjectivism develops as its 'left wing' antinomianism. In literature, its left wing is romanticism. And in practical life it is either a nerveless sentimentality or a sensualism without bounds.

Everywhere it fosters the fatalistic mood of mind. It makes those who are already too inert more passive still; it renders wholly reckless those whose energy is already in excess. All through history we find how subjectivism, as soon as it has a free career, exhausts itself in every sort of spiritual, moral, and practical license. Its optimism turns to an ethical indifference, which infallibly brings dissolution in its train. It is perfectly safe to say now that if the Hegelian gnosticism, which has begun to show itself here and in Great Britain, were to become a popular philosophy, as it once was in Germany, it would certainly develop its left wing here as there, and produce a reaction of disgust. Already I have heard a graduate of this very school express in the pulpit his willingness to sin like David, if only he might repent like David. You may tell me he was only sowing his wild, or rather his tame, oats; and perhaps he was. But the point is

that in the subjectivistic or gnostical philosophy oat-
sowing, wild or tame, becomes a systematic necessity
and the chief function of life. After the pure and
classic truths, the exciting and rancid ones must be
experienced; and if the stupid virtues of the philistine
herd do not then come in and save society from the
influence of the children of light, a sort of inward
putrefaction becomes its inevitable doom.

Look at the last runnings of the romantic school, as
we see them in that strange contemporary Parisian
literature, with which we of the less clever countries
are so often driven to rinse out our minds after they
have become clogged with the dulness and heaviness
of our native pursuits. The romantic school began
with the worship of subjective sensibility and the re-
volt against legality of which Rousseau was the first
great prophet: and through various fluxes and re-
fluxes, right wings and left wings, it stands to-day
with two men of genius, M. Renan and M. Zola, as its
principal exponents, — one speaking with its mascu-
line, and the other with what might be called its fem-
inine, voice. I prefer not to think now of less noble
members of the school, and the Renan I have in mind
is of course the Renan of latest dates. As I have
used the term gnostic, both he and Zola are gnostics
of the most pronounced sort. Both are athirst for
the facts of life, and both think the facts of human
sensibility to be of all facts the most worthy of attention. Both agree, moreover, that sensibility seems to
be there for no higher purpose, — certainly not, as
the Philistines say, for the sake of bringing mere outward rights to pass and frustrating outward wrongs.
One dwells on the sensibilities for their energy, the
other for their sweetness; one speaks with a voice of

bronze, the other with that of an Æolian harp; one
ruggedly ignores the distinction of good and evil, the
other plays the coquette between the craven unman-
liness of his Philosophic Dialogues and the butterfly
optimism of his Souvenirs de Jeunesse. But under the
pages of both there sounds incessantly the hoarse bass
of *vanitas vanitatum, omnia vanitas*, which the reader
may hear, whenever he will, between the lines. No
writer of this French romantic school has a word of
rescue from the hour of satiety with the things of life,
— the hour in which we say, "I take no pleasure in
them," — or from the hour of terror at the world's
vast meaningless grinding, if perchance such hours
should come. For terror and satiety are facts of sensibility like any others; and at their own hour they
reign in their own right. The heart of the romantic
utterances, whether poetical, critical, or historical, is
this inward remedilessness, what Carlyle calls this far-
off whimpering of wail and woe. And from this romantic state of mind there is absolutely no possible
theoretic escape. Whether, like Renan, we look upon
life in a more refined way, as a romance of the spirit;
or whether, like the friends of M. Zola, we pique ourselves on our ' scientific ' and ' analytic ' character, and
prefer to be cynical, and call the world a ' roman ex-
périmental ' on an infinite scale, — in either case the
world appears to us potentially as what the same Carlyle once called it, a vast, gloomy, solitary Golgotha
and mill of death.

The only escape is by the practical way. And
since I have mentioned the nowadays much-reviled
name of Carlyle, let me mention it once more, and
say it is the way of his teaching. No matter for
Carlyle's life, no matter for a great deal of his writ-

ing. What was the most important thing he said to us? He said: "Hang your sensibilities! Stop your snivelling complaints, and your equally snivelling raptures! Leave off your general emotional tomfoolery, and get to WORK like men!" But this means a complete rupture with the subjectivist philosophy of things. It says conduct, and not sensibility, is the ultimate fact for our recognition. With the vision of certain works to be done, of certain outward changes to be wrought or resisted, it says our intellectual horizon terminates. No matter how we succeed in doing these outward duties, whether gladly and spontaneously, or heavily and unwillingly, do them we somehow must; for the leaving of them undone is perdition. No matter how we feel; if we are only faithful in the outward act and refuse to do wrong, the world will in so far be safe, and we quit of our debt toward it. Take, then, the yoke upon our shoulders; bend our neck beneath the heavy legality of its weight; regard something else than our feeling as our limit, our master, and our law; be willing to live and die in its service, — and, at a stroke, we have passed from the subjective into the objective philosophy of things, much as one awakens from some feverish dream, full of bad lights and noises, to find one's self bathed in the sacred coolness and quiet of the air of the night.

But what is the essence of this philosophy of objective conduct, so old-fashioned and finite, but so chaste and sane and strong, when compared with its romantic rival? It is the recognition of limits, foreign and opaque to our understanding. It is the willingness, after bringing about some external good, to feel at peace; for our responsibility ends with the

performance of that duty, and the burden of the rest
we may lay on higher powers.[1]

> " Look to thyself, O Universe,
> Thou art better and not worse,"

we may say in that philosophy, the moment we have
done our stroke of conduct, however small. For in
the view of that philosophy the universe belongs to
a plurality of semi-independent forces, each one of
which may help or hinder, and be helped or hindered
by, the operations of the rest.

But this brings us right back, after such a long
détour, to the question of indeterminism and to the
conclusion of all I came here to say to-night. For
the only consistent way of representing a pluralism and
a world whose parts may affect one another through
their conduct being either good or bad is the inde-
terministic way. What interest, zest, or excitement
can there be in achieving the right way, unless we
are enabled to feel that the wrong way is also a possible and a natural way, — nay, more, a menacing
and an imminent way? And what sense can there
be in condemning ourselves for taking the wrong
way, unless we need have done nothing of the sort,
unless the right way was open to us as well? I cannot understand the willingness to act, no matter how
we feel, without the belief that acts are really good
and bad. I cannot understand the belief that an act
is bad, without regret at its happening. I cannot
understand regret without the admission of real,
genuine possibilities in the world. Only *then* is it

---

[1] The burden, for example, of seeing to it that the *end* of all our
righteousness be some positive universal gain.

other than a mockery to feel, after we have failed to do our best, that an irreparable opportunity is gone from the universe, the loss of which it must forever after mourn.

If you insist that this is all superstition, that possibility is in the eye of science and reason impossibility, and that if I act badly 't is that the universe was foredoomed to suffer this defect, you fall right back into the dilemma, the labyrinth, of pessimism and subjectivism, from out of whose toils we have just wound our way.

Now, we are of course free to fall back, if we please. For my own part, though, whatever difficulties may beset the philosophy of objective right and wrong, and the indeterminism it seems to imply, determinism, with its alternative of pessimism or romanticism, contains difficulties that are greater still. But you will remember that I expressly repudiated awhile ago the pretension to offer any arguments which could be coercive in a so-called scientific fashion in this matter. And I consequently find myself, at the end of this long talk, obliged to state my conclusions in an altogether personal way. This personal method of appeal seems to be among the very conditions of the problem; and the most any one can do is to confess as candidly as he can the grounds for the faith that is in him, and leave his example to work on others as it may.

Let me, then, without circumlocution say just this. The world is enigmatical enough in all conscience, whatever theory we may take up toward it. The indeterminism I defend, the free-will theory of popular sense based on the judgment of regret, represents that world as vulnerable, and liable to be injured by certain of its parts if they act wrong. And it represents their acting wrong as a matter of possibility or accident, neither inevitable nor yet to be infallibly warded off. In all this, it is a theory devoid either of transparency or of stability. It gives us a pluralistic, restless universe, in which no single point of view can ever take in the whole scene; and to a mind possessed of the love of unity at any cost, it will, no doubt, remain forever inacceptable. A friend with such a mind once told me that the thought of my universe made him sick, like the sight of the horrible motion of a mass of maggots in their carrion bed.

But while I freely admit that the pluralism and the restlessness are repugnant and irrational in a certain way, I find that every alternative to them is irrational in a deeper way. The indeterminism with its maggots, if you please to speak so about it, offends only the native absolutism of my intellect, — an absolutism which, after all, perhaps, deserves to be snubbed and kept in check. But the determinism with its necessary carrion, to continue the figure of speech, and with no possible maggots to eat the latter up, violates my sense of moral reality through and through. When, for example, I imagine such carrion as the Brockton murder, I cannot conceive it as an act by which the universe, as a whole, logically and necessarily expresses its nature without shrinking from complicity with such a whole. And I deliberately refuse to keep on terms of loyalty with the universe by saying blankly that the murder, since it does flow from the nature of the whole, is not carrion. There are *some* instinctive reactions which

I, for one, will not tamper with. The only remaining alternative, the attitude of gnostical romanticism, wrenches my personal instincts in quite as violent a way. It falsifies the simple objectivity of their deliverance. It makes the goose-flesh the murder excites in me a sufficient reason for the perpetration of the crime. It transforms life from a tragic reality into an insincere melodramatic exhibition, as foul or as tawdry as any one's diseased curiosity pleases to carry it out. And with its consecration of the ' roman naturaliste' state of mind, and its enthronement of the baser crew of Parisian *littérateurs* among the eternally indispensable organs by which the infinite spirit of things attains to that subjective illumination which is the task of its life, it leaves me in presence of a sort of subjective carrion considerably more noisome than the objective carrion I called it in to take away.

No! better a thousand times, than such systematic corruption of our moral sanity, the plainest pessimism, so that it be straightforward; but better far than that the world of chance. Make as great an uproar about chance as you please, I know that chance means pluralism and nothing more. If some of the members of the pluralism are bad, the philosophy of pluralism, whatever broad views it may deny me, permits me, at least, to turn to the other members with a clean breast of affection and an unsophisticated moral sense. And if I still wish to think of the world as a totality, it lets me feel that a world with a *chance* in it of being altogether good, even if the chance never come to pass, is better than a world with no such chance at all. That ' chance' whose very notion I am exhorted and conjured to banish

from my view of the future as the suicide of reason
concerning it, that ' chance ' is — what?   Just this, —
the chance that in moral respects the future may be
other and better than the past has been.   This is the
only chance we have any motive for supposing to
exist.   Shame, rather, on its repudiation and its denial!   For its presence is the vital air which lets the
world live, the salt which keeps it sweet.

And here I might legitimately stop, having expressed all I care to see admitted by others to-night.
But I know that if I do stop here, misapprehensions
will remain in the minds of some of you, and keep
all I have said from having its effect; so I judge it
best to add a few more words.

In the first place, in spite of all my explanations, the
word ' chance ' will still be giving trouble.   Though
you may yourselves be adverse to the deterministic
doctrine, you wish a pleasanter word than ' chance '
to name the opposite doctrine by; and you very
likely consider my preference for such a word a per-
verse sort of a partiality on my part.   It certainly *is*
a bad word to make converts with; and you wish I
had not thrust it so butt-foremost at you, — you wish
to use a milder term.

Well, I admit there may be just a dash of perversity in its choice.   The spectacle of the mere word-
grabbing game played by the soft determinists has
perhaps driven me too violently the other way; and,
rather than be found wrangling with them for the
good words, I am willing to take the first bad one
which comes along, provided it be unequivocal.   The
question is of things, not of eulogistic names for them;
and the best word is the one that enables men to

know the quickest whether they disagree or not about the things. But the word 'chance,' with its singular negativity, is just the word for this purpose. Whoever uses it instead of 'freedom,' squarely and resolutely gives up all pretence to control the things he says are free. For *him*, he confesses that they are no better than mere chance would be. It is a word of *impotence*, and is therefore the only sincere word we can use, if, in granting freedom to certain things, we grant it honestly, and really risk the game. "Who chooses me must give and forfeit all he hath." Any other word permits of quibbling, and lets us, after the fashion of the soft determinists, make a pretence of restoring the caged bird to liberty with one hand, while with the other we anxiously tie a string to its leg to make sure it does not get beyond our sight.

But now you will bring up your final doubt. Does not the admission of such an unguaranteed chance or freedom preclude utterly the notion of a Providence governing the world? Does it not leave the fate of the universe at the mercy of the chance-possibilities, and so far insecure? Does it not, in short, deny the craving of our nature for an ultimate peace behind all tempests, for a blue zenith above all clouds?

To this my answer must be very brief. The belief in free-will is not in the least incompatible with the belief in Providence, provided you do not restrict the Providence to fulminating nothing but *fatal* decrees. If you allow him to provide possibilities as well as actualities to the universe, and to carry on his own thinking in those two categories just as we do ours, chances may be there, uncontrolled even by him, and the course of the universe be really ambiguous;

and yet the end of all things may be just what he intended it to be from all eternity.

An analogy will make the meaning of this clear. Suppose two men before a chessboard, — the one a novice, the other an expert player of the game. The expert intends to beat. But he cannot foresee exactly what any one actual move of his adversary may be. He knows, however, all the *possible* moves of the latter; and he knows in advance how to meet each of them by a move of his own which leads in the direction of victory. And the victory infallibly arrives, after no matter how devious a course, in the one predestined form of check-mate to the novice's king.

Let now the novice stand for us finite free agents, and the expert for the infinite mind in which the universe lies. Suppose the latter to be thinking out his universe before he actually creates it. Suppose him to say, I will lead things to a certain end, but I will not *now* [1] decide on all the steps thereto. At various points, ambiguous possibilities shall be left

---

[1] This of course leaves the creative mind subject to the law of time. And to any one who insists on the timelessness of that mind I have no reply to make. A mind to whom all time is simultaneously present must see all things under the form of actuality, or under some form to us unknown. If he thinks certain moments as ambiguous in their content while future, he must simultaneously know how the ambiguity will have been decided when they are past. So that none of his mental judgments can possibly be called hypothetical, and his world is one from which chance is excluded. Is not, however, the timeless mind rather a gratuitous fiction? And is not the notion of eternity being given at a stroke to omniscience only just another way of whacking upon us the block-universe, and of denying that possibilities exist? — just the point to be proved. To say that time is an illusory appearance is only a roundabout manner of saying there is no real plurality, and that the frame of things is an absolute unit. Admit plurality, and time may be its form.

open, *either* of which, at a given instant, may become actual. But whichever branch of these bifurcations become real, I know what I shall do at the *next* bifurcation to keep things from drifting away from the final result I intend.[1]

The creator's plan of the universe would thus be left blank as to many of its actual details, but all possibilities would be marked down. The realization of some of these would be left absolutely to chance; that is, would only be determined when the moment of realization came. Other possibilities would be *contingently* determined; that is, their decision would have to wait till it was seen how the matters of absolute chance fell out. But the rest of the plan, including its final upshot, would be rigorously determined once for all. So the creator himself would not need to know *all* the details of actuality until they came; and at any time his own view of the world would be a view partly of facts and partly of possibilities, exactly as ours is now. Of one thing, however, he might be certain; and that is that his world was safe, and that no matter how much it might zigzag he could surely bring it home at last.

---

[1] And this of course means 'miraculous' interposition, but not necessarily of the gross sort our fathers took such delight in representing, and which has so lost its magic for us. Emerson quotes some Eastern sage as saying that if evil were really done under the sun, the sky would incontinently shrivel to a snakeskin and cast it out in spasms. But, says Emerson, the spasms of Nature are years and centuries; and it will tax man's patience to wait so long. We may think of the reserved possibilities God keeps in his own hand, under as invisible and molecular and slowly self-summating a form as we please. We may think of them as counteracting human agencies which he inspires *ad hoc*. In short, signs and wonders and convulsions of the earth and sky are not the only neutralizers of obstruction to a god's plans of which it is possible to think.

Now, it is entirely immaterial, in this scheme, whether the creator leave the absolute chance-possibilities to be decided by himself, each when its proper moment arrives, or whether, on the contrary, he alienate this power from himself, and leave the decision out and out to finite creatures such as we men are. The great point is that the possibilities are really *here*. Whether it be we who solve them, or he working through us, at those soul-trying moments when fate's scales seem to quiver, and good snatches the victory from evil or shrinks nerveless from the fight, is of small account, so long as we admit that the issue is decided nowhere else than *here* and *now*. *That* is what gives the palpitating reality to our moral life and makes it tingle, as Mr. Mallock says, with so strange and elaborate an excitement.   This reality, this excitement, are what the determinisms, hard and soft alike, suppress by their denial that *anything* is decided here and now, and their dogma that all things were foredoomed and settled long ago.   If it be so, may you and I then have been foredoomed to the error of continuing to believe in liberty.[1]   It is fortunate for the winding up of controversy that in every discussion with determinism this *argumentum ad hominem* can be its adversary's last word.

[1] As long as languages contain a future perfect tense, determinists, following the bent of laziness or passion, the lines of least resistance, can reply in that tense, saying, "It will have been fated," to the still small voice which urges an opposite course; and thus excuse themselves from effort in a quite unanswerable way.

THE MORAL PHILOSOPHER AND THE
MORAL LIFE.[1]

THE main purpose of this paper is to show that there is no such thing possible as an ethical philosophy dogmatically made up in advance. We all help to determine the content of ethical philosophy so far as we contribute to the race's moral life. In other words, there can be no final truth in ethics any more than in physics, until the last man has had his experience and said his say. In the one case as in the other, however, the hypotheses which we now make while waiting, and the acts to which they prompt us, are among the indispensable conditions which determine what that 'say' shall be.

First of all, what is the position of him who seeks an ethical philosophy? To begin with, he must be distinguished from all those who are satisfied to be ethical sceptics. He *will* not be a sceptic; therefore so far from ethical scepticism being one possible fruit of ethical philosophizing, it can only be regarded as that residual alternative to all philosophy which from the outset menaces every would-be philosopher who may give up the quest discouraged, and renounce his original aim. That aim is to find an account of the moral relations that obtain among things, which

[1] An Address to the Yale Philosophical Club, published in the International Journal of Ethics, April, 1891.

will weave them into the unity of a stable system, and make of the world what one may call a genuine universe from the ethical point of view. So far as the world resists reduction to the form of unity, so far as ethical propositions seem unstable, so far does the philosopher fail of his ideal. The subject-matter of his study is the ideals he finds existing in the world; the purpose which guides him is this ideal of his own, of getting them into a certain form. This ideal is thus a factor in ethical philosophy whose legitimate presence must never be overlooked; it is a positive contribution which the philosopher himself necessarily makes to the problem. But it is his only positive contribution. At the outset of his inquiry he ought to have no other ideals. Were he interested peculiarly in the triumph of any one kind of good, he would *pro tanto* cease to be a judicial investigator, and become an advocate for some limited element of the case.

There are three questions in ethics which must be kept apart. Let them be called respectively the *psychological* question, the *metaphysical* question, and the *casuistic* question. The psychological question asks after the historical *origin* of our moral ideas and judgments; the metaphysical question asks what the very *meaning* of the words 'good,' 'ill,' and 'obligation' are; the casuistic question asks what is the *measure* of the various goods and ills which men recognize, so that the philosopher may settle the true order of human obligations.

I.

The psychological question is for most disputants the only question. When your ordinary doctor of divinity has proved to his own satisfaction that an altogether unique faculty called 'conscience' must be postulated to tell us what is right and what is wrong; or when your popular-science enthusiast has proclaimed that 'apriorism' is an exploded superstition, and that our moral judgments have gradually resulted from the teaching of the environment, each of these persons thinks that ethics is settled and nothing more is to be said.   The familiar pair of names, Intuitionist and Evolutionist, so commonly used now to connote all possible differences in ethical opinion, really refer to the psychological question alone.   The discussion of this question hinges so much upon particular details that it is impossible to enter upon it at all within the limits of this paper.   I will therefore only express dogmatically my own belief, which is this, — that the Benthams, the Mills, and the Bains have done a lasting service in taking so many of our human ideals and showing how they must have arisen from the association with acts of simple bodily pleasures and reliefs from pain.   Association with many remote pleasures will unquestionably make a thing significant of goodness in our minds; and the more vaguely the goodness is conceived of, the more mysterious will its source appear to be.   But it is surely impossible to explain all our sentiments and preferences in this simple way.   The more minutely psychology studies human nature, the more clearly it finds there traces of secondary affections, relating the impressions of the environment with one another and with our impulses in quite different ways from those mere associations of coexistence and succession which are practically all that pure empiricism can admit.   Take the love of drunkenness; take bashfulness, the terror of high places, the tendency to sea-sickness, to faint at the sight of blood, the susceptibility to musical sounds; take the emotion of the comical, the passion for poetry, for mathematics, or for metaphysics, — no one of these things can be wholly explained by either association or utility. They *go with* other things that can be so explained, no doubt; and some of them are prophetic of future utilities, since there is nothing in us for which some use may not be found. But their origin is in incidental complications to our cerebral structure, a structure whose original features arose with no reference to the perception of such discords and harmonies as these.

Well, a vast number of our moral perceptions also are certainly of this secondary and brain-born kind. They deal with directly felt fitnesses between things, and often fly in the teeth of all the prepossessions of habit and presumptions of utility. The moment you get beyond the coarser and more commonplace moral maxims, the Decalogues and Poor Richard's Almanacs, you fall into schemes and positions which to the eye of common-sense are fantastic and overstrained. The sense for abstract justice which some persons have is as excentric a variation, from the natural-history point of view, as is the passion for music or for the higher philosophical consistencies which consumes the soul of others. The feeling of the inward dignity of certain spiritual attitudes, as peace, serenity, simplicity, veracity; and of the essential vulgarity of others, as querulousness, anxiety, egoistic fussiness, etc., — are quite inexplicable except by an innate preference of the more ideal attitude for its own pure sake. The nobler thing *tastes* better, and that is all that we can say. 'Ex-

perience' of consequences may truly teach us what
things are *wicked*, but what have consequences to
do with what is *mean* and *vulgar?*   If a man has
shot his wife's paramour, by reason of what subtile repugnancy in things is it that we are so dis-
gusted when we hear that the wife and the husband
have made it up and are living comfortably together
again?   Or if the hypothesis were offered us of a
world in which Messrs. Fourier's and Bellamy's and
Morris's utopias should all be outdone, and millions
kept permanently happy on the one simple condition
that a certain lost soul on the far-off edge of things
should lead a life of lonely torture, what except a
specifical and independent sort of emotion can it be
which would make us immediately feel, even though
an impulse arose within us to clutch at the happiness
so offered, how hideous a thing would be its enjoyment when deliberately accepted as the fruit of such
a bargain?   To what, once more, but subtile brain-
born feelings of discord can be due all these recent
protests against the entire race-tradition of retributive
justice? — I refer to Tolstoï with his ideas of non-
resistance, to Mr. Bellamy with his substitution of
oblivion for repentance (in his novel of Dr. Heiden-
hain's Process), to M. Guyau with his radical condemnation of the punitive ideal.   All these subtileties
of the moral sensibility go as much beyond what can
be ciphered out from the 'laws of association' as
the delicacies of sentiment possible between a pair
of young lovers go beyond such precepts of the
'etiquette to be observed during engagement' as
are printed in manuals of social form.

No! Purely inward forces are certainly at work
here. All the higher, more penetrating ideals are

revolutionary. They present themselves far less in the guise of effects of past experience than in that of probable causes of future experience, factors to which the environment and the lessons it has so far taught us must learn to bend.

This is all I can say of the psychological question now. In the last chapter of a recent work [1] I have sought to prove in a general way the existence, in our thought, of relations which do not merely repeat the couplings of experience. Our ideals have certainly many sources. They are not all explicable as signifying corporeal pleasures to be gained, and pains to be escaped. And for having so constantly perceived this psychological fact, we must applaud the intuitionist school. Whether or not such applause must be extended to that school's other characteristics will appear as we take up the following questions.

The next one in order is the metaphysical question, of what we mean by the words ' obligation,' ' good,' and ' ill.'

II.

First of all, it appears that such words can have no application or relevancy in a world in which no sentient life exists. Imagine an absolutely material world, containing only physical and chemical facts, and existing from eternity without a God, without even an inteɪ ͻted spectator : would there be any sense in saying of that world that one of its states is better than another? Or if there were two such worlds possible, would there be any rhyme or reason in calling one good and the other bad, — good or

[1] The Principles of Psychology, New York, H. Holt & Co., 1890.

bad positively, I mean, and apart from the fact that one might relate itself better than the other to the philosopher's private interests? But we must leave these private interests out of the account, for the philosopher is a mental fact, and we are asking whether goods and evils and obligations exist in physical facts *per se.* Surely there is no *status* for good and evil to exist in, in a purely insentient world. How can one physical fact, considered simply as a physical fact, be 'better' than another? Betterness is not a physical relation. In its mere material capacity, a thing can no more be good or bad than it can be pleasant or painful. Good for what? Good for the production of another physical fact, do you say? But what in a purely physical universe demands the production of that other fact? Physical facts simply *are* or are *not;* and neither when present or absent, can they be supposed to make demands. If they do, they can only do so by having desires; and then they have ceased to be purely physical facts, and have become facts of conscious sensibility. Goodness, badness, and obligation must be *realized* somewhere in order really to exist; and the first step in ethical philosophy is to see that no merely inorganic 'nature of things' can realize them. Neither moral relations nor the moral law can swing *in vacuo.* Their only habitat can be a mind which feels them; and no world composed of merely physical facts can possibly be a world to which ethical propositions apply.

The moment one sentient being, however, is made a part of the universe, there is a chance for goods and evils really to exist. Moral relations now have their *status*, in that being's consciousness. So far as he feels anything to be good, he *makes* it good. It *is* good, for him; and being good for him, is absolutely good, for he is the sole creator of values in that universe, and outside of his opinion things have no moral character at all.

In such a universe as that it would of course be absurd to raise the question of whether the solitary thinker's judgments of good and ill are true or not. Truth supposes a standard outside of the thinker to which he must conform; but here the thinker is a sort of divinity, subject to no higher judge. Let us call the supposed universe which he inhabits a *moral solitude*. In such a moral solitude it is clear that there can be no outward obligation, and that the only trouble the god-like thinker is liable to have will be over the consistency of his own several ideals with one another. Some of these will no doubt be more pungent and appealing than the rest, their goodness will have a profounder, more penetrating taste; they will return to haunt him with more obstinate regrets if violated. So the thinker will have to order his life with them as its chief determinants, or else remain inwardly discordant and unhappy. Into whatever equilibrium he may settle, though, and however he may straighten out his system, it will be a right system; for beyond the facts of his own subjectivity there is nothing moral in the world.

If now we introduce a second thinker with his likes and dislikes into the universe, the ethical situation becomes much more complex, and several possibilities are immediately seen to obtain.

One of these is that the thinkers may ignore each other's attitude about good and evil altogether, and each continue to indulge his own preferences, indifferent to what the other may feel or do. In such a case we have a world with twice as much of the ethical quality in it as our moral solitude, only it is without ethical unity. The same object is good or bad there, according as you measure it by the view which this one or that one of the thinkers takes. Nor can you find any possible ground in such a world for saying that one thinker's opinion is more correct than the other's, or that either has the trurer moral sense. Such a world, in short, is not a moral universe but a moral dualism. Not only is there no single point of view within it from which the values of things can be une-quivocally judged, but there is not even a demand for such a point of view, since the two thinkers are supposed to be indifferent to each other's thoughts and acts. Multiply the thinkers into a pluralism, and we find realized for us in the ethical sphere something like that world which the antique sceptics conceived of, — in which individual minds are the measures of all things, and in which no one ‘ objective ’ truth, but only a multitude of ‘ subjective ’ opinions, can be found.

But this is the kind of world with which the philo-sopher, so long as he holds to the hope of a philoso-phy, will not put up. Among the various ideals rep-resented, there must be, he thinks, some which have the more truth or authority; and to these the others *ought* to yield, so that system and subordination may reign. Here in the word ‘ ought ’ the notion of *obligation* comes emphatically into view, and the next thing in order must be to make its meaning clear.

Since the outcome of the discussion so far has been to show us that nothing can be good or right except so far as some consciousness feels it to be good or thinks it to be right, we perceive on the very threshold that the real superiority and authority which are postulated by the philosopher to reside in some of the opinions, and the really inferior character which he supposes must belong to others, cannot be explained by any abstract moral 'nature of things' existing antecedently to the concrete thinkers themselves with their ideals. Like the positive attributes good and bad, the comparative ones better and worse must be *realized* in order to be real. If one ideal judgment be objectively better than another, that betterness must be made flesh by being lodged concretely in some one's actual perception. It cannot float in the atmosphere, for it is not a sort of meteorological phenomenon, like the aurora borealis or the zodiacal light. Its *esse* is *percipi*, like the *esse* of the ideals themselves between which it obtains. The philosopher, therefore, who seeks to know which ideal ought to have supreme weight and which one ought to be subordinated, must trace the *ought* itself to the *de facto* constitution of some existing consciousness, behind which, as one of the data of the universe, he as a purely ethical philosopher is unable to go. This consciousness must make the one ideal right by feeling it to be right, the other wrong by feeling it to be wrong. But now what particular consciousness in the universe *can* enjoy this prerogative of obliging others to conform to a rule which it lays down?

If one of the thinkers were obviously divine, while all the rest were human, there would probably be no practical dispute about the matter. The divine thought would be the model, to which the others should conform. But still the theoretic question would remain, What is the ground of the obligation, even here?

In our first essays at answering this question, there is an inevitable tendency to slip into an assumption which ordinary men follow when they are disputing with one another about questions of good and bad. They imagine an abstract moral order in which the objective truth resides; and each tries to prove that this pre-existing order is more accurately reflected in his own ideas than in those of his adversary. It is because one disputant is backed by this overarching abstract order that we think the other should submit. Even so, when it is a question no longer of two finite thinkers, but of God and ourselves, — we follow our usual habit, and imagine a sort of *de jure* relation, which antedates and overarches the mere facts, and would make it right that we should conform our thoughts to God's thoughts, even though he made no claim to that effect, and though we preferred *de facto* to go on thinking for ourselves.

But the moment we take a steady look at the question, *we see not only that without a claim actually made by some concrete person there can be no obligation, but that there is some obligation wherever there is a claim.* Claim and obligation are, in fact, coextensive terms; they cover each other exactly. Our ordinary attitude of regarding ourselves as subject to an overarching system of moral relations, true ' in themselves,' is therefore either an out-and-out superstition, or else it must be treated as a merely provisional abstraction from that real Thinker in whose actual demand upon us to think as he does our obligation must be ultimately based. In a theistic-ethical philosophy that thinker in question is, of course, the Deity to whom the existence of the universe is due.

I know well how hard it is for those who are accustomed to what I have called the superstitious view, to realize that every *de facto* claim creates in so far forth an obligation. We inveterately think that something which we call the 'validity' of the claim is what gives to it its obligatory character, and that this validity is something outside of the claim's mere existence as a matter of fact. It rains down upon the claim, we think, from some sublime dimension of being, which the moral law inhabits, much as upon the steel of the compass-needle the influence of the Pole rains down from out of the starry heavens. But again, how can such an inorganic abstract character of imperativeness, additional to the imperativeness which is in the concrete claim itself, *exist?* Take any demand, however slight, which any creature, however weak, may make. Ought it not, for its own sole sake, to be satisfied? If not, prove why not. The only possible kind of proof you could adduce would be the exhibition of another creature who should make a demand that ran the other way. The only possible reason there can be why any phenomenon ought to exist is that such a phenomenon actually is desired. Any desire is imperative to the extent of its amount; it *makes* itself valid by the fact that it exists at all. Some desires, truly enough, are small desires; they are put forward by insignificant persons, and we customarily make light of the obligations which they bring. But the fact that such personal demands as these impose small obligations does not keep the largest obligations from being personal demands.

If we must talk impersonally, to be sure we can say

that 'the universe' requires, exacts, or makes obligatory such or such an action, whenever it expresses itself through the desires of such or such a creature. But it is better not to talk about the universe in this personified way, unless we believe in a universal or divine consciousness which actually exists. If there be such a consciousness, then its demands carry the most of obligation simply because they are the greatest in amount. But it is even then not *abstractly* right that we should respect them. It is only *concretely* right, — or right after the fact, and by virtue of the fact, that they are actually made. Suppose we do not respect them, as seems largely to be the case in this queer world. That ought not to be, we say; that is wrong. But in what way is this fact of wrongness made more acceptable or intelligible when we imagine it to consist rather in the laceration of an *à priori* ideal order than in the disappointment of a living personal God? Do we, perhaps, think that we cover God and protect him and make his impotence over us less ultimate, when we back him up with this *à priori* blanket from which he may draw some warmth of further appeal? But the only force of appeal to *us*, which either a living God or an abstract ideal order can wield, is found in the 'everlasting ruby vaults' of our own human hearts, as they happen to beat responsive and not irresponsive to the claim. So far as they do feel it when made by a living consciousness, it is life answering to life. A claim thus livingly acknowledged is acknowledged with a solidity and fulness which no thought of an 'ideal' backing can render more complete; while if, on the other hand, the heart's response is withheld, the stubborn phenomenon is there of an impotence in the claims

which the universe embodies, which no talk about
an eternal nature of things can gloze over or dispel.
An ineffective *à priori* order is as impotent a thing
as an ineffective God; and in the eye of philosophy,
it is as hard a thing to explain.

We may now consider that what we distinguished
as the metaphysical question in ethical philosophy
is sufficiently answered, and that we have learned
what the words 'good,' ' bad,' and ' obligation' severally mean. They mean no absolute natures, independent of personal support. They are objects of
feeling and desire, which have no foothold or anchorage in Being, apart from the existence of actually
living minds.
Wherever such minds exist, with judgments of
good and ill, and demands upon one another, there
is an ethical world in its essential features. Were
all other things, gods and men and starry heavens,
blotted out from this universe, and were there left
but one rock with two loving souls upon it, that rock
would have as thoroughly moral a constitution as any
possible world which the eternities and immensities
could harbor. It would be a tragic constitution, because the rock's inhabitants would die. But while
they lived, there would be real good things and real
bad things in the universe; there would be obligations, claims, and expectations; obediences, refusals,
and disappointments; compunctions and longings for
harmony to come again, and inward peace of conscience when it was restored; there would, in short,
be a moral life, whose active energy would have no
limit but the intensity of interest in each other with
which the hero and heroine might be endowed

We, on this terrestrial globe, so far as the visible facts go, are just like the inhabitants of such a rock. Whether a God exist, or whether no God exist, in yon blue heaven above us bent, we form at any rate an ethical republic here below. And the first reflection which this leads to is that ethics have as genuine and real a foothold in a universe where the highest consciousness is human, as in a universe where there is a God as well. 'The religion of humanity' affords a basis for ethics as well as theism does. Whether the purely human system can gratify the philosopher's demand as well as the other is a different question, which we ourselves must answer ere we close.

III.

The last fundamental question in Ethics was, it will be remembered, the *casuistic* question. Here we are, in a world where the existence of a divine thinker has been and perhaps always will be doubted by some of the lookers-on, and where, in spite of the presence of a large number of ideals in which human beings agree, there are a mass of others about which no general consensus obtains. It is hardly necessary to present a literary picture of this, for the facts are too well known. The wars of the flesh and the spirit in each man, the concupiscences of different individuals pursuing the same unshareable material or social prizes, the ideals which contrast so according to races, circumstances, temperaments, philosophical beliefs, etc., — all form a maze of apparently inextricable confusion with no obvious Ariadne's thread to lead one out. Yet the philosopher, just because he is a philosopher, adds his own peculiar ideal to the confusion (with which if he were willing to be a sceptic he would be passably content), and insists that over all these individual opinions there is a *system of truth* which he can discover if he only takes sufficient pains.

We stand ourselves at present in the place of that philosopher, and must not fail to realize all the features that the situation comports. In the first place we will not be sceptics; we hold to it that there is a truth to be ascertained. But in the second place we have just gained the insight that that truth cannot be a self-proclaiming set of laws, or an abstract ' moral reason,' but can only exist in act, or in the shape of an opinion held by some thinker really to be found There is, however, no visible thinker invested with authority. Shall we then simply proclaim our own ideals as the lawgiving ones? No; for if we are true philosophers we must throw our own spontaneous ideals, even the dearest, impartially in with that total mass of ideals which are fairly to be judged. But how then can we as philosophers ever find a test; how avoid complete moral scepticism on the one hand, and on the other escape bringing a wayward personal standard of our own along with us, on which we simply pin our faith?

The dilemma is a hard one, nor does it grow a bit more easy as we revolve it in our minds. The entire undertaking of the philosopher obliges him to seek an impartial test. That test, however, must be incarnated in the demand of some actually existent person; and how can he pick out the person save by an act in which his own sympathies and prepossessions are implied?

One method indeed presents itself, and has as a matter of history been taken by the more serious

ethical schools. If the heap of things demanded
proved on inspection less chaotic than at first they
seemed, if they furnished their own relative test and
measure, then the casuistic problem would be solved.
If it were found that all goods *quâ* goods contained a
common essence, then the amount of this essence
involved in any one good would show its rank in the
scale of goodness, and order could be quickly made;
for this essence would be *the* good upon which all
thinkers were agreed, the relatively objective and
universal good that the philosopher seeks. Even his
own private ideals would be measured by their share
of it, and find their rightful place among the rest.

Various essences of good have thus been found and
proposed as bases of the ethical system. Thus, to be
a mean between two extremes; to be recognized by
a special intuitive faculty; to make the agent happy
for the moment; to make others as well as him
happy in the long run; to add to his perfection or
dignity; to harm no one; to follow from reason or
flow from universal law; to be in accordance with the
will of God; to promote the survival of the human
species on this planet, — are so many tests, each of
which has been maintained by somebody to constitute the essence of all good things or actions so far
as they are good.

No one of the measures that have been actually
proposed has, however, given general satisfaction.
Some are obviously not universally present in all
cases, — *e. g.*, the character of harming no one, or
that of following a universal law; for the best course
is often cruel; and many acts are reckoned good on
the sole condition that they be exceptions, and serve
not as examples of a universal law. Other charac-

ters, such as following the will of God, are unascertainable and vague. Others again, like survival, are quite indeterminate in their consequences, and leave us in the lurch where we most need their help: a philosopher of the Sioux Nation, for example, will be certain to use the survival-criterion in a very different way from ourselves. The best, on the whole, of these marks and measures of goodness seems to be the capacity to bring happiness. But in order not to break down fatally, this test must be taken to cover innumerable acts and impulses that never *aim* at happiness; so that, after all, in seeking for a universal principle we inevitably are carried onward to the *most* universal principle, — that *the essence of good is simply to satisfy demand.* The demand may be for anything under the sun. There is really no more ground for supposing that all our demands can be accounted for by one universal underlying kind of motive than there is ground for supposing that all physical phenomena are cases of a single law. The elementary forces in ethics are probably as plural as those of physics are. The various ideals have no common character apart from the fact that they are ideals. No single abstract principle can be so used as to yield to the philosopher anything like a scientifically accurate and genuinely useful casuistic scale.

A look at another peculiarity of the ethical universe, as we find it, will still further show us the philosopher's perplexities. As a purely theoretic problem, namely, the casuistic question would hardly ever come up at all. If the ethical philosopher were only asking after the best *imaginable* system of goods he would indeed have an easy task; for all demands as such are *primâ facie* respectable, and the best simply imaginary world would be one in which *every* demand was gratified as soon as made. Such a world would, however, have to have a physical constitution entirely different from that of the one which we inhabit. It would need not only a space, but a time, ' of *n*–dimensions,' to include all the acts and experiences incompatible with one another here below, which would then go on in conjunction, — such as spending our money, yet growing rich; taking our holiday, yet getting ahead with our work; shooting and fishing, yet doing no hurt to the beasts; gaining no end of experience, yet keeping our youthful freshness of heart; and the like. There can be no question that such a system of things, however brought about, would be the absolutely ideal system; and that if a philosopher could create universes *à priori*, and provide all the mechanical conditions, that is the sort of universe which he should unhesitatingly create.

But this world of ours is made on an entirely different pattern, and the casuistic question here is most tragically practical. The actually possible in this world is vastly narrower than all that is demanded; and there is always a *pinch* between the ideal and the actual which can only be got through by leaving part of the ideal behind. There is hardly a good which we can imagine except as competing for the possession of the same bit of space and time with some other imagined good. Every end of desire that presents itself appears exclusive of some other end of desire. Shall a man drink and smoke, *or* keep his nerves in condition? — he cannot do both. Shall he follow his fancy for Amelia, *or* for Henrietta? — both cannot be the choice of his heart. Shall he have the dear old Republican party, *or* a spirit of unsophistication in public affairs? — he cannot have both, etc. So that the ethical philosopher's demand for the right scale of subordination in ideals is the fruit of an altogether practical need. Some part of the ideal must be butchered, and he needs to know which part. It is a tragic situation, and no mere speculative conundrum, with which he has to deal.

Now *we* are blinded to the real difficulty of the philosopher's task by the fact that we are born into a society whose ideals are largely ordered already. If we follow the ideal which is conventionally highest, the others which we butcher either die and do not return to haunt us; or if they come back and accuse us of murder, every one applauds us for turning to them a deaf ear. In other words, our environment encourages us not to be philosophers but partisans. The philosopher, however, cannot, so long as he clings to his own ideal of objectivity, rule out any ideal from being heard. He is confident, and rightly confident, that the simple taking counsel of his own intuitive preferences would be certain to end in a mutilation of the fulness of the truth. The poet Heine is said to have written 'Bunsen' in the place of 'Gott' in his copy of that author's work entitled "God in History," so as to make it read 'Bunsen in der Geschichte.' Now, with no disrespect to the good and learned Baron, is it not safe to say that any single philosopher, however wide his sympathies, must be just such a Bunsen in der Geschichte of the moral world, so soon as he attempts to put his own ideas of order into that howling mob of desires, each struggling to get breathing-room for the ideal to which it clings? The very best of men must not only be insensible, but be ludicrously and peculiarly insensible, to many goods. As a militant, fighting free-handed that the goods to which he *is* sensible may not be submerged and lost from out of life, the philosopher, like every other human being, is in a natural position. But think of Zeno and of Epicurus, think of Calvin and of Paley, think of Kant and Schopenhauer, of Herbert Spencer and John Henry Newman, no longer as one-sided champions of special ideals, but as schoolmasters deciding what all must think, — and what more grotesque topic could a satirist wish for on which to exercise his pen? The fabled attempt of Mrs. Partington to arrest the rising tide of the North Atlantic with her broom was a reasonable spectacle compared with their effort to substitute the content of their clean-shaven systems for that exuberant mass of goods with which all human nature is in travail, and groaning to bring to the light of day. Think, furthermore, of such individual moralists, no longer as mere schoolmasters, but as pontiffs armed with the temporal power, and having authority in every concrete case of conflict to order which good shall be butchered and which shall be suffered to survive, — and the notion really turns one pale. All one's slumbering revolutionary instincts waken at the thought of any single moralist wielding such powers of life and death. Better chaos forever than an order based on any closet-philosopher's rule, even though he were the most enlightened possible member of his tribe. No! if the philosopher is to keep his judicial position, he must never become one of the parties to the fray.

What can he do, then, it will now be asked, except to fall back on scepticism and give up the notion of being a philosopher at all?

But do we not already see a perfectly definite path of escape which is open to him just because he is a philosopher, and not the champion of one particular ideal? Since everything which is demanded is by that fact a good, must not the guiding principle for ethical philosophy (since all demands conjointly cannot be satisfied in this poor world) be simply to satisfy at all times *as many demands as we can?* That act must be the best act, accordingly, which makes for the *best whole*, in the sense of awakening the least sum of dissatisfactions. In the casuistic scale, therefore, those ideals must be written highest which *prevail at the least cost*, or by whose realization the least possible number of other ideals are destroyed. Since victory and defeat there must be, the victory to be philosophically prayed for is that of the more inclusive side, — of the side which even in the hour of triumph will to some degree do justice to the ideals in which the vanquished party's interests lay. The course of history is nothing but the story of men's struggles from generation to generation to find the more and more inclusive order. *Invent some manner* of realizing your own ideals which will also satisfy the alien demands, — that and that only is the path of peace! Following this path, society has shaken itself into one sort of relative equilibrium after another by a series of social discoveries quite analogous to those of science. Polyandry and polygamy and slavery, private warfare and liberty to kill, judicial torture and arbitrary royal power have slowly succumbed to actually aroused complaints; and though some one's ideals are unquestionably the worse off for each improvement, yet a vastly greater total number of them find shelter in our civilized society than in the older savage ways. So far then, and up to date, the casuistic scale is made for the philosopher already far better than he can ever make it for himself. An experiment of the most searching kind has proved that the laws and usages of the land are what yield the maximum of satisfaction to the thinkers taken all together. The presumption in cases of conflict must always be in favor of the conventionally recognized good. The philosopher must be a conservative, and in the construction of his casuistic scale must put the things most in accordance with the customs of the community on top.

And yet if he be a true philosopher he must see that there is nothing final in any actually given equilibrium of human ideals, but that, as our present laws and customs have fought and conquered other past ones, so they will in their turn be overthrown by any newly discovered order which will hush up the complaints that they still give rise to, without producing others louder still. "Rules are made for man, not man for rules," — that one sentence is enough to immortalize Green's Prolegomena to Ethics. And although a man always risks much when he breaks away from established rules and strives to realize a larger ideal whole than they permit, yet the philosopher must allow that it is at all times open to any one to make the experiment, provided he fear not to stake his life and character upon the throw. The pinch is always here. Pent in under every system of moral rules are innumerable persons whom it weighs upon, and goods which it represses; and these are always rumbling and grumbling in the background, and ready for any issue by which they may get free. See the abuses which the

institution of private property covers, so that even
to-day it is shamelessly asserted among us that one
of the prime functions of the national government is
to help the adroiter citizens to grow rich. See the
unnamed and unnamable sorrows which the tyranny,
on the whole so beneficent, of the marriage-institu-
tion brings to so many, both of the married and the
unwed. See the wholesale loss of opportunity under
our *régime* of so-called equality and industrialism,
with the drummer and the counter-jumper in the
saddle, for so many faculties and graces which could
flourish in the feudal world. See our kindliness for
the humble and the outcast, how it wars with that
stern weeding-out which until now has been the
condition of every perfection in the breed. See
everywhere the struggle and the squeeze; and ever-
lastingly the problem how to make them less. The
anarchists, nihilists, and free-lovers; the free-silver-
ites, socialists, and single-tax men; the free-traders
and civil-service reformers; the prohibitionists and
anti-vivisectionists; the radical darwinians with their
idea of the suppression of the weak, — these and
all the conservative sentiments of society arrayed
against them, are simply deciding through actual
experiment by what sort of conduct the maximum
amount of good can be gained and kept in this world.
These experiments are to be judged, not *à priori*,
but by actually finding, after the fact of their making,
how much more outcry or how much appeasement
comes about. What closet-solutions can possibly
anticipate the result of trials made on such a scale?
Or what can any superficial theorist's judgment be
worth, in a world where every one of hundreds of
ideals has its special champion already provided

in the shape of some genius expressly born to feel it, and to fight to death in its behalf? The pure philosopher can only follow the windings of the spectacle, confident that the line of least resistance will always be towards the richer and the more inclusive arrangement, and that by one tack after another some approach to the kingdom of heaven is incessantly made.

IV.

All this amounts to saying that, so far as the casuistic question goes, ethical science is just like physical science, and instead of being deducible all at once from abstract principles, must simply bide its time, and be ready to revise its conclusions from day to day. The presumption of course, in both sciences, always is that the vulgarly accepted opinions are true, and the right casuistic order that which public opinion believes in; and surely it would be folly quite as great, in most of us, to strike out independently and to aim at originality in ethics as in physics. Every now and then, however, some one is born with the right to be original, and his revolutionary thought or action may bear prosperous fruit. He may replace old 'laws of nature' by better ones; he may, by breaking old moral rules in a certain place, bring in a total condition of things more ideal than would have followed had the rules been kept.

On the whole, then, we must conclude that no philosophy of ethics is possible in the old-fashioned absolute sense of the term. Everywhere the ethical philosopher must wait on facts. The thinkers who create the ideals come he knows not whence, their sensibilities are evolved he knows not how; and the question as to which of two conflicting ideals will give the best universe then and there, can be answered by him only through the aid of the experience of other men. I said some time ago, in treating of the 'first' question, that the intuitional moralists deserve credit for keeping most clearly to the psychological facts. They do much to spoil this merit on the whole, however, by mixing with it that dogmatic temper which, by absolute distinctions and unconditional 'thou shalt nots,' changes a growing, elastic, and continuous life into a superstitious system of relics and dead bones. In point of fact, there are no absolute evils, and there are no non-moral goods; and the *highest* ethical life — however few may be called to bear its burdens — consists at all times in the breaking of rules which have grown too narrow for the actual case. There is but one unconditional commandment, which is that we should seek incessantly, with fear and trembling, so to vote and to act as to bring about the very largest total universe of good which we can see. Abstract rules indeed can help; but they help the less in proportion as our intuitions are more piercing, and our vocation is the stronger for the moral life. For every real dilemma is in literal strictness a unique situation; and the exact combination of ideals realized and ideals disappointed which each decision creates is always a universe without a precedent, and for which no adequate previous rule exists. The philosopher, then, *quâ* philosopher, is no better able to determine the best universe in the concrete emergency than other men. He sees, indeed, somewhat better than most men what the question always is, — not a question of this good or that good simply taken, but of the two total

14

universes with which these goods respectively belong. He knows that he must vote always for the richer universe, for the good which seems most organizable, most fit to enter into complex combinations, most apt to be a member of a more inclusive whole. But which particular universe this is he cannot know for certain in advance; he only knows that if he makes a bad mistake the cries of the wounded will soon inform him of the fact. In all this the philosopher is just like the rest of us non-philosophers, so far as we are just and sympathetic instinctively, and so far as we are open to the voice of complaint. His function is in fact indistinguishable from that of the best kind of statesman at the present day. His books upon ethics, therefore, so far as they truly touch the moral life, must more and more ally themselves with a literature which is confessedly tentative and suggestive rather than dogmatic, — I mean with novels and dramas of the deeper sort, with sermons, with books on statecraft and philanthropy and social and economical reform. Treated in this way ethical treatises may be voluminous and luminous as well; but they never can be *final*, except in their abstractest and vaguest features; and they must more and more abandon the old-fashioned, clear-cut, and would-be ' scientific ' form.

V.

The chief of all the reasons why concrete ethics cannot be final is that they have to wait on metaphysical and theological beliefs. I said some time back that real ethical relations existed in a purely human world. They would exist even in what we called a moral solitude if the thinker had various ideals which took hold of him in turn. His self of one day would make demands on his self of another; and some of the demands might be urgent and tyrannical, while others were gentle and easily put aside. We call the tyrannical demands *imperatives*. If we ignore these we do not hear the last of it. The good which we have wounded returns to plague us with interminable crops of consequential damages, compunctions, and regrets. Obligation can thus exist inside a single thinker's consciousness; and perfect peace can abide with him only so far as he lives according to some sort of a casuistic scale which keeps his more imperative goods on top. It is the nature of these goods to be cruel to their rivals. Nothing shall avail when weighed in the balance against them. They call out all the mercilessness in our disposition, and do not easily forgive us if we are so soft-hearted as to shrink from sacrifice in their behalf.

The deepest difference, practically, in the moral life of man is the difference between the easy-going and the strenuous mood. When in the easy-going mood the shrinking from present ill is our ruling consideration. The strenuous mood, on the contrary, makes us quite indifferent to present ill, if only the greater ideal be attained. The capacity for the strenuous mood probably lies slumbering in every man, but it has more difficulty in some than in others in waking up. It needs the wilder passions to arouse it, the big fears, loves, and indignations; or else the deeply penetrating appeal of some one of the higher fidelities, like justice, truth, or freedom. Strong relief is a necessity of its vision; and a world where all the mountains are brought down and all the valleys are

exalted is no congenial place for its habitation. This
is why in a solitary thinker this mood might slumber
on forever without waking. His various ideals, known
to him to be mere preferences of his own, are too
nearly of the same denominational value: he can
play fast or loose with them at will. This too is why,
in a merely human world without a God, the appeal
to our moral energy falls short of its maximal stimulating power. Life, to be sure, is even in such a
world a genuinely ethical symphony; but it is played
in the compass of a couple of poor octaves, and the
infinite scale of values fails to open up. Many of us,
indeed, — like Sir James Stephen in those eloquent
' Essays by a Barrister,' — would openly laugh at the
very idea of the strenuous mood being awakened in
us by those claims of remote posterity which constitute the last appeal of the religion of humanity. We
do not love these men of the future keenly enough;
and we love them perhaps the less the more we hear
of their evolutionized perfection, their high average
longevity and education, their freedom from war and
crime, their relative immunity from pain and zymotic
disease, and all their other negative superiorities.
This is all too finite, we say; we see too well the
vacuum beyond. It lacks the note of infinitude and
mystery, and may all be dealt with in the don't-care
mood. No need of agonizing ourselves or making
others agonize for these good creatures just at present.

When, however, we believe that a God is there, and
that he is one of the claimants, the infinite perspective
opens out. The scale of the symphony is incalculably
prolonged. The more imperative ideals now begin
to speak with an altogether new objectivity and significance, and to utter the penetrating, shattering,

tragically challenging note of appeal.   They ring out like the call of Victor Hugo's alpine eagle, "qui parle au précipice et que le gouffre entend," and the strenuous mood awakens at the sound.   It saith among the trumpets, ha, ha! it smelleth the battle afar off, the thunder of the captains and the shouting.   Its blood is up; and cruelty to the lesser claims, so far from being a deterrent element, does but add to the stern joy with which it leaps to answer to the greater. All through history, in the periodical conflicts of puritanism with the don't-care temper, we see the antagonism of the strenuous and genial moods, and the contrast between the ethics of infinite and mysterious obligation from on high, and those of prudence and the satisfaction of merely finite need.

The capacity of the strenuous mood lies so deep down among our natural human possibilities that even if there were no metaphysical or traditional grounds for believing in a God, men would postulate one simply as a pretext for living hard, and getting out of the game of existence its keenest possibilities of zest. Our attitude towards concrete evils is entirely different in a world where we believe there are none but finite demanders, from what it is in one where we joyously face tragedy for an infinite demander's sake. Every sort of energy and endurance, of courage and capacity for handling life's evils, is set free in those who have religious faith.   For this reason the strenuous type of character will on the battle-field of human history always outwear the easy-going type, and religion will drive irreligion to the wall.

It would seem, too, — and this is my final conclusion, — that the stable and systematic moral universe for which the ethical philosopher asks is fully possible only in a world where there is a divine thinker with all-enveloping demands. If such a thinker existed, his way of subordinating the demands to one another would be the finally valid casuistic scale; his claims would be the most appealing; his ideal universe would be the most inclusive realizable whole. If he now exist, then actualized in his thought already must be that ethical philosophy which we seek as the pattern which our own must evermore approach.[1] In the interests of our own ideal of systematically unified moral truth, therefore, we, as would-be philosophers, must postulate a divine thinker, and pray for the victory of the religious cause. Meanwhile, exactly what the thought of the infinite thinker may be is hidden from us even were we sure of his existence; so that our postulation of him after all serves only to let loose in us the strenuous mood. But this is what it does in all men, even those who have no interest in philosophy. The ethical philosopher, therefore, whenever he ventures to say which course of action is the best, is on no essentially different level from the common man. " See, I have set before thee this day life and good, and death and evil; therefore, choose life that thou and thy seed may live," — when this challenge comes to us, it is simply our total character and personal genius that are on trial; and if we invoke any so-called philosophy, our choice and use of that also are but revelations of our personal aptitude or incapacity for moral life. From this unsparing practical ordeal no professor's lectures and no array of books

---

[1] All this is set forth with great freshness and force in the work of my colleague, Professor Josiah Royce: " The Religious Aspect of Philosophy." Boston, 1885.

can save us. The solving word, for the learned and the unlearned man alike, lies in the last resort in the dumb willingnesses and unwillingnesses of their interior characters, and nowhere else. It is not in heaven, neither is it beyond the sea; but the word is very nigh unto thee, in thy mouth and in thy heart, that thou mayest do it.

GREAT MEN AND THEIR ENVIRONMENT.[1]

A REMARKABLE parallel, which I think has never been noticed, obtains between the facts of social evolution on the one hand, and of zoölogical evolution as expounded by Mr. Darwin on the other. It will be best to prepare the ground for my thesis by a few very general remarks on the method of getting at scientific truth. It is a common platitude that a complete acquaintance with any one thing, however small, would require a knowledge of the entire universe. Not a sparrow falls to the ground but some of the remote conditions of his fall are to be found in the milky way, in our federal constitution, or in the early history of Europe. That is to say, alter the milky way, alter the federal constitution, alter the facts of our barbarian ancestry, and the universe would so far be a different universe from what it now is. One fact involved in the difference might be that the particular little street-boy who threw the stone which brought down the sparrow might not find himself opposite the sparrow at that particular moment; or, finding himself there, he might not be in that particular serene and disengaged mood of mind which expressed itself in throwing the stone. But, true as all this is, it would be very foolish for any one who

---

[1] A lecture before the Harvard Natural History Society; published in the Atlantic Monthly, October, 1880.

was inquiring the cause of the sparrow's fall to overlook the boy as too personal, proximate, and so to
speak anthropomorphic an agent, and to say that the
true cause is the federal constitution, the westward
migration of the Celtic race, or the structure of the
milky way. If we proceeded on that method, we
might say with perfect legitimacy that a friend of
ours, who had slipped on the ice upon his door-step
and cracked his skull, some months after dining with
thirteen at the table, died because of that ominous
feast. I know, in fact, one such instance; and I
might, if I chose, contend with perfect logical propriety that the slip on the ice was no real accident.
"There are no accidents," I might say, " for science.
The whole history of the world converged to produce
that slip. If anything had been left out, the slip
would not have occurred just there and then. To say
it would is to deny the relations of cause and effect
throughout the universe. The real cause of the death
was not the slip, *but the conditions which engendered
the slip,* — and among them his having sat at a table,
six months previous, one among thirteen. *That* is
truly the reason why he died within the year."

It will soon be seen whose arguments I am, in form,
reproducing here. I would fain lay down the truth
without polemics or recrimination. But unfortunately
we never fully grasp the import of any true statement
until we have a clear notion of what the opposite untrue statement would be. The error is needed to set
off the truth, much as a dark background is required
for exhibiting the brightness of a picture. And the
error which I am going to use as a foil to set off what
seems to me the truth of my own statements is contained in the philosophy of Mr. Herbert Spencer and

his disciples. Our problem is, What are the causes that make communities change from generation to generation, — that make the England of Queen Anne so different from the England of Elizabeth, the Harvard College of to-day so different from that of thirty years ago?

I shall reply to this problem, The difference is due to the accumulated influences of individuals, of their examples, their initiatives, and their decisions. The Spencerian school replies, The changes are irrespective of persons, and independent of individual control. They are due to the environment, to the circumstances, the physical geography, the ancestral conditions, the increasing experience of outer relations; to everything, in fact, except the Grants and the Bismarcks, the Joneses and the Smiths.

Now, I say that these theorizers are guilty of precisely the same fallacy as he who should ascribe the death of his friend to the dinner with thirteen, or the fall of the sparrow to the milky way. Like the dog in the fable, who drops his real bone to snatch at its image, they drop the real causes to snatch at others, which from no possible human point of view are available or attainable. Their fallacy is a practical one. Let us see where it lies. Although I believe in free-will myself, I will waive that belief in this discussion, and assume with the Spencerians the predestination of all human actions. On that assumption I gladly allow that were the intelligence investigating the man's or the sparrow's death omniscient and omnipresent, able to take in the whole of time and space at a single glance, there would not be the slightest objection to the milky way or the fatal feast being in-

voked among the sought-for causes.   Such a divine
intelligence would see instantaneously all the infinite
lines of convergence towards a given result, and it
would, moreover, see impartially: it would see the
fatal feast to be as much a condition of the sparrow's
death as of the man's; it would see the boy with the
stone to be as much a condition of the man's fall as
of the sparrow's.

The human mind, however, is constituted on an
entirely different plan.   It has no such power of universal intuition.   Its finiteness obliges it to see but
two or three things at a time.   If it wishes to take
wider sweeps it has to use 'general ideas,' as they are
called, and in so doing to drop all concrete truths.
Thus, in the present case, if we as men wish to feel
the connection between the milky way and the boy
and the dinner and the sparrow and the man's death,
we can do so only by falling back on the enormous
emptiness of what is called an abstract proposition.
We must say, All things in the world are fatally predetermined, and hang together in the adamantine fixity of a system of natural law.   But in the vagueness
of this vast proposition we have lost all the concrete
facts and links; and in all practical matters the concrete links are the only things of importance.   The
human mind is essentially partial.   It can be efficient
at all only by *picking out* what to attend to, and ignoring everything else, — by narrowing its point of view.
Otherwise, what little strength it has is dispersed,
and it loses its way altogether.   Man always wants
his curiosity gratified for a particular purpose.   If, in
the case of the sparrow, the purpose is punishment, it
would be idiotic to wander off from the cats, boys,
and other possible agencies close by in the street, to

survey the early Celts and the milky way: the boy would meanwhile escape. And if, in the case of the unfortunate man, we lose ourselves in contemplation of the thirteen-at-table mystery, and fail to notice the ice on the step and cover it with ashes, some other poor fellow, who never dined out in his life, may slip on it in coming to the door, and fall and break his head too.

It is, then, a necessity laid upon us as human beings to limit our view. In mathematics we know how this method of ignoring and neglecting quantities lying outside of a certain range has been adopted in the differential calculus. The calculator throws out all the 'infinitesimals' of the quantities he is considering. He treats them (under certain rules) as if they did not exist. In themselves they exist perfectly all the while; but they are as if they did not exist for the purposes of his calculation. Just so an astronomer, in dealing with the tidal movements of the ocean, takes no account of the waves made by the wind, or by the pressure of all the steamers which day and night are moving their thousands of tons upon its surface. Just so the marksman, in sighting his rifle, allows for the motion of the wind, but not for the equally real motion of the earth and solar system. Just so a business man's punctuality may overlook an error of five minutes, while a physicist, measuring the velocity of light, must count each thousandth of a second.

There are, in short, *different cycles of operation* in nature; different departments, so to speak, relatively independent of one another, so that what goes on at any moment in one may be compatible with almost any condition of things at the same time in the next. The mould on the biscuit in the store-room of a man-of-war vegetates in absolute indifference to the nationality of the flag, the direction of the voyage, the weather, and the human dramas that may go on on board; and a mycologist may study it in complete abstraction from all these larger details. Only by so studying it, in fact, is there any chance of the mental concentration by which alone he may hope to learn something of its nature. On the other hand, the captain who in manœuvring the vessel through a naval fight should think it necessary to bring the mouldy biscuit into his calculations would very likely lose the battle by reason of the excessive 'thoroughness' of his mind.

The causes which operate in these incommensurable cycles are connected with one another only *if we take the whole universe into account.* For all lesser points of view it is lawful — nay, more, it is for human wisdom necessary — to regard them as disconnected and irrelevant to one another.

And this brings us nearer to our special topic. If we look at an animal or a human being, distinguished from the rest of his kind by the possession of some extraordinary peculiarity, good or bad, we shall be able to discriminate between the causes which originally *produced* the peculiarity in him and the causes that *maintain* it after it is produced; and we shall see, if the peculiarity be one that he was born with, that these two sets of causes belong to two such irrelevant cycles. It was the triumphant originality of Darwin to see this, and to act accordingly. Separating the causes of production under the title of 'tendencies to spontaneous variation,' and relegating them to a physiological cycle which he forthwith agreed to ignore altogether,[1] he confined his attention to the causes of preservation, and under the names of natural selection and sexual selection studied them exclusively as functions of the cycle of the environment.

Pre-Darwinian philosophers had also tried to establish the doctrine of descent with modification; but they all committed the blunder of clumping the two cycles of causation into one. What preserves an animal with his peculiarity, if it be a useful one, they saw to be the nature of the environment to which the peculiarity was adjusted. The giraffe with his peculiar neck is preserved by the fact that there are in his environment tall trees whose leaves he can digest. But these philosophers went further, and said that the presence of the trees not only maintained an animal with a long neck to browse upon their branches, but also produced him. They *made* his neck long by the constant striving they aroused in him to reach up to them. The environment, in short, was supposed by these writers to mould the animal by a kind of direct pressure, very much as a seal presses the wax into harmony with itself. Numerous instances were given of the way in which this goes on under our eyes. The exercise of the forge makes the right arm strong, the palm grows callous to the oar, the mountain air distends the chest, the chased fox grows cunning and the chased bird shy, the arctic cold stimulates the animal combustion, and so forth. Now these changes, of which many more examples might be adduced, are

[1] Darwin's theory of pangenesis is, it is true, an attempt to account (among other things) for variation. But it occupies its own separate place, and its author no more invokes the environment when he talks of the adhesions of gemmules than he invokes these adhesions when he talks of the relations of the whole animal to the environment. *Divide et impera!*

at present distinguished by the special name of *adaptive* changes. Their peculiarity is that that very feature in the environment to which the animal's nature grows adjusted, itself produces the adjustment. The 'inner relation,' to use Mr. Spencer's phrase, 'corresponds' with its own efficient cause.

Darwin's first achievement was to show the utter insignificance in amount of these changes produced by direct adaptation, the immensely greater mass of changes being produced by internal molecular accidents, of which we know nothing. His next achievement was to define the true problem with which we have to deal when we study the effects of the visible environment on the animal. That problem is simply this: Is the environment more likely to *preserve or to destroy him*, on account of this or that peculiarity with which he may be born? In giving the name 'of accidental variations' to those peculiarities with which an animal is born, Darwin does not for a moment mean to suggest that they are not the fixed outcome of natural law. If the total system of the universe be taken into account, the causes of these variations and the visible environment which preserves or destroys them, undoubtedly do, in some remote and roundabout way, hang together. What Darwin means is, that, since that environment is a perfectly known thing, and its relations to the organism in the way of destruction or preservation are tangible and distinct, it would utterly confuse our finite understandings and frustrate our hopes of science to mix in with it facts from such a disparate and incommensurable cycle as that in which the variations are produced. This last cycle is that of occurrences before the animal is born. It is the cycle of influences upon ova and embryos;

in which lie the causes that tip them and tilt them towards masculinity or femininity, towards strength or weakness, towards health or disease, and towards divergence from the parent type. What are the causes there?

In the first place, they are molecular and invisible, — inaccessible, therefore, to direct observation of any kind. Secondly, their operations are compatible with any social, political, and physical conditions of environment. The same parents, living in the same environing conditions, may at one birth produce a genius, at the next an idiot or a monster. The visible external conditions are therefore not direct determinants of this cycle; and the more we consider the matter, the more we are forced to believe that two children of the same parents are made to differ from each other by causes as disproportionate to their ultimate effects as is the famous pebble on the Rocky Mountain crest, which separates two rain-drops, to the Gulf of St. Lawrence and the Pacific Ocean toward which it makes them severally flow.

The great mechanical distinction between transitive forces and discharging forces is nowhere illustrated on such a scale as in physiology. Almost all causes there are forces of *detent*, which operate by simply unlocking energy already stored up. They are upsetters of unstable equilibria, and the resultant effect depends infinitely more on the nature of the materials upset than on that of the particular stimulus which joggles them down. Galvanic work, equal to unity, done on a frog's nerve will discharge from the muscle to which the nerve belongs mechanical work equal to seventy thousand; and exactly the same muscular effect will emerge if other irritants than galvanism are employed. The irritant has merely started or provoked something which then went on of itself, — as a match may start a fire which consumes a whole town. And qualitatively as well as quantitatively the effect may be absolutely incommensurable with the cause. We find this condition of things in all organic matter. Chemists are distracted by the difficulties which the instability of albuminoid compounds opposes to their study. Two specimens, treated in what outwardly seem scrupulously identical conditions, behave in quite different ways. You know about the invisible factors of fermentation, and how the fate of a jar of milk — whether it turn into a sour clot or a mass of koumiss — depends on whether the lactic acid ferment or the alcoholic is introduced first, and gets ahead of the other in starting the process. Now, when the result is the tendency of an ovum, itself invisible to the naked eye, to tip towards this direction or that in its further evolution, — to bring forth a genius or a dunce, even as the rain-drop passes east or west of the pebble, — is it not obvious that the deflecting cause must lie in a region so recondite and minute, must be such a ferment of a ferment, an infinitesimal of so high an order, that surmise itself may never succeed even in attempting to frame an image of it?

Such being the case, was not Darwin right to turn his back upon that region altogether, and to keep his own problem carefully free from all entanglement with matters such as these? The success of his work is a sufficiently affirmative reply.

And this brings us at last to the heart of our subject. The causes of production of great men lie in a

15

sphere wholly inaccessible to the social philosopher.
He must simply accept geniuses as data, just as Darwin accepts his spontaneous variations. For him, as
for Darwin, the only problem is, these data being
given, How does the environment affect them, and
how do they affect the environment? Now, I affirm
that the relation of the visible environment to the
great man is in the main exactly what it is to the
'variation' in the Darwinian philosophy. It chiefly
adopts or rejects, preserves or destroys, in short *selects*
him.[1] And whenever it adopts and preserves the
great man, it becomes modified by his influence in
an entirely original and peculiar way. He acts as a
ferment, and changes its constitution, just as the ad-
vent of a new zoölogical species changes the faunal
and floral equilibrium of the region in which it appears. We all recollect Mr. Darwin's famous statement of the influence of cats on the growth of clover
in their neighborhood. We all have read of the
effects of the European rabbit in New Zealand, and
we have many of us taken part in the controversy
about the English sparrow here, — whether he kills
most canker-worms, or drives away most native
birds. Just so the great man, whether he be an im-
portation from without like Clive in India or Agassiz
here, or whether he spring from the soil like Maho-
met or Franklin, brings about a rearrangement, on
a large or a small scale, of the pre-existing social
relations.

---

[1] It is true that it remodels him, also, to some degree, by its edu-
cative influence, and that this constitutes a considerable difference
between the social case and the zoölogical case. I neglect this aspect
of the relation here, for the other is the more important. At the end
of the article I will return to it incidentally.

The mutations of societies, then, from generation to generation, are in the main due directly or indirectly to the acts or the example of individuals whose genius was so adapted to the receptivities of the moment, or whose accidental position of authority was so critical that they became ferments, initiators of movement, setters of precedent or fashion, centres of corruption, or destroyers of other persons, whose gifts, had they had free play, would have led society in another direction.

We see this power of individual initiative exemplified on a small scale all about us, and on a large scale in the case of the leaders of history. It is only following the common-sense method of a Lyell, a Darwin, and a Whitney to interpret the unknown by the known, and reckon up cumulatively the only causes of social change we can directly observe. Societies of men are just like individuals, in that both at any given moment offer ambiguous potentialities of development. Whether a young man enters business or the ministry may depend on a decision which has to be made before a certain day. He takes the place offered in the counting-house, and is *committed*. Little by little, the habits, the knowledges, of the other career, which once lay so near, cease to be reckoned even among his possibilities. At first, he may sometimes doubt whether the self he murdered in that decisive hour might not have been the better of the two ; but with the years such questions themselves expire, and the old alternative *ego*, once so vivid, fades into something less substantial than a dream. It is no otherwise with nations. They may be committed by kings and ministers to peace or war, by generals to victory or defeat, by prophets to this religion or to that, by various geniuses to fame in art, science, or industry. A war is a true point of bifurcation of future possibilities. Whether it fail or succeed, its declaration must be the starting-point of new policies. Just so does a revolution, or any great civic precedent, become a deflecting influence, whose operations widen with the course of time. Communities obey their ideals; and an accidental success fixes an ideal, as an accidental failure blights it.

Would England have to-day the 'imperial' ideal which she now has, if a certain boy named Bob Clive had shot himself, as he tried to do, at Madras? Would she be the drifting raft she is now in European affairs [1] if a Frederic the Great had inherited her throne instead of a Victoria, and if Messrs. Bentham, Mill, Cobden, and Bright had all been born in Prussia? England has, no doubt, to-day precisely the same intrinsic value relatively to the other nations that she ever had. There is no such fine accumulation of human material upon the globe. But in England the material has lost effective form, while in Germany it has found it. Leaders give the form. Would England be crying forward and backward at once, as she does now, 'letting I will not wait upon I would,' wishing to conquer but not to fight, if her ideal had in all these years been fixed by a succession of statesmen of supremely commanding personality, working in one direction? Certainly not. She would have espoused, for better or worse, either one course or another. Had Bismarck died in his cradle, the Germans would still be satisfied with appearing to themselves as a race of spectacled *Gelehrten* and political herbivora, and to the French as *ces bons*, or *ces naïfs*,

---

[1] The reader will remember when this was written.

Allemands.   Bismarck's will showed them, to their
own great astonishment, that they could play a far
livelier game.   The lesson will not be forgotten.
Germany may have many vicissitudes, but they —

> "will never do away, I ween,
> The marks of that which once hath been" —

of Bismarck's initiative, namely, from 1860 to 1873.

The fermentative influence of geniuses must be
admitted as, at any rate, one factor in the changes
that constitute social evolution.   The community
may evolve in many ways.   The accidental presence
of this or that ferment decides in which way it *shall*
evolve.   Why, the very birds of the forest, the par-
rot, the mino, have the power of human speech, but
never develop it of themselves; some one must be
there to teach them.   So with us individuals.   Rembrandt must teach us to enjoy the struggle of light
with darkness, Wagner to enjoy peculiar musical
effects; Dickens gives a twist to our sentimentality,
Artemus Ward to our humor; Emerson kindles a
new moral light within us.   But it is like Columbus's
egg.   "All can raise the flowers now, for all have got
the seed."   But if this be true of the individuals in
the community, how can it be false of the community
as a whole?   If shown a certain way, a community
may take it; if not, it will never find it.   And the
ways are to a large extent indeterminate in advance.
A nation may obey either of many alternative impulses given by different men of genius, and still live
and be prosperous, just as a man may enter either of
many businesses.   Only, the prosperities may differ in
their type.

But the indeterminism is not absolute.   Not every

' man ' fits every ' hour.' Some incompatibilities there
are. A given genius may come either too early or
too late. Peter the Hermit would now be sent to a
lunatic asylum. John Mill in the tenth century
would have lived and died unknown. Cromwell and
Napoleon need their revolutions, Grant his civil war.
An Ajax gets no fame in the day of telescopic-sighted
rifles; and, to express differently an instance which
Spencer uses, what could a Watt have effected in a
tribe which no precursive genius had taught to smelt
iron or to turn a lathe?

Now, the important thing to notice is that what
makes a certain genius now incompatible with his
surroundings is usually the fact that some previous
genius of a different strain has warped the community
away from the sphere of his possible effectiveness.
After Voltaire, no Peter the Hermit; after Charles
IX. and Louis XIV., no general protestantization of
France; after a Manchester school, a Beaconsfield's
success is transient; after a Philip II., a Castelar
makes little headway; and so on. Each bifurcation
cuts off certain sides of the field altogether, and limits
the future possible angles of deflection. A community is a living thing, and in words which I can do no
better than quote from Professor Clifford,[1] " it is the
peculiarity of living things not merely that they
change under the influence of surrounding circumstances, but that any change which takes place in
them is not lost but retained, and as it were built into
the organism to serve as the foundation for future
actions. If you cause any distortion in the growth
of a tree and make it crooked, whatever you may do
afterwards to make the tree straight the mark of your

[1] Lectures and Essays, i. 82.

distortion is there; it is absolutely indelible; it has become part of the tree's nature. . . . Suppose, however, that you take a lump of gold, melt it, and let it cool. . . . No one can tell by examining a piece of gold how often it has been melted and cooled in geologic ages, or even in the last year by the hand of man. Any one who cuts down an oak can tell by the rings in its trunk how many times winter has frozen it into widowhood, and how many times summer has warmed it into life. A living being must always contain within itself the history, not merely of its own existence, but of all its ancestors."

Every painter can tell us how each added line deflects his picture in a certain sense. Whatever lines follow must be built on those first laid down. Every author who starts to rewrite a piece of work knows how impossible it becomes to use any of the first-written pages again. The new beginning has already excluded the possibility of those earlier phrases and transitions, while it has at the same time created the possibility of an indefinite set of new ones, no one of which, however, is completely determined in advance. Just so the social surroundings of the past and present hour exclude the possibility of accepting certain contributions from individuals; but they do not positively define what contributions shall be accepted, for in themselves they are powerless to fix what the nature of the individual offerings shall be.[1]

[1] Mr. Grant Allen himself, in an article from which I shall presently quote, admits that a set of people who, if they had been exposed ages ago to the geographical agencies of Timbuctoo, would have developed into negroes might now, after a protracted exposure to the conditions of Hamburg, never become negroes if transplanted to Timbuctoo.

Thus social evolution is a resultant of the inter-action of two wholly distinct factors, — the individual, deriving his peculiar gifts from the play of physiolog-ical and infra-social forces, but bearing all the power of initiative and origination in his hands; and, second, the social environment, with its power of adopting or rejecting both him and his gifts. Both factors are essential to change. The community stagnates with-out the impulse of the individual. The impulse dies away without the sympathy of the community.

All this seems nothing more than common-sense. All who wish to see it developed by a man of genius should read that golden little work, Bagehot's Physics and Politics, in which (it seems to me) the complete sense of the way in which concrete things grow and change is as livingly present as the straining after a pseudo-philosophy of evolution is livingly absent. But there are never wanting minds to whom such views seem personal and contracted, and allied to an anthropomorphism long exploded in other fields of knowledge. "The individual withers, and the world is more and more," to these writers; and in a Buckle, a Draper, and a Taine we all know how much the 'world' has come to be almost synonymous with the *climate*. We all know, too, how the controversy has been kept up between the partisans of a 'science of history' and those who deny the existence of any-thing like necessary 'laws' where human societies are concerned. Mr. Spencer, at the opening of his Study of Sociology, makes an onslaught on the 'great-man theory' of history, from which a few passages may be quoted: —

"The genesis of societies by the action of great men may be comfortably believed so long as, resting in general notions, you do not ask for particulars. But now, if, dissatisfied with vagueness, we demand that our ideas shall be brought into focus and exactly defined, we discover the hypothesis to be utterly incoherent. If, not stopping at the explanation of social progress as due to the great man, we go back a step, and ask, Whence comes the great man? we find that the theory breaks down completely. The question has two conceivable answers : his origin is supernatural, or it is natural. Is his origin supernatural? Then he is a deputy god, and we have theocracy once removed, — or, rather, not removed at all. . . . Is this an unacceptable solution? Then the origin of the great man is natural; and immediately this is recognized, he must be classed with all other phenomena in the society that gave him birth as a product of its antecedents. Along with the whole generation of which he forms a minute part, along with its institutions, language, knowledge, manners, and its multitudinous arts and appliances, he is a *resultant*. . . . You must admit that the genesis of the great man depends on the long series of complex influences which has produced the race in which he appears, and the social state into which that race has slowly grown. . . . Before he can remake his society, his society must make him. All those changes of which he is the proximate initiator have their chief causes in the generations he descended from. If there is to be anything like a real explanation of those changes, it must be sought in that aggregate of conditions out of which both he and they have arisen." [1]

Now, it seems to me that there is something which one might almost call impudent in the attempt which Mr. Spencer makes, in the first sentence of this extract, to pin the reproach of vagueness upon those who believe in the power of initiative of the great man.

[1] Study of Sociology, pages 33–35.

Suppose I say that the singular moderation which now distinguishes social, political, and religious discussion in England, and contrasts so strongly with the bigotry and dogmatism of sixty years ago, is largely due to J. S. Mill's example. I may possibly be wrong about the facts; but I am, at any rate, ' asking for particulars,' and not ' resting in general notions.' And if Mr. Spencer should tell me it started from no personal influence whatever, but from the ' aggregate of conditions,' the ' generations,' Mill and all his contemporaries ' descended from,' the whole past order of nature in short, surely he, not I, would be the person ' satisfied with vagueness.'

The fact is that Mr. Spencer's sociological method is identical with that of one who would invoke the zodiac to account for the fall of the sparrow, and the thirteen at table to explain the gentleman's death. It is of little more scientific value than the Oriental method of replying to whatever question arises by the unimpeachable truism, " God is great." *Not* to fall back on the gods, where a proximate principle may be found, has with us Westerners long since become the sign of an efficient as distinguished from an inefficient intellect.

To believe that the cause of everything is to be found in its antecedents is the starting-point, the initial postulate, not the goal and consummation, of science. If she is simply to lead us out of the labyrinth by the same hole we went in by three or four thousand years ago, it seems hardly worth while to have followed her through the darkness at all. If anything is humanly certain it is that the great man's society, properly so called, does *not* make him before he can remake it. Physiological forces, with which

the social, political, geographical, and to a great
extent anthropological conditions have just as much
and just as little to do as the condition of the crater
of Vesuvius has to do with the flickering of this gas by
which I write, are what make him.   Can it be that Mr.
Spencer holds the convergence of sociological pres-
sures to have so impinged on Stratford-upon-Avon
about the 26th of April, 1564, that a W. Shakespeare,
with all his mental peculiarities, had to be born there,
— as the pressure of water outside a certain boat will
cause a stream of a certain form to ooze into a particular leak?   And does he mean to say that if the
aforesaid W. Shakespeare had died of cholera infan-
tum, another mother at Stratford-upon-Avon would
needs have engendered a duplicate copy of him, to
restore the sociologic equilibrium, — just as the same
stream of water will reappear, no matter how often
you pass a sponge over the leak, so long as the outside level remains unchanged?   Or might the substitute arise at 'Stratford-atte-Bowe'?   Here, as elsewhere, it is very hard, in the midst of Mr. Spencer's
vagueness, to tell what he does mean at all.

We have, however, in his disciple, Mr. Grant Allen,
one who leaves us in no doubt whatever of his precise
meaning.   This widely informed, suggestive, and brilliant writer published last year a couple of articles in
the Gentleman's Magazine, in which he maintained that
individuals have no initiative in determining social
change.

"The differences between one nation and another,
whether in intellect, commerce, art, morals, or general temperament, ultimately depend, not upon any mysterious
properties of race, nationality, or any other unknown and
unintelligible abstractions, but simply and solely upon the

physical circumstances to which they are exposed. If it be a fact, as we know it to be, that the French nation differs recognizably from the Chinese, and the people of Hamburg differ recognizably from the people of Timbuctoo, then the notorious and conspicuous differences between them are wholly due to the geographical position of the various races. If the people who went to Hamburg had gone to Timbuctoo, they would now be indistinguishable from the semi-barbarian negroes who inhabit that central African metropolis ;[1] and if the people who went to Timbuctoo had gone to Hamburg, they would now have been white-skinned merchants driving a roaring trade in imitation sherry and indigestible port. . . . The differentiating agency must be sought in the great permanent geographical features of land and sea ; . . . these have necessarily and inevitably moulded the characters and histories of every nation upon the earth. . . . We cannot regard any nation as an active agent in differentiating itself. Only the surrounding circumstances can have any effect in such a direction. [These two sentences dogmatically deny the existence of the relatively independent physiological cycle of causation.] To suppose otherwise is to suppose that the mind of man is exempt from the universal law of causation. There is no caprice, no spontaneous impulse, in human endeavors. Even tastes and inclinations *must* themselves be the result of surrounding causes."[2]

---

[1] No! not even though they were bodily brothers ! The geographical factor utterly vanishes before the ancestral factor. The difference between Hamburg and Timbuctoo as a cause of ultimate divergence of two races is as nothing to the difference of constitution of the ancestors of the two races, even though as in twin brothers, this difference might be invisible to the naked eye. No two couples of the most homogeneous race could possibly be found so identical as, if set in identical environments, to give rise to two identical lineages. The minute divergence at the start grows broader with each generation, and ends with entirely dissimilar breeds.

[2] Article 'Nation Making,' in Gentleman's Magazine, 1878. I

Elsewhere Mr. Allen, writing of the Greek culture, says : —

" It was absolutely and unreservedly the product of the geographical Hellas, acting upon the given factor of the undifferentiated Aryan brain. . . . To me it seems a self-evident proposition that nothing whatsoever can differentiate one body of men from another, except the physical conditions in which they are set, — including, of course, under the term *physical conditions* the relations of place and time in which they stand with regard to other bodies of men. To suppose otherwise is to deny the primordial law of causation. To imagine that the mind can differentiate itself is to imagine that it can be differentiated without a cause." [1]

This outcry about the law of universal causation being undone, the moment we refuse to invest in the kind of causation which is peddled round by a particular school, makes one impatient. These writers have no imagination of alternatives. With them there is no *tertium quid* between outward environment and miracle. *Aut Cæsar, aut nullus! Aut* Spencerism, *aut* catechism !

If by ' physical conditions ' Mr. Allen means what he does mean, the outward cycle of visible nature and man, his assertion is simply physiologically false. For a national mind differentiates ' itself ' whenever a genius is born in its midst by causes acting in the invisible and molecular cycle. But if Mr. Allen means by ' physical conditions ' the whole of nature, his assertion, though true, forms but the vague Asiatic

quote from the reprint in the Popular Science Monthly Supplement, December, 1878, pages 121, 123, 126.

[1] Article ' Hellas,' in Gentleman's Magazine, 1878. Reprint in Popular Science Monthly Supplement, September, 1878.

profession of belief in an all-enveloping fate, which certainly need not plume itself on any specially advanced or scientific character.

And how can a thinker so clever as Mr. Allen fail to have distinguished in these matters between *necessary* conditions and *sufficient* conditions of a given result? The French say that to have an omelet we must break our eggs; that is, the breaking of eggs is a necessary condition of the omelet. But is it a sufficient condition? Does an omelet appear whenever three eggs are broken? So of the Greek mind. To get such versatile intelligence it may be that such commercial dealings with the world as the geographical Hellas afforded are a necessary condition. But if they are a sufficient condition, why did not the Phœnicians outstrip the Greeks in intelligence? No geographical environment can produce a given type of mind. It can only foster and further certain types fortuitously produced, and thwart and frustrate others. Once again, its function is simply selective, and determines what shall actually be only by destroying what is positively incompatible. An Arctic environment is incompatible with improvident habits in its denizens; but whether the inhabitants of such a region shall unite with their thrift the peacefulness of the Eskimo or the pugnacity of the Norseman is, so far as the climate is concerned, an accident. Evolutionists should not forget that we all have five fingers not because four or six would not do just as well, but merely because the first vertebrate above the fishes *happened* to have that number. He owed his prodigious success in founding a line of descent to some entirely other quality, — we know not which, — but the inessential five fingers were taken in tow and preserved to the present day. So of most social peculiarities. Which of them shall be taken in tow by the few qualities which the environment necessarily exacts is a matter of what physiological accidents shall happen among individuals. Mr. Allen promises to prove his thesis in detail by the examples of China, India, England, Rome, etc. I have not the smallest hesitation in predicting that he will do no more with these examples than he has done with Hellas. He will appear upon the scene after the fact, and show that the quality developed by each race was, naturally enough, not incompatible with its habitat. But he will utterly fail to show that the particular form of compatibility fallen into in each case was the one necessary and only possible form.

Naturalists know well enough how indeterminate the harmonies between a fauna and its environment are. An animal may better his chances of existence in either of many ways, — growing aquatic, arboreal, or subterranean; small and swift, or massive and bulky; spiny, horny, slimy, or venomous; more timid or more pugnacious; more cunning or more fertile of offspring; more gregarious or more solitary; or in other ways besides, — and any one of these ways may suit him to many widely different environments.

Readers of Mr. A. R. Wallace will well remember the striking illustrations of this in his Malay Archipelago : —

"Borneo closely resembles New Guinea not only in its vast size and its freedom from volcanoes, but in its variety of geological structure, its uniformity of climate, and the general aspect of the forest vegetation that clothes its surface ; the Moluccas are the counterpart of the Philippines in their volcanic structure, their extreme fertility, their luxuriant forests, and their frequent earthquakes; and Bali, with the east end of Java, has a climate almost as dry and a soil almost as arid as that of Timor. Yet between these corresponding groups of islands, constructed, as it were, after the same pattern, subjected to the same climate, and bathed by the same oceans, there exists the greatest possible contrast when we compare their animal productions. Nowhere does the ancient doctrine that differences or similarities in the various forms of life that inhabit different countries are due to corresponding physical differences or similarities in the countries themselves, meet with so direct and palpable a contradiction. Borneo and New Guinea, as alike physically as two distinct countries can be, are zoölogically wide as the poles asunder; while Australia, with its dry winds, its open plains, its stony deserts, and its temperate climate, yet produces birds and quadrupeds which are closely related to those inhabiting the hot, damp, luxuriant forests which everywhere clothe the plains and mountains of New Guinea."

Here we have similar physical-geography environments harmonizing with widely differing animal lives, and similar animal lives harmonizing with widely differing geographical environments. A singularly accomplished writer, E. Gryzanowski, in the North American Review,[1] uses the instances of Sardinia and Corsica in support of this thesis with great effect. He says: —

" These sister islands, lying in the very centre of the Mediterranean, at almost equal distances from the centres of Latin and Neo-Latin civilization, within easy reach of the Phœnician, the Greek, and the Saracen, with a coast-

[1] Vol. cxiii. p. 318 (October, 1871).

line of more than a thousand miles, endowed with obvious and tempting advantages, and hiding untold sources of agricultural and mineral wealth, have nevertheless remained unknown, unheeded, and certainly uncared for during the thirty centuries of European history. . . . These islands have dialects, but no language ; records of battles, but no history. They have customs, but no laws ; the *vendetta*, but no justice. They have wants and wealth, but no commerce ; timber and ports, but no shipping. They have legends, but no poetry ; beauty, but no art ; and twenty years ago it could still be said that they had universities, but no students. . . . That Sardinia, with all her emotional and picturesque barbarism, has never produced a single artist is almost as strange as her barbarism itself. . . . Near the focus of European civilization, in the very spot which an *à priori* geographer would point out as the most favorable place for material and intellectual, commercial, and political development, these strange sister islands have slept their secular sleep, like *nodes* on the sounding-board of history."

This writer then goes on to compare Sardinia and Sicily with some detail. All the material advantages are in favor of Sardinia, "and the Sardinian population, being of an ancestry more mixed than that of the English race, would justify far higher expectations than that of Sicily." Yet Sicily's past history has been brilliant in the extreme, and her commerce to-day is great. Dr. Gryzanowiski has his own theory of the historic torpor of these favored isles. He thinks they stagnated because they never gained political autonomy, being always owned by some Continental power. I will not dispute the theory ; but I will ask, Why did they not gain it? and answer immediately : Simply because no individuals were born there with patriotism and ability enough to inflame their countrymen with national pride, ambition, and thirst for independent life. Corsicans and Sardinians are probably as good stuff as any of their neighbors. But the best wood-pile will not blaze till a torch is applied, and the appropriate torches seem to have been wanting.[1]

Sporadic great men come everywhere. But for a community to get vibrating through and through

[1] I am well aware that in much that follows (though in nothing that precedes) I seem to be crossing the heavily shotted bows of Mr. Galton, for whose laborious investigations into the heredity of genius I have the greatest respect. Mr. Galton inclines to think that genius of intellect and passion is bound to express itself, whatever the outward opportunity, and that within any given race an equal number of geniuses of each grade must needs be born in every equal period of time; a subordinate race cannot possibly engender a large number of high-class geniuses, etc. He would, I suspect, infer the suppositions I go on to make — of great men fortuitously assembling around a given epoch and making it great, and of their being fortuitously absent from certain places and times (from Sardinia, from Boston now, etc.) — to be radically vicious. I hardly think, however, that he does justice to the great complexity of the conditions of *effective* greatness, and to the way in which the physiological averages of production may be masked entirely during long periods, either by the accidental mortality of geniuses in infancy, or by the fact that the particular geniuses born happened not to find tasks. I doubt the truth of his assertion that *intellectual* genius, like murder, 'will out.' It is true that certain types are irrepressible. Voltaire, Shelley, Carlyle, can hardly be conceived leading a dumb and vegetative life in any epoch. But take Mr. Galton himself, take his cousin Mr. Darwin, and take Mr. Spencer: nothing is to me more conceivable than that at another epoch all three of these men might have died 'with all their music in them,' known only to their friends as persons of strong and original character and judgment. What has started them on their career of effective greatness is simply the accident of each stumbling upon a task vast, brilliant, and congenial enough to call out the convergence of all his passions and powers. I see no more reason why, in case they had not fallen in with their several hobbies at propitious periods in their life, they need

with intensely active life, many geniuses coming together and in rapid succession are required. This is why great epochs are so rare, — why the sudden bloom of a Greece, an early Rome, a Renaissance, is such a mystery. Blow must follow blow so fast that no cooling can occur in the intervals. Then the mass of the nation grows incandescent, and may continue to glow by pure inertia long after the originators of its internal movement have passed away. We often hear surprise expressed that in these high tides of human affairs not only the people should be filled with stronger life, but that individual geniuses should seem so exceptionally abundant. This mystery is just about as deep as the time-honored conundrum as to why great rivers flow by great towns. It is true that great public fermentations awaken and adopt many geniuses, who in more torpid times would have had no chance to work. But over and above this there must be an exceptional concourse of genius about a time, to make the fermentation begin at all. The unlikeliness of the concourse is far greater than the unlikeliness of any particular genius; hence the rarity of these periods and the exceptional aspect which they always wear.

necessarily have hit upon other hobbies, and made themselves equally great. Their case seems similar to that of the Washingtons, Cromwells, and Grants, who simply rose to their occasions. But apart from these causes of fallacy, I am strongly disposed to think that where transcendent geniuses are concerned the numbers anyhow are so small that their appearance will not fit into any scheme of averages. That is, two or three might appear together, just as the two or three balls nearest the target centre might be fired consecutively. Take longer epochs and more firing, and the great geniuses and near balls would on the whole be more spread out.

It is folly, then, to speak of the 'laws of history' as of something inevitable, which science has only to discover, and whose consequences any one can then foretell but do nothing to alter or avert. Why, the very laws of physics are conditional, and deal with *ifs*. The physicist does not say, "The water will boil anyhow;" he only says it will boil if a fire be kindled beneath it. And so the utmost the student of sociology can ever predict is that *if* a genius of a certain sort show the way, society will be sure to follow. It might long ago have been predicted with great confidence that both Italy and Germany would reach a stable unity if some one could but succeed in starting the process. It could not have been predicted, however, that the *modus operandi* in each case would be subordination to a paramount state rather than federation, because no historian could have calculated the freaks of birth and fortune which gave at the same moment such positions of authority to three such peculiar individuals as Napoleon III., Bismarck, and Cavour. So of our own politics. It is certain now that the movement of the independents, reformers, or whatever one please to call them, will triumph. But whether it do so by converting the Republican party to its ends, or by rearing a new party on the ruins of both our present factions, the historian cannot say. There can be no doubt that the reform movement would make more progress in one year with an adequate personal leader than as now in ten without one. Were there a great citizen, splendid with every civic gift, to be its candidate, who can doubt that he would lead us to victory? But, at present, we, his environment, who sigh for him and would so gladly preserve and adopt him if he came, can neither move without him, nor yet do anything to bring him forth.[1]

To conclude: The evolutionary view of history, when it denies the vital importance of individual initiative, is, then, an utterly vague and unscientific conception, a lapse from modern scientific determinism into the most ancient oriental fatalism. The lesson of the analysis that we have made (even on the completely deterministic hypothesis with which we started) forms an appeal of the most stimulating sort to the energy of the individual. Even the dogged resistance of the reactionary conservative to changes which he cannot hope entirely to defeat is justified and shown to be effective. He retards the movement; deflects it a little by the concessions he extracts; gives it a resultant momentum, compounded of his inertia and his adversaries' speed; and keeps up, in short, a constant lateral pressure, which, to be sure, never heads it round about, but brings it up at last at a goal far to the right or left of that to which it would have drifted had he allowed it to drift alone.

I now pass to the last division of my subject, the function of the environment in *mental* evolution. After what I have already said, I may be quite concise. Here, if anywhere, it would seem at first sight as if that school must be right which makes the mind passively plastic, and the environment actively productive of the form and order of its conceptions; which, in a word, thinks that all mental progress must result from

[1] Since this paper was written, President Cleveland has to a certain extent met the need. But who can doubt that if he had certain other qualities which he has not yet shown, his influence would have been still more decisive? (1896.)

a series of adaptive changes, in the sense already defined of that word. We know what a vast part of our mental furniture consists of purely remembered, not reasoned, experience. The entire field of our habits and associations by contiguity belongs here. The entire field of those abstract conceptions which were taught us with the language into which we were born belongs here also. And, more than this, there is reason to think that the order of 'outer relations' experienced by the individual may itself determine the order in which the general characters imbedded therein shall be noticed and extracted by his mind.[1] The pleasures and benefits, moreover, which certain parts of the environment yield, and the pains and hurts which other parts inflict, determine the direction of our interest and our attention, and so decide at which points the accumulation of mental experiences shall begin. It might, accordingly, seem as if there were no room for any other agency than this; as if the distinction we have found so useful between 'spontaneous variation,' as the producer of changed forms, and the environment, as their preserver and destroyer, did not hold in the case of mental progress; as if, in a word, the parallel with darwinism might no longer obtain, and Spencer might be quite right with his fundamental law of intelligence, which says, "The cohesion between psychical states is proportionate to the frequency with which the relation between the answering external pheonmena has been repeated in experience."[2]

---

[1] That is, if a certain general character be rapidly repeated in our outer experience with a number of strongly contrasted concomitants, it will be sooner abstracted than if its associates are invariable or monotonous.

[2] Principles of Psychology, i. 460. See also pp. 463, 464, 500. On

But, in spite of all these facts, I have no hesitation whatever in holding firm to the darwinian distinction even here. I maintain that the facts in question are all drawn from the lower strata of the mind, so to speak, — from the sphere of its least evolved functions, from the region of intelligence which man possesses in common with the brutes. And I can easily show that throughout the whole extent of those mental departments which are highest, which are most characteristically human, Spencer's law is violated at every step; and that as a matter of fact the new conceptions, emotions, and active tendencies which evolve are originally produced in the shape of random images, fancies, accidental out-births of spontaneous variation in the functional activity of the excessively instable human brain, which the outer environment simply confirms or refutes, adopts or rejects, preserves or destroys, — selects, in short, just as it selects morphological and social variations due to molecular accidents of an analogous sort.

It is one of the tritest of truisms that human intelligences of a simple order are very literal. They are slaves of habit, doing what they have been taught without variation; dry, prosaic, and matter-of-fact in their remarks; devoid of humor, except of the coarse physical kind which rejoices in a practical joke; taking the world for granted; and possessing in their faithfulness and honesty the single gift by which they are sometimes able to warm us into admiration. But

---

page 408 the law is formulated thus : The *persistence* of the connection in consciousness is proportionate to the *persistence* of the outer connection. Mr. Spencer works most with the law of frequency. Either law, from my point of view, is false; but Mr. Spencer ought not to think them synonymous.

even this faithfulness seems to have a sort of inorganic ring, and to remind us more of the immutable properties of a piece of inanimate matter than of the steadfastness of a human will capable of alternative choice. When we descend to the brutes, all these peculiarities are intensified. No reader of Schopenhauer can forget his frequent allusions to the *trockener ernst* of dogs and horses, nor to their *ehrlichkeit*. And every noticer of their ways must receive a deep impression of the fatally literal character of the few, simple, and treadmill-like operations of their minds.

But turn to the highest order of minds, and what a change! Instead of thoughts of concrete things patiently following one another in a beaten track of habitual suggestion, we have the most abrupt cross-cuts and transitions from one idea to another, the most rarefied abstractions and discriminations, the most unheard-of combinations of elements, the subtlest associations of analogy; in a word, we seem suddenly introduced into a seething caldron of ideas, where everything is fizzling and bobbing about in a state of bewildering activity, where partnerships can be joined or loosened in an instant, treadmill routine is unknown, and the unexpected seems the only law. According to the idiosyncrasy of the individual, the scintillations will have one character or another. They will be sallies of wit and humor; they will be flashes of poetry and eloquence; they will be constructions of dramatic fiction or of mechanical device, logical or philosophic abstractions, business projects, or scientific hypotheses, with trains of experimental consequences based thereon; they will be musical sounds, or images of plastic beauty or picturesqueness, or visions of moral harmony. But, whatever their differences may be, they will all agree in this, — that their genesis is sudden and, as it were, spontaneous. That is to say, the same premises would not, in the mind of another individual, have engendered just that conclusion; although, when the conclusion is offered to the other individual, he may thoroughly accept and enjoy it, and envy the brilliancy of him to whom it first occurred.

To Professor Jevons is due the great credit of having emphatically pointed out [1] how the genius of discovery depends altogether on the number of these random notions and guesses which visit the investigator's mind. To be fertile in hypotheses is the first requisite, and to be willing to throw them away the moment experience contradicts them is the next. The Baconian method of collating tables of instances may be a useful aid at certain times. But one might as well expect a chemist's note-book to write down the name of the body analyzed, or a weather table to sum itself up into a prediction of probabilities of its own accord, as to hope that the mere fact of mental confrontation with a certain series of facts will be sufficient to make *any* brain conceive their law. The conceiving of the law is a spontaneous variation in the strictest sense of the term. It flashes out of one brain, and no other, because the instability of that brain is such as to tip and upset itself in just that particular direction. But the important thing to notice is that the good flashes and the bad flashes, the triumphant hypotheses and the absurd conceits, are on an exact equality in respect of their origin. Aristotle's absurd Physics and his immortal Logic flow from one source: the forces that produce the one produce the other.

[1] In his Principles of Science, chapters xi. xii. xxvi.

When walking along the street, thinking of the blue sky or the fine spring weather, I may either smile at some grotesque whim which occurs to me, or I may suddenly catch an intuition of the solution of a long-unsolved problem, which at that moment was far from my thoughts. Bóth notions are shaken out of the same reservoir, — the reservoir of a brain in which the reproduction of images in the relations of their outward persistence or frequency has long ceased to be the dominant law. But to the thought, when it is once engendered, the consecration of agreement with outward relations may come. The conceit perishes in a moment, and is forgotten. The scientific hypothesis arouses in me a fever of desire for verification. I read, write, experiment, consult experts. Everything corroborates my notion, which being then published in a book spreads from review to review and from mouth to mouth, till at last there is no doubt I am enshrined in the Pantheon of the great diviners of nature's ways. The environment *preserves* the conception which it was unable to *produce* in any brain less idiosyncratic than my own.

Now, the spontaneous upsettings of brains this way and that at particular moments into particular ideas and combinations are matched by their equally spontaneous permanent tiltings or saggings towards determinate directions. The humorous bent is quite characteristic; the sentimental one equally so. And the personal tone of each mind, which makes it more alive to certain classes of experience than others, more attentive to certain impressions, more open to certain reasons, is equally the result of that invisible and unimaginable play of the forces of growth within the nervous system which, irresponsibly to the environment, makes the brain peculiarly apt to function in a certain way.   Here again the selection goes on. The products of the mind with the determined æsthetic bent please or displease the community.   We adopt Wordsworth, and grow unsentimental and serene.   We are fascinated by Schopenhauer, and learn from him the true luxury of woe.   The adopted bent becomes a ferment in the community, and alters its tone.   The alteration may be a benefit or a misfortune, for it is (*pace* Mr. Allen) a differentiation from within, which has to run the gauntlet of the larger environment's selective power.   Civilized Languedoc, taking the tone of its scholars, poets, princes, and theologians, fell a prey to its rude Catholic environment in the Albigensian crusade.   France in 1792, taking the tone of its St. Justs and Marats, plunged into its long career of unstable outward relations.   Prussia in 1806, taking the tone of its Humboldts and its Steins, proved itself in the most signal way ' adjusted ' to its environment in 1872.

Mr. Spencer, in one of the strangest chapters of his Psychology,[1] tries to show the necessary order in which the development of conceptions in the human race occurs.   No abstract conception can be developed, according to him, until the outward experiences have reached a certain degree of heterogeneity, definiteness, coherence, and so forth.

"Thus the belief in an unchanging order, the belief in *law*, is a belief of which the primitive man is absolutely incapable. . . . Experiences such as he receives furnish but few data for the conception of uniformity, whether as displayed in things or in relations. . . . The daily impres-

[1] Part viii. chap. iii.

sions which the savage gets yield the notion very imperfectly, and in but few cases. Of all the objects around, — trees, stones, hills, pieces of water, clouds, and so forth, — most differ widely, . . . and few approach complete likeness so nearly as to make discrimination difficult. Even between animals of the same species it rarely happens that, whether alive or dead, they are presented in just the same attitudes. . . . It is only along with a gradual development of the arts . . . that there come frequent experiences of perfectly straight lines admitting of complete apposition, bringing the perceptions of equality and inequality. Still more devoid is savage life of the experiences which generate the conception of the uniformity of succession. The sequences observed from hour to hour and day to day seem anything but uniform ; difference is a far more conspicuous trait among them. . . . So that if we contemplate primitive human life as a whole, we see that multiformity of sequence, rather than uniformity, is the notion which it tends to generate. . . . Only as fast as the practice of the arts develops the idea of measure can the consciousness of uniformity become clear. . . . Those conditions furnished by advancing civilization which make possible the notion of uniformity simultaneously make possible the notion of *exactness*. . . . Hence the primitive man has little experience which cultivates the consciousness of what we call *truth*. How closely allied this is to the consciousness which the practice of the arts cultivates is implied even in language. We speak of a true surface as well as a true statement. Exactness describes perfection in a mechanical fit, as well as perfect agreement between the results of calculations."

The whole burden of Mr. Spencer's book is to show the fatal way in which the mind, supposed passive, is moulded by its experiences of ' outer relations.' In this chapter the yard-stick, the balance, the chronometer, and other machines and instruments come to figure among the ' relations' external to the mind. Surely they are so, after they have been manufactured; but only because of the preservative power of the social environment. Originally all these things and all other institutions were flashes of genius in an individual head, of which the outer environment showed no sign. Adopted by the race and become its heritage, they then supply instigations to new geniuses whom they environ to make new inventions and discoveries; and so the ball of progress rolls. But take out the geniuses, or alter their idiosyncrasies, and what increasing uniformities will the environment show? We defy Mr. Spencer or any one else to reply.

The plain truth is that the ' philosophy' of evolution (as distinguished from our special information about particular cases of change) is a metaphysical creed, and nothing else. It is a mood of contemplation, an emotional attitude, rather than a system of thought, — a mood which is old as the world, and which no refutation of any one incarnation of it (such as the spencerian philosophy) will dispel; the mood of fatalistic pantheism, with its intuition of the One and All, which was, and is, and ever shall be, and from whose womb each single thing proceeds. Far be it from us to speak slightingly here of so hoary and mighty a style of looking on the world as this. What we at present call scientific discoveries had nothing to do with bringing it to birth, nor can one easily conceive that they should ever give it its *quietus*, no matter how logically incompatible with its spirit the ultimate phenomenal distinctions which science accumulates should turn out to be. It can laugh at the phenomenal distinctions on which science is based, for it draws its vital breath from a region which — whether above or below — is at least altogether different from that in which science dwells. A critic, however, who cannot disprove the truth of the metaphysic creed, can at least raise his voice in protest against its disguising itself in ' scientific ' plumes. I think that all who have had the patience to follow me thus far will agree that the spencerian ' philosophy ' of social and intellectual progress is an obsolete anachronism, reverting to a pre-darwinian type of thought, just as the spencerian philosophy of ' Force,' effacing all the previous distinctions between actual and potential energy, momentum, work, force, mass, etc., which physicists have with so much agony achieved, carries us back to a pre-galilean age.

THE IMPORTANCE OF INDIVIDUALS.

THE previous Essay, on Great Men, etc., called forth two replies, — one by Mr. Grant Allen, entitled the ' Genesis of Genius,' in the Atlantic Monthly, vol. xlvii. p. 351; the other entitled 'Sociology and Hero Worship,' by Mr. John Fiske, *ibidem,* p. 75. The article which follows is a rejoinder to Mr. Allen's article. It was refused at the time by the Atlantic, but saw the day later in the Open Court for August, 1890. It appears here as a natural supplement to the foregoing article, on which it casts some explanatory light.

Mr. Allen's contempt for hero-worship is based on very simple considerations. A nation's great men, he says, are but slight deviations from the general level. The hero is merely a special complex of the ordinary qualities of his race. The petty differences impressed upon ordinary Greek minds by Plato or Aristotle or Zeno, are nothing at all compared with the vast differences between every Greek mind and every Egyptian or Chinese mind. We may neglect them in a philosophy of history, just as in calculating the impetus of a locomotive we neglect the extra impetus given by a single piece of better coal. What each man adds is but an infinitesimal fraction compared with what he derives from his parents, or indirectly from his earlier ancestry. And if what the past gives to the hero is so much bulkier than what the future receives from him, it is what really calls for philosophical treatment. The problem for the sociologist is as to what produces the average man; the extraordinary men and what they produce may by the philosophers be taken for granted, as too trivial variations to merit deep inquiry.

Now, as I wish to vie with Mr. Allen's unrivalled polemic amiability and be as conciliatory as possible, I will not cavil at his facts or try to magnify the chasm between an Aristotle, a Goethe, or a Napoleon and the average level of their respective tribes. Let it be as small as Mr. Allen thinks. All that I object to is that he should think the mere *size* of a difference is capable of deciding whether that difference be or be not a fit subject for philosophic study. Truly enough, the details vanish in the bird's-eye view; but so does the bird's-eye view vanish in the details. Which is the right point of view for philosophic vision? Nature gives no reply, for both points of view, being equally real, are equally natural; and no one natural reality *per se* is any more emphatic than any other. Accentuation, foreground, and background are created solely by the interested attention of the looker-on; and if the small difference between the genius and his tribe interests me most, while the large one between that tribe and another tribe interests Mr. Allen, our controversy cannot be ended until a complete philosophy, accounting for all differences impartially, shall justify us both.

An unlearned carpenter of my acquaintance once said in my hearing: "There is very little difference between one man and another; but what little there

is, *is very important.*" This distinction seems to me
to go to the root of the matter.   It is not only the size
of the difference which concerns the philosopher, but
also its place and its kind.   An inch is a small thing,
but we know the proverb about an inch on a man's
nose.   Messrs. Allen and Spencer, in inveighing
against hero-worship, are thinking exclusively of the
size of the inch; I, as a hero-worshipper, attend to its
seat and function.

Now, there is a striking law over which few people
seem to have pondered.   It is this: That among all
the differences which exist, the only ones that interest
us strongly are those *we do not take for granted.*   We
are not a bit elated that our friend should have two
hands and the power of speech, and should practise
the matter-of-course human virtues; and quite as
little are we vexed that our dog goes on all fours and
fails to understand our conversation.   Expecting no
more from the latter companion, and no less from
the former, we get what we expect and are satisfied.
We never think of communing with the dog by discourse of philosophy, or with the friend by head-
scratching or the throwing of crusts to be snapped
at.   But if either dog or friend fall above or below
the expected standard, they arouse the most lively
emotion.   On our brother's vices or genius we never
weary of descanting; to his bipedism or his hairless
skin we do not consecrate a thought.   *What* he says
may transport us; that he is able to speak at all leaves
us stone cold.   The reason of all this is that his virtues and vices and utterances might, compatibly with
the current range of variation in our tribe, be just the
opposites of what they are, while his zoölogically
human attributes cannot possibly go astray.   There

is thus a zone of insecurity in human affairs in which all the dramatic interest lies; the rest belongs to the dead machinery of the stage. This is the formative zone, the part not yet ingrained into the race's average, not yet a typical, hereditary, and constant factor of the social community in which it occurs. It is like the soft layer beneath the bark of the tree in which all the year's growth is going on. Life has abandoned the mighty trunk inside, which stands inert and belongs almost to the inorganic world. Layer after layer of human perfection separates me from the central Africans who pursued Stanley with cries of "meat, meat!" This vast difference ought, on Mr. Allen's principles, to rivet my attention far more than the petty one which obtains between two such birds of a feather as Mr. Allen and myself. Yet while I never feel proud that the sight of a passer-by awakens in me no cannibalistic waterings of the mouth, I am free to confess that I shall feel very proud if I do not publicly appear inferior to Mr. Allen in the conduct of this momentous debate. To me as a teacher the intellectual gap between my ablest and my dullest student counts for infinitely more than that between the latter and the amphioxus: indeed, I never thought of the latter chasm till this moment. Will Mr. Allen seriously say that this is all human folly, and tweedledum and tweedledee?

To a Veddah's eyes the differences between two white literary men seem slight indeed, — same clothes, same spectacles, same harmless disposition, same habit of scribbling on paper and poring over books, etc. "Just two white fellows," the Veddah will say, "with no perceptible difference." But what a difference to the literary men themselves! Think, Mr. Allen, of confounding our philosophies together merely because both are printed in the same magazines and are indistinguishable to the eye of a Veddah ! Our flesh creeps at the thought.

But in judging of history Mr. Allen deliberately prefers to place himself at the Veddah's point of view, and to see things *en gros* and out of focus, rather than minutely.   It is quite true that there are things and differences enough to be seen either way.   But which are the humanly important ones, those most worthy to arouse our interest, — the large distinctions or the small ?   In the answer to this question lies the whole divergence of the hero-worshippers from the sociologists.   As I said at the outset, it is merely a quarrel of emphasis; and the only thing I can do is to state my personal reasons for the emphasis I prefer.

The zone of the individual differences, and of the social ' twists' which by common confession they initiate, is the zone of formative processes, the dynamic belt of quivering uncertainty, the line where past and future meet.   It is the theatre of all we do not take for granted, the stage of the living drama of life; and however narrow its scope, it is roomy enough to lodge the whole range of human passions. The sphere of the race's average, on the contrary, no matter how large it may be, is a dead and stagnant thing, an achieved possession, from which all insecurity has vanished.   Like the trunk of a tree, it has been built up by successive concretions of successive active zones.   The moving present in which we live with its problems and passions, its individual rivalries, victories, and defeats, will soon pass over to the majority and leave its small deposit on this static mass, to make room for fresh actors and a newer play.

And though it may be true, as Mr. Spencer predicts, that each later zone shall fatally be narrower than its forerunners; and that when the ultimate lady-like tea-table elysium of the Data of Ethics shall prevail, such questions as the breaking of eggs at the large or the small end will span the whole scope of possible human warfare, — still even in this shrunken and enfeebled generation, *spatio aetatis defessa vetusto*, what eagerness there will be! Battles and defeats will occur, the victors will be glorified and the vanquished dishonored just as in the brave days of yore, the human heart still withdrawing itself from the much it has in safe possession, and concentrating all its passion upon those evanescent possibilities of fact which still quiver in fate's scale.

And is not its instinct right? Do not we here grasp the race-differences *in the making*, and catch the only glimpse it is allotted to us to attain of the working units themselves, of whose differentiating action the race-gaps form but the stagnant sum? What strange inversion of scientific procedure does Mr. Allen practise when he teaches us to neglect elements and attend only to aggregate resultants? On the contrary, simply because the active ring, whatever its bulk, *is elementary*, I hold that the study of its conditions (be these never so 'proximate') is the highest of topics for the social philosopher. If individual variations determine its ups and downs and hair-breadth escapes and twists and turns, as Mr. Allen and Mr. Fiske both admit, Heaven forbid us from tabooing the study of these in favor of the average! On the contrary, let us emphasize these, and the importance of these; and in picking out from history our heroes, and communing with their kindred spirits, — in imagining as strongly as possible what differences their individualities brought about in this world, while its surface was still plastic in their hands, and what whilom feasibilities they made impossible, — each one of us may best fortify and inspire what creative energy may lie in his own soul.[1]

This is the lasting justification of hero-worship, and the pooh-poohing of it by 'sociologists' is the everlasting excuse for popular indifference to their general laws and averages. The difference between an America rescued by a Washington or by a 'Jenkins' may, as Mr. Allen says, be 'little,' but it is, in the words of my carpenter friend, 'important.' Some organizing genius must in the nature of things have emerged from the French Revolution; but what Frenchman will affirm it to have been an accident of no consequence that he should have had the supernumerary idiosyncrasies of a Bonaparte? What animal, domestic or wild, will call it a matter of no moment that scarce a word of sympathy with brutes should have survived from the teachings of Jesus of Nazareth?

The preferences of sentient creatures are what *create* the importance of topics. They are the absolute and ultimate law-giver here. And I for my part cannot but consider the talk of the contemporary sociological school about averages and general laws and predetermined tendencies, with its obligatory undervaluing of the importance of individual differ-

---

[1] M. G. Tarde's book (itself a work of genius), Les Lois de l'Imitation, Étude Sociologique (2me Édition, Paris, Alcan, 1895), is the best possible commentary on this text, — 'invention' on the one hand, and 'imitation' on the other, being for this author the two sole factors of social change.

ences, as the most pernicious and immoral of fatal-
isms.   Suppose there is a social equilibrium fated to
be, whose is it to be, — that of your preference, or
mine?   There lies the question of questions, and it
is one which no study of averages can decide.

ON SOME HEGELISMS.[1]

WE are just now witnessing a singular phenomenon in British and American philosophy. Hegelism, so defunct on its native soil that I believe but a single youthful disciple of the school is to be counted among the privat-docenten and younger professors of Germany, and whose older champions are all passing off the stage, has found among us so zealous and able a set of propagandists that to-day it may really be reckoned one of the most powerful influences of the time in the higher walks of thought. And there is no doubt that, as a movement of reaction against the traditional British empiricism, the hegelian influence represents expansion and freedom, and is doing service of a certain kind. Such service, however, ought not to make us blindly indulgent. Hegel's philosophy mingles mountain-loads of corruption with its scanty merits, and must, now that it has become quasi-official, make ready to defend itself as well as to attack others. It is with no hope of converting independent thinkers, but rather with the sole aspiration of showing some chance youthful disciple that there *is* another point of view in philosophy that I fire this skirmisher's shot, which may, I hope, soon be followed by somebody else's heavier musketry.

[1] Reprinted from Mind, April, 1882.

The point of view I have in mind will become clearer if I begin with a few preparatory remarks on the motives and difficulties of philosophizing in general.

To show that the real is identical with the ideal may roughly be set down as the mainspring of philosophic activity. The atomic and mechanical conception of the world is as ideal from the point of view of some of our faculties as the teleological one is from the point of view of others. In the realm of every ideal we can begin anywhere and roam over the field, each term passing us to its neighbor, each member calling for the next, and our reason rejoicing in its glad activity. Where the parts of a conception seem thus to belong together by inward kinship, where the whole is defined in a way congruous with our powers of reaction, to see is to approve and to understand.

Much of the real seems at the first blush to follow a different law. The parts seem, as Hegel has said, to be shot out of a pistol at us. Each asserts itself as a simple brute fact, uncalled for by the rest, which, so far as we can see, might even make a better system without it. Arbitrary, foreign, jolting, discontinuous — are the adjectives by which we are tempted to describe it. And yet from out the bosom of it a partial ideality constantly arises which keeps alive our aspiration that the whole may some day be construed in ideal form. Not only do the materials lend themselves under certain circumstances to æsthetic manipulation, but underlying their worst disjointedness are three great continua in which for each of us reason's ideal is actually reached. I mean the continua of memory or personal consciousness, of time and of space. In

these great matrices of all we know, we are absolutely
at home. The things we meet are many, and yet are
one; each is itself, and yet all belong together; continuity reigns, yet individuality is not lost.

Consider, for example, space. It is a unit. No
force can in any way break, wound, or tear it. It has
no joints between which you can pass your amputat-
ing knife, for it penetrates the knife and is not split.
Try to make a hole in space by annihilating an inch
of it. To make a hole you must drive something else
through. But what can you drive through space except what is itself spatial?

But notwithstanding it is this very paragon of unity,
space in its parts contains an infinite variety, and the
unity and the variety do not contradict each other,
for they obtain in different respects. The one is the
whole, the many are the parts. Each part is one
again, but only one fraction; and part lies beside part
in absolute nextness, the very picture of peace and
non-contradiction. It is true that the space between
two points both unites and divides them, just as the
bar of a dumb-bell both unites and divides the two
balls. But the union and the division are not *secundum idem :* it divides them by keeping them out of
the space between, it unites them by keeping them
out of the space beyond; so the double function presents no inconsistency. Self-contradiction in space
could only ensue if one part tried to oust another
from its position; but the notion of such an absurdity
vanishes in the framing, and cannot stay to vex the
mind.[1] Beyond the parts we, see or think at any

[1] The seeming contradiction between the infinitude of space and
the fact that it is all finished and given and there, can be got over
in more than one way. The simplest way is by idealism, which dis-

given time extend further parts; but the beyond is homogeneous with what is embraced, and follows the same law; so that no surprises, no foreignness, can ever emerge from space's womb.

Thus with space our intelligence is absolutely intimate; it is rationality and transparency incarnate. The same may be said of the ego and of time. But if for simplicity's sake we ignore them, we may truly say that when we desiderate rational knowledge of the world the standard set by our knowledge of space is what governs our desire.[1] Cannot the breaks, the jolts, the margin of foreignness, be exorcised from other things and leave them unitary like the space they fill? Could this be done, the philosophic kingdom of heaven would be at hand.

But the moment we turn to the material qualities

tinguishes between space as actual and space as potential. For idealism, space only exists so far as it is represented; but all actually represented spaces are finite; it is only possibly representable spaces that are infinite.

[1] Not only for simplicity's sake do we select space as the paragon of a rationalizing continuum. Space determines the relations of the items that enter it in a far more intricate way than does time; in a far more fixed way than does the ego. By this last clause I mean that if things are in space at all, they must conform to geometry; while the being in an ego at all need not make them conform to logic or any other manner of rationality. Under the sheltering wings of a self the matter of unreason can lodge itself as safely as any other kind of content. One cannot but respect the devoutness of the ego-worship of some of our English-writing Hegelians, But at the same time one cannot help fearing lest the monotonous contemplation of so barren a principle as that of the pure formal self (which, be it never so essential a condition of the existence of a world of organized experience at all, must notwithstanding take its own *character* from, not give the character to, the separate empirical data over which its mantle is cast), one cannot but fear, I say, lest the religion of the transcendental ego should, like all religions of the 'one thing needful,' end by sterilizing and occluding the minds of its believers.

of being, we find the continuity ruptured on every side. A fearful jolting begins. Even if we simplify the world by reducing it to its mechanical bare poles, — atoms and their motions, — the discontinuity is bad enough. The laws of clash, the effects of distance upon attraction and repulsion, all seem arbitrary collocations of data. The atoms themselves are so many independent facts, the existence of any one of which in no wise seems to involve the existence of the rest. We have not banished discontinuity, we have only made it finer-grained. And to get even that degree of rationality into the universe we have had to butcher a great part of its contents. The secondary qualities we stripped off from the reality and swept into the dust-bin labelled 'subjective illusion,' still *as such* are facts, and must themselves be rationalized in some way.

But when we deal with facts believed to be purely subjective, we are farther than ever from the goal. We have not now the refuge of distinguishing between the 'reality' and its appearances. Facts of thought being the only facts, differences of thought become the only differences, and identities of thought the only identities there are. Two thoughts that seem different are different to all eternity. We can no longer speak of heat and light being reconciled in any *tertium quid* like wave-motion. For motion is motion, and light is light, and heat heat forever, and their discontinuity is as absolute as their existence. Together with the other attributes and things we conceive, they make up Plato's realm of immutable ideas. Neither *per se* calls for the other, hatches it out, is its 'truth,' creates it, or has any sort of inward community with it except that of being comparable in an ego and found more or less differing, or more or less resembling, as the case may be. The world of qualities is a world of things almost wholly discontinuous *inter se*. Each only says, " I am that I am," and each says it on its own account and with absolute monotony. The continuities of which they *partake*, in Plato's phrase, the ego, space, and time, are for most of them the only grounds of union they possess.

It might seem as if in the mere 'partaking' there lay a contradiction of the discontinuity. If the white must partake of space, the heat of time, and so forth, —do not whiteness and space, heat and time, mutually call for or help to create each other?

Yes; a few such *à priori* couplings must be admitted. They are the axioms: no feeling except as occupying some space and time, or as a moment in some ego; no motion but of something moved; no thought but of an object; no time without a previous time, — and the like. But they are limited in number, and they obtain only between excessively broad genera of concepts, and leave quite undetermined what the specifications of those genera shall be. What feeling shall fill *this* time, what substance execute *this* motion, what qualities combine in *this* being, are as much unanswered questions as if the metaphysical axioms never existed at all.

The existence of such syntheses as they are does then but slightly mitigate the jolt, jolt, jolt we get when we pass over the facts of the world. Everywhere indeterminate variables, subject only to these few vague enveloping laws, independent in all besides, — such seems the truth.

In yet another way, too, ideal and real are so far

apart that their conjunction seems quite hopeless.
To eat our cake and have it, to lose our soul and
save it, to enjoy the physical privileges of selfishness
and the moral luxury of altruism at the same time,
would be the ideal. But the real offers us these
terms in the shape of mutually exclusive alternatives
of which only one can be true at once; so that we
must choose, and in choosing murder one possibility.
The wrench is absolute: "Either — or!" Just as
whenever I bet a hundred dollars on an event, there
comes an instant when I am a hundred dollars richer
or poorer without any intermediate degrees passed
over; just as my wavering between a journey to
Portland or to New York does not carry me from
Cambridge in a resultant direction in which both
motions are compounded, say to Albany, but at a
given moment results in the conjunction of reality in
all its fulness for one alternative and impossibility in
all its fulness for the other, — so the bachelor joys
are utterly lost from the face of being for the married
man, who must henceforward find his account in
something that is not them but is good enough to
make him forget them; so the careless and irrespon-
sible living in the sunshine, the 'unbuttoning after
supper and sleeping upon benches in the afternoon,'
are stars that have set upon the path of him who in
good earnest makes himself a moralist. The transitions are abrupt, absolute, truly shot out of a pistol;
for while many possibilities are called, the few that are
chosen are chosen in all their sudden completeness.

Must we then think that the world that fills space
and time can yield us no acquaintance of that high
and perfect type yielded by empty space and time
themselves? Is what unity there is in the world

mainly derived from the fact that the world is *in* space and time and 'partakes' of them? Can no vision of it forestall the facts of it, or know from some fractions the others before the others have arrived? Are there real logically indeterminate possibilities which forbid there being any equivalent for the happening of it all but the happening itself? Can we gain no anticipatory assurance that what is to come will have no strangeness? Is there no substitute, in short, for life but the living itself in all its long-drawn weary length and breadth and thickness?

In the negative reply to all these questions, a modest common-sense finds no difficulty in acquiescing. To such a way of thinking the notion of 'partaking' has a deep and real significance. Whoso partakes of a thing enjoys his share, and comes into contact with the thing and its other partakers. But he claims no more. His share in no wise negates the thing or their share; nor does it preclude his possession of reserved and private powers with which they have nothing to do, and which are not all absorbed in the mere function of sharing. Why may not the world be a sort of republican banquet of this sort, where all the qualities of being respect one another's personal sacredness, yet sit at the common table of space and time?

To me this view seems deeply probable. Things cohere, but the act of cohesion itself implies but few conditions, and leaves the rest of their qualifications indeterminate. As the first three notes of a tune comport many endings, all melodious, but the tune is not named till a particular ending has actually come, — so the parts actually known of the universe may comport many ideally possible complements. But as

the facts are not the complements, so the knowledge of
the one is not the knowledge of the other in anything
but the few necessary elements of which all must partake in order to be together at all. Why, if one act of
knowledge could from one point take in the total perspective, with all mere possibilities abolished, should
there ever have been anything more than that act?
Why duplicate it by the tedious unrolling, inch by
inch, of the foredone reality? No answer seems possible. On the other hand, if we stipulate only a partial
community of partially independent powers, we see
perfectly why no one part controls the whole view, but
each detail must come and be actually given, before,
in any special sense, it can be said to be determined
at all. This is the moral view, the view that gives to
other powers the same freedom it would have itself,
— not the ridiculous ' freedom to do right,' which in
my mouth can only mean the freedom to do as *I* think
right, but the freedom to do as *they* think right, or
wrong either. After all, what accounts do the nether-
most bounds of the universe owe to me? By what
insatiate conceit and lust of intellectual despotism do
I arrogate the right to know their secrets, and from
my philosophic throne to play the only airs they shall
march to, as if I were the Lord's anointed? Is not
my knowing them at all a gift and not a right? And
shall it be given before they are given? *Data: gifts!*
something to be thankful for! It is a gift that we can
approach things at all, and, by means of the time and
space of which our minds and they partake, alter our
actions so as to meet them.

There are ' bounds of ord'nance ' set for all things,
where they must pause or rue it. 'Facts' are the
bounds of human knowledge, set for it, not by it.

Now, to a mind like Hegel's such pusillanimous twaddle sounds simply loathsome. Bounds that we can't overpass! Data! facts that say, "Hands off, till we are given"! possibilities we can't control! a banquet of which we merely share! Heavens, this is intolerable; such a world is no world for a philosopher to have to do with. He must have all or nothing. If the world cannot be rational in my sense, in the sense of unconditional surrender, I refuse to grant that it is rational at all. It is pure incoherence, a chaos, a nulliverse, to whose haphazard sway I will not truckle. But, no! this is not the world. The world is philosophy's own, — a single block, of which, if she once get her teeth on any part, the whole shall inevitably become her prey and feed her all-devouring theoretic maw. Naught shall be but the necessities she creates and impossibilities; freedom shall mean freedom to obey her will; ideal and actual shall be one: she, and I as her champion, will be satisfied on no lower terms.

The insolence of sway, the ὕβρις on which gods take vengeance, is in temporal and spiritual matters usually admitted to be a vice. A Bonaparte and a Philip II. are called monsters. But when an *intellect* is found insatiate enough to declare that all existence must bend the knee to its requirements, we do not call its owner a monster, but a philosophic prophet. May not this be all wrong? Is there any one of our functions exempted from the common lot of liability to excess? And where everything else must be contented with its part in the universe, shall the theorizing faculty ride rough-shod over the whole?

I confess I can see no *à priori* reason for the exception. He who claims it must be judged by the consequences of his acts, and by them alone. Let Hegel then confront the universe with his claim, and see how he can make the two match.

The universe absolutely refuses to let him travel without jolt. Time, space, and his ego are continuous; so are degrees of heat, shades of light and color, and a few other serial things; so too do potatoes call for salt, and cranberries for sugar, in the taste of one who knows what salt and sugar are. But on the whole there is nought to soften the shock of surprise to his intelligence, as it passes from one quality of being to another. Light is not heat, heat is not light; and to him who holds the one the other is not given till it give itself. Real being comes moreover and goes from any concept at its own sweet will, with no permission asked of the conceiver. In despair must Hegel lift vain hands of imprecation; and since he will take nothing but the whole, he must throw away even the part he might retain, and call the nature of things an *absolute* muddle and incoherence.

But, hark! What wondrous strain is this that steals upon his ear? Incoherence itself, may it not be the very sort of coherence I require? Muddle! is it anything but a peculiar sort of transparency? Is not jolt passage? Is friction other than a kind of lubrication? Is not a chasm a filling? — a queer kind of filling, but a filling still. Why seek for a glue to hold things together when their very falling apart is the only glue you need? Let all that negation which seemed to disintegrate the universe be the mortar that combines it, and the problem stands solved. The paradoxical character of the notion could not fail to please a mind monstrous even in its native

Germany, where mental excess is endemic. Richard, for a moment brought to bay, is himself again. He vaults into the saddle, and from that time his career is that of a philosophic desperado, — one series of outrages upon the chastity of thought.

And can we not ourselves sympathize with his mood in some degree? The old receipts of squeezing the thistle and taking the bull by the horns have many applications. An evil frankly accepted loses half its sting and all its terror. The Stoics had their cheap and easy way of dealing with evil. *Call* your woes goods, they said; refuse to *call* your lost blessings by that name, — and you are happy. So of the unintelligibilities: call them means of intelligibility, and what further do you require? There is even a more legitimate excuse than that. In the exceedingness of the facts of life over our formulas lies a standing temptation at certain times to give up trying to say anything adequate about them, and to take refuge in wild and whirling words which but confess our impotence before their ineffability. Thus Baron Bunsen writes to his wife: "Nothing is near but the far; nothing true but the highest; nothing credible but the inconceivable; nothing so real as the impossible; nothing clear but the deepest; nothing so visible as the invisible; and no life is there but through death." Of these ecstatic moments the *credo quia impossibile* is the classical expression. Hegel's originality lies in his making their mood permanent and sacramental, and authorized to supersede all others, — not as a mystical bath and refuge for feeling when tired reason sickens of her intellectual responsibilities (thank Heaven! that bath is always ready), but as the very form of intellectual responsibility itself.

And now after this long introduction, let me trace some of Hegel's ways of applying his discovery. His system resembles a mouse-trap, in which if you once pass the door you may be lost forever. Safety lies in not entering. Hegelians have anointed, so to speak, the entrance with various considerations which, stated in an abstract form, are so plausible as to slide us unresistingly and almost unwittingly through the fatal arch. It is not necessary to drink the ocean to know that it is salt; nor need a critic dissect a whole system after proving that its premises are rotten. I shall accordingly confine myself to a few of the points that captivate beginners most; and assume that if they break down, so must the system which they prop.

First of all, Hegel has to do utterly away with the sharing and partaking business he so much loathes. He will not call contradiction the glue in one place and identity in another; that is too half-hearted. Contradiction must be a glue universal, and must derive its credit from being shown to be latently involved in cases that we hitherto supposed to embody pure continuity. Thus, the relations of an ego with its objects, of one time with another time, of one place with another place, of a cause with its effect, of a thing with its properties, and especially of parts with wholes, must be shown to involve contradiction. Contradiction, shown to lurk in the very heart of coherence and continuity, cannot after that be held to defeat them, and must be taken as the universal solvent, — or, rather, there is no longer any need of a solvent. To 'dissolve' things in identity was the dream of earlier cruder schools. Hegel will show that their very difference is their identity, and that

in the act of detachment the detachment is undone,
and they fall into each other's arms.

Now, at the very outset it seems rather odd that a
philosopher who pretends that the world is absolutely
rational, or in other words that it can be completely
understood, should fall back on a principle (the identity of contradictories) which utterly defies understanding, and obliges him in fact to use the word
'understanding,' whenever it occurs in his pages, as a
term of contempt. Take the case of space we used
above. The common man who looks at space believes there is nothing in it to be acquainted with
beyond what he sees; no hidden machinery, no
secrets, nothing but the parts as they lie side by side
and make the static whole. His intellect is satisfied
with accepting space as an ultimate genus of the
given. But Hegel cries to him: "Dupe! dost thou
not see it to be one nest of incompatibilities? Do
not the unity of its wholeness and the diversity of its
parts stand in patent contradiction? Does it not both
unite and divide things; and but for this strange and
irreconcilable activity, would it be at all? The hidden
dynamism of self-contradiction is what incessantly
produces the static appearance by which your sense
is fooled."

But if the man ask how self-contradiction *can* do
all this, and how its dynamism may be seen to work,
Hegel can only reply by showing him the space itself
and saying: "Lo, *thus*." In other words, instead of
the principle of explanation being more intelligible
than the thing to be explained, it is absolutely unintelligible if taken by itself, and must appeal to its
pretended product to prove its existence. Surely,
such a system of explaining *notum per ignotum*, of

making the *explicans* borrow credentials from the *explicand*, and of creating paradoxes and impossibilities where none were suspected, is a strange candidate for the honor of being a complete rationalizer of the world.

The principle of the contradictoriness of identity and the identity of contradictories is the essence of the hegelian system. But what probably washes this principle down most with beginners is the combination in which its author works it with another principle which is by no means characteristic of his system, and which, for want of a better name, might be called the ' principle of totality.' This principle says that you cannot adequately know even a part until you know of what whole it forms a part. As Aristotle writes and Hegel loves to quote, an amputated hand is not even a hand. And as Tennyson says, —

> " Little flower — but if I could understand
> What you are, root and all, and all in all,
> I should know what God and man is."

Obviously, until we have taken in all the relations, immediate or remote, into which the thing actually enters or potentially may enter, we do not know all *about* the thing.

And obviously for such an exhaustive acquaintance with the thing, an acquaintance with every other thing, actual and potential, near and remote, is needed; so that it is quite fair to say that omniscience alone can completely know any one thing as it stands. Standing in a world of relations, that world must be known before the thing is fully known. This doctrine is of course an integral part of empiricism, an integral part of common-sense. Since when could good men not apprehend the passing hour in the light of life's larger sweep, — not grow dispassionate the more they stretched their view? Did the 'law of sharing' so little legitimate their procedure that a law of identity of contradictories, forsooth, must be trumped up to give it scope? Out upon the idea!

Hume's account of causation is a good illustration of the way in which empiricism may use the principle of totality. We call something a cause; but we at the same time deny its effect to be in any latent way contained in or substantially identical with it. We thus cannot tell what its causality amounts to until its effect has actually supervened. The effect, then, or something beyond the thing is what makes the thing to be so far as it is a cause. Humism thus says that its causality is something adventitious and not necessarily given when its other attributes are there. Generalizing this, empiricism contends that we must everywhere distinguish between the intrinsic being of a thing and its relations, and, among these, between those that are essential to our knowing it at all and those that may be called adventitious. The thing as actually present in a given world is there with *all* its relations; for it to be known as it *there* exists, they must be known too, and it and they form a single fact for any consciousness large enough to embrace that world as a unity. But what constitutes this singleness of fact, this unity? Empiricism says, Nothing but the relation-yielding matrix in which the several items of the world find themselves embedded, — time, namely, and space, and the mind of the knower. And it says that were some of the items quite different from what they are and others the same, still, for aught we can see, an equally unitary world might be, provided each

item were an object for consciousness and occupied a
determinate point in space and time. All the adventitious relations would in such a world be changed,
along with the intrinsic natures and places of the
beings between which they obtained; but the 'principle of totality' in knowledge would in no wise be
affected.

But Hegelism dogmatically denies all this to be
possible. In the first place it says there are no intrinsic natures that may change; in the second it
says there are no adventitious relations. When the
relations of what we call a thing are told, no *caput
mortuum* of intrinsicality, no 'nature,' is left. The
relations soak up all there is of the thing; the 'items'
of the world are but *foci* of relation with other *foci* of
relation; and all the relations are necessary. The
unity of the world has nothing to do with any
'matrix.' The matrix and the items, each with all,
make a unity, simply because each in truth *is* all the
rest. The proof lies in the *hegelian* principle of totality, which demands that if any one part be posited
alone all the others shall forthwith *emanate* from it and
infallibly reproduce the whole. In the *modus operandi*
of the emanation comes in, as I said, that partnership
of the principle of totality with that of the identity of
contradictories which so recommends the latter to
beginners in Hegel's philosophy. To posit one item
alone is to deny the rest; to deny them is to refer to
them; to refer to them is to begin, at least, to bring
them on the scene; and to begin is in the fulness of
time to end.

If we call this a monism, Hegel is quick to cry,
Not so! To say simply that the one item is the rest

of the universe is as false and one-sided as to say that it is simply itself. It is both and neither; and the only condition on which we gain the right to affirm that it is, is that we fail not to keep affirming all the while that it is not, as well. Thus the truth refuses to be expressed in any single act of judgment or sentence. The world appears as a monism *and* a pluralism, just as it appeared in our own introductory exposition.

But the trouble that keeps us and Hegel from ever joining hands over this apparent formula of brotherhood is that we distinguish, or try to distinguish, the respects in which the world is one from those in which it is many, while all such stable distinctions are what he most abominates. The reader may decide which procedure helps his reason most. For my own part, the time-honored formula of empiricist pluralism, that the world cannot be set down in any single proposition, grows less instead of more intelligible when I add, " And yet the different propositions that express it are one ! " The unity of the propositions is that of the mind that harbors them. Any one who insists that their diversity is in any way itself their unity, can only do so because he loves obscurity and mystification for their own pure sakes.

Where you meet with a contradiction among realities, Herbart used to say, it shows you have failed to make a real distinction. Hegel's sovereign method of going to work and saving all possible contradictions, lies in pertinaciously refusing to distinguish. He takes what is true of a term *secundum quid*, treats it as true of the same term *simpliciter*, and then, of course, applies it to the term *secundum aliud*. A

good example of this is found in the first triad. This
triad shows that the mutability of the real world is
due to the fact that being constantly negates itself;
that whatever *is* by the same act *is not*, and gets undone and swept away ; and that thus the irremediable
torrent of life about which so much rhetoric has been
written has its roots in an ineluctable necessity which
lies revealed to our logical reason. This notion of a
being which forever stumbles over its own feet, and
has to change in order to exist at all, is a very picturesque symbol of the reality, and is probably one of
the points that make young readers feel as if a deep
core of truth lay in the system.

But how is the reasoning done? Pure being is assumed, without determinations, being *secundum quid*.
In this respect it agrees with nothing. Therefore
simpliciter it is nothing; wherever we find it, it is nothing; crowned with complete determinations then,
or *secundum aliud*, it is nothing still, and *hebt sich
auf*.

It is as if we said, Man without his clothes may be
named 'the naked.' Therefore man *simpliciter* is
the naked; and finally man with his hat, shoes, and
overcoat on is the naked still.

Of course we may in this instance or any other
repeat that the conclusion is strictly true, however
comical it seems. Man within the clothes is naked,
just as he is without them. Man would never have
invented the clothes had he not been naked. The
fact of his being clad at all does prove his essential
nudity. And so in general, — the form of any judgment, being the addition of a predicate to a subject,
shows that the subject has been conceived without
the predicate, and thus by a strained metaphor may

be called the predicate's negation. Well and good! let the expression pass. But we must notice this. The judgment has now created a new subject, the naked-clad, and all propositions regarding this must be judged on their own merits; for those true of the old subject, 'the naked,' are no longer true of this one. For instance, we cannot say because the naked pure and simple must not enter the drawing-room or is in danger of taking cold, that the naked with his clothes on will also take cold or must stay in his bedroom. Hold to it eternally that the clad man *is* still naked if it amuse you, — 't is designated in the bond; but the so-called contradiction is a sterile boon. Like Shylock's pound of flesh, it leads to no consequences. It does not entitle you to one drop of his Christian blood either in the way of catarrh, social exclusion, or what further results pure nakedness may involve.

In a version of the first step given by our foremost American Hegelian,[1] we find this playing with the necessary form of judgment. Pure being, he says, has no determinations. But the having none is itself a determination. Wherefore pure being contradicts its own self, and so on. Why not take heed to the *meaning* of what is said? When we make the predication concerning pure being, our meaning is merely the denial of all other determinations than the particular one we make. The showman who advertised his elephant as 'larger than any elephant in the world except himself' must have been in an hegelian country where he was afraid that if he were less explicit the audience would dialectically proceed to say:

[1] Journal of Speculative Philosophy, viii. 37.

"This elephant, larger than any in the world, involves a contradiction; for he himself is in the world, and so stands endowed with the virtue of being both larger and smaller than himself, — a perfect hegelian elephant, whose immanent self-contradictoriness can only be removed in a higher synthesis. Show us the higher synthesis! We don't care to see such a mere abstract creature as your elephant." It may be (and it was indeed suggested in antiquity) that all things are of their own size by being both larger and smaller than themselves. But in the case of this elephant the scrupulous showman nipped such philosophizing and all its inconvenient consequences in the bud, by explicitly intimating that larger than any *other* elephant was all he meant.

Hegel's quibble with this word *other* exemplifies the same fallacy. All ' others,' as such, are according to him identical. That is, ' otherness,' which can only be predicated of a given thing *A*, *secundum quid* (as other than *B*, etc.), is predicated *simpliciter*, and made to identify the *A* in question with *B*, which is other only *secundum aliud*, — namely other than *A*.

Another maxim that Hegelism is never tired of repeating is that "to know a limit is already to be beyond it." "Stone walls do not a prison make, nor iron bars a cage." The inmate of the penitentiary shows by his grumbling that he is still in the stage of abstraction and of separative thought. The more keenly he thinks of the fun he might be having outside, the more deeply he ought to feel that the walls identify him with it. They set him beyond them *secundum quid*, in imagination, in longing, in despair; *argal* they take him there *simpliciter* and in every way, — in flesh, in power, in deed. Foolish convict, to ignore his blessings!

Another mode of stating his principle is this: "To know the finite as such, is also to know the infinite." Expressed in this abstract shape, the formula is as insignificant as it is unobjectionable. We can cap every word with a negative particle, and the word *finished* immediately suggests the word *unfinished*, and we know the two words together.

But it is an entirely different thing to take the knowledge of a concrete case of ending, and to say that it virtually makes us acquainted with other concrete facts *in infinitum*. For, in the first place, the end may be an absolute one. The *matter* of the universe, for instance, is according to all appearances in finite amount; and if we knew that we had counted the last bit of it, infinite knowledge in that respect, so far from being given, would be impossible. With regard to *space*, it is true that in drawing a bound we are aware of more. But to treat this little fringe as the equal of infinite space is ridiculous. It resembles infinite space *secundum quid*, or in but one respect, — its spatial quality. We believe it homogeneous with whatever spaces may remain; but it would be fatuous to say, because one dollar in my pocket is homogeneous with all the dollars in the country, that to have it is to have them. The further points of space are as numerically distinct from the fringe as the dollars from the dollar, and not until we have actually intuited them can we be said to 'know' them *simpliciter*. The hegelian reply is that the *quality* of space constitutes its only *worth*; and that there is nothing true, good, or beautiful to be known

in the spaces beyond which is not already known in
the fringe. This introduction of a eulogistic term
into a mathematical question is original. The 'true'
and the 'false' infinite are about as appropriate distinctions in a discussion of cognition as the good and
the naughty rain would be in a treatise on meteor-
ology. But when we grant that all the worth of the
knowledge of distant spaces is due to the knowledge
of what they may carry in them, it then appears more
than ever absurd to say that the knowledge of the
fringe is an equivalent for the infinitude of the distant
knowledge. The distant spaces even *simpliciter* are
not yet yielded to our thinking; and if they were
yielded *simpliciter*, would not be yielded *secundum
aliud*, or in respect to their material filling out.

Shylock's bond was an omnipotent instrument compared with this knowledge of the finite, which remains
the ignorance it always was, till the infinite by its own
act has piece by piece placed itself in our hands.

Here Hegelism cries out: "By the identity of the
knowledges of infinite and finite I never meant that
one could be a *substitute* for the other; nor does true
philosophy ever mean by identity capacity for substitution." This sounds suspiciously like the good and
the naughty infinite, or rather like the mysteries of
the Trinity and the Eucharist. To the unsentimental
mind there are but two sorts of identity, — total identity and partial identity. Where the identity is total,
the things can be substituted wholly for one another.
Where substitution is impossible, it must be that the
identity is incomplete. It is the duty of the student
then to ascertain the exact *quid, secundum* which it
obtains, as we have tried to do above. Even the
Catholic will tell you that when he believes in the

identity of the wafer with Christ's body, he does not mean in all respects, — so that he might use it to exhibit muscular fibre, or a cook make it smell like baked meat in the oven. He means that in the one sole respect of nourishing his being in a certain way, it is identical with and *can* be substituted for the very body of his Redeemer.

'The knowledge of opposites is one,' is one of the hegelian first principles, of which the preceding are perhaps only derivatives. Here again Hegelism takes 'knowledge' *simpliciter*, and substituting it for knowledge in a particular respect, avails itself of the confusion to cover other respects never originally implied. When the knowledge of a thing is given us, we no doubt think that the thing may or must have an opposite. This postulate of something opposite we may call a 'knowledge of the opposite' if we like; but it is a knowledge of it in only that one single respect, that it is something opposite. No number of opposites to a quality we have never directly experienced could ever lead us positively to infer what that quality is. There is a jolt between the negation of them and the actual positing of it in its proper shape, that twenty logics of Hegel harnessed abreast cannot drive us smoothly over.

The use of the maxim 'All determination is negation' is the fattest and most full-blown application of the method of refusing to distinguish. Taken in its vague confusion, it probably does more than anything else to produce the sort of flicker and dazzle which are the first mental conditions for the reception of Hegel's system. The word 'negation' taken *simpliciter* is treated as if it covered an indefinite number of *secundums*, culminating in the very peculiar one of self-negation. Whence finally the conclusion is drawn that assertions are universally self-contradictory. As this is an important matter, it seems worth while to treat it a little minutely.

When I measure out a pint, say of milk, and so determine it, what do I do? I virtually make two assertions regarding it, — it *is* this pint; it is *not* those other gallons. One of these is an affirmation, the other a negation. Both have a common subject; but the predicates being mutually exclusive, the two assertions lie beside each other in endless peace.

I may with propriety be said to make assertions more remote still, — assertions of which those other gallons are the subject. As it is not they, so are they not the pint which it is. The determination "this is the pint" carries with it the negation, — "those are not the pints." Here we have the same predicate; but the subjects are exclusive of each other, so there is again endless peace. In both couples of propositions negation and affirmation are *secundum aliud:* this is *a;* this is n't not-*a*. This kind of negation involved in determination cannot possibly be what Hegel wants for his purposes. The table is not the chair, the fireplace is not the cupboard, — these are literal expressions of the law of identity and contradiction, those principles of the abstracting and separating understanding for which Hegel has so sovereign a contempt, and which his logic is meant to supersede.

And accordingly Hegelians pursue the subject further, saying there is in every determination an element of real conflict. Do you not in determining the milk to be this pint exclude it forever from the chance of being those gallons, frustrate it from expansion? And so do you not equally exclude them from the being which it now maintains as its own?

Assuredly if you had been hearing of a land flowing with milk and honey, and had gone there with unlimited expectations of the rivers the milk would fill; and if you found there was but this single pint in the whole country, — the determination of the pint would exclude another determination which your mind had previously made of the milk. There would be a real conflict resulting in the victory of one side. The rivers would be negated by the single pint being affirmed; and as rivers and pint are affirmed of the same milk (first as supposed and then as found), the contradiction would be complete.

But it is a contradiction that can never by any chance occur in real nature or being. It can only occur between a false representation of a being and the true idea of the being when actually cognized. The first got into a place where it had no rights and had to be ousted. But in *rerum naturâ* things do not get into one another's logical places. The gallons first spoken of never say, "We are the pint;" the pint never says, "I am the gallons." It never tries to expand; and so there is no chance for anything to exclude or negate it. It thus remains affirmed absolutely.

Can it be believed in the teeth of these elementary truths that the principle *determinatio negatio* is held throughout Hegel to imply an active contradiction, conflict, and exclusion? Do the horse-cars jingling outside negate me writing in this room? Do I, reader, negate you? Of course, if I say, "Reader, we are two, and therefore I am two," I negate you, for I am actually thrusting a part into the seat of the whole.

The orthodox logic expresses the fallacy by saying the *we* is taken by me distributively instead of collectively; but as long as I do not make this blunder, and am content with my part, we all are safe. In *rerum naturâ*, parts remain parts. Can you imagine one position in space trying to get into the place of another position and having to be 'contradicted' by that other? Can you imagine your thought of an object trying to dispossess the real object from its being, and so being negated by it? The great, the sacred law of partaking, the noiseless step of continuity, seems something that Hegel cannot possibly understand. All or nothing is his one idea. For him each point of space, of time, each feeling in the ego, each quality of being, is clamoring, "I am the all,—there is nought else but me." This clamor is its essence, which has to be negated in another act which gives it its true determination. What there is of affirmative in this determination is thus the mere residuum left from the negation by others of the negation it originally applied to them.

But why talk of residuum? The Kilkenny cats of fable could leave a residuum in the shape of their undevoured tails. But the Kilkenny cats of existence as it appears in the pages of Hegel are all-devouring, and leave no residuum. Such is the unexampled fury of their onslaught that they get clean out of themselves and into each other, nay more, pass right through each other, and then "return into themselves" ready for another round, as insatiate, but as inconclusive, as the one that went before.

If I characterized Hegel's own mood as ὕβρις, the insolence of excess, what shall I say of the mood he ascribes to being? Man makes the gods in his image; and Hegel, in daring to insult the spotless σωφροσύνη of space and time, the bound-respecters, in branding as strife that law of sharing under whose sacred keeping, like a strain of music, like an odor of incense (as Emerson says), the dance of the atoms goes forward still, seems to me but to manifest his own deformity.

This leads me to animadvert on an erroneous inference which hegelian idealism makes from the form of the negative judgment. Every negation, it says, must be an intellectual act. Even the most *naïf* realism will hardly pretend that the non-table as such exsists *in se* after the same fashion as the table does. But table and non-table, since they are given to our thought together, must be consubstantial. Try to make the position or affirmation of the table as simple as you can, it is also the negation of the non-table; and thus positive being itself seems after all but a function of intelligence, like negation. Idealism is proved, realism is unthinkable. Now I have not myself the least objection to idealism, — an hypothesis which voluminous considerations make plausible, and whose difficulties may be cleared away any day by new discriminations or discoveries. But I object to proving by these patent ready-made *à priori* methods that which can only be the fruit of a wide and patient induction. For the truth is that our affirmations and negations do not stand on the same footing at all, and are anything but consubstantial. An affirmation says something about an objective existence. A negation says something *about an affirmation,* — namely, that it is false. There are no negative predicates or falsities in nature. Being makes no false hypotheses that have to be contradicted. The only denials she can be in any way construed to perform are denials of our errors. This shows plainly enough that denial must be of something mental, since the thing denied is always a fiction. "The table is not the chair" supposes the speaker to have been playing with the false notion that it may have been the chair. But affirmation may perfectly well be of something having no such necessary and constitutive relation to thought. Whether it really is of such a thing is for harder considerations to decide.

If idealism be true, the great question that presents itself is whether its truth involve the necessity of an infinite, unitary, and omniscient consciousness, or whether a republic of semi-detached consciousnesses will do, — consciousnesses united by a certain common fund of representations, but each possessing a private store which the others do not share. Either hypothesis is to me conceivable. But whether the egos be one or many, the *nextness* of representations to one another within them is the principle of unification of the universe. To be thus consciously next to some other representation is the condition to which each representation must submit, under penalty of being excluded from this universe, and like Lord Dundreary's bird ' flocking all alone,' and forming a separate universe by itself. But this is only a condition of which the representations *partake;* it leaves all their other determinations undecided. To say, because representation b cannot be in the same universe with a without being a's *neighbor;* that therefore a possesses, involves, or necessitates b, hide and hair, flesh and fell, all appurtenances and belongings, — is only the silly hegelian all-or-nothing insatiateness once more.

Hegel's own logic, with all the senseless hocus-pocus of its triads, utterly fails to prove his position. The only evident compulsion which representations exert upon one another is compulsion to submit to the conditions of entrance into the same universe with them — the conditions of continuity, of selfhood, space, and time — under penalty of being excluded. But what this universe shall be is a matter of fact which we cannot decide till we know what representations *have* submitted to these its sole conditions. The conditions themselves impose no further requirements. In short, the notion that real contingency and ambiguity may be features of the real world is a perfectly unimpeachable hypothesis. Only in such a world can moral judgments have a claim to be. For the bad is that which takes the place of something else which possibly might have been where *it* now is, and the better is that which absolutely might be where it absolutely is not. In the universe of Hegel — the absolute block whose parts have no loose play, the pure plethora of necessary being with the oxygen of possibility all suffocated out of its lungs — there can be neither good nor bad, but one dead level of mere fate.

But I have tired the reader out. The worst of criticising Hegel is that the very arguments we use against him give forth strange and hollow sounds that make them seem almost as fantastic as the errors to which they are addressed. The sense of a universal mirage, of a ghostly unreality, steals over us, which is the very moonlit atmosphere of Hegelism itself. What wonder then if, instead of converting, our words do but rejoice and delight, those already baptized in the faith of confusion? To their charmed senses we all seem children of Hegel together, only some of us have not the wit to know our own father. Just as Romanists are sure to inform us that our reasons against Papal Christianity unconsciously breathe the purest spirit of Catholicism, so Hegelism benignantly smiles at our exertions, and murmurs, "If the red slayer think he slays;" "When me they fly, I am the wings," etc.

To forefend this unwelcome adoption, let me recapitulate in a few propositions the reasons why I am *not* an hegelian.

1. We cannot eat our cake and have it; that is, the only real contradiction there can be between thoughts is where one is true, the other false. When this happens, one must go forever; nor is there any 'higher synthesis' in which both can wholly revive.

2. A chasm is not a bridge in any utilizable sense; that is, no mere negation can be the instrument of a positive advance in thought.

3. The continua, time, space, and the ego, are bridges, because they are without chasm.

4. But they bridge over the chasms between represented qualities only partially.

5. This partial bridging, however, makes the qualities share in a common world.

6. The other characteristics of the qualities are separate facts.

7. But the same quality appears in many times and spaces. Generic sameness of the quality wherever found becomes thus a further means by which the jolts are reduced.

8. But between different qualities jolts remain.

Each, as far as the other is concerned, is an absolutely separate and contingent being.

9. The moral judgment may lead us to postulate as irreducible the contingencies of the world.

10. Elements mutually contingent are not in conflict so long as they partake of the continua of time, space, etc., — partaking being the exact opposite of strife. They conflict only when, as mutually exclusive possibilities, they strive to possess themselves of the same parts of time, space, and ego.

11. That there are such real conflicts, irreducible to any intelligence, and giving rise to an excess of possibility over actuality, is an hypothesis, but a credible one. No philosophy should pretend to be anything more.

NOTE. — Since the preceding article was written, some observations on the effects of nitrous-oxide-gas-intoxication which I was prompted to make by reading the pamphlet called The Anæsthetic Revelation and the Gist of Philosophy, by Benjamin Paul Blood, Amsterdam, N. Y., 1874, have made me understand better than ever before both the strength and the weakness of Hegel's philosophy. I strongly urge others to repeat the experiment, which with pure gas is short and harmless enough. The effects will of course vary with the individual, just as they vary in the same individual from time to time; but it is probable that in the former case, as in the latter, a generic resemblance will obtain. With me, as with every other person of whom I have heard, the keynote of the experience is the tremendously exciting sense of an intense metaphysical illumination. Truth lies open to the view in depth beneath depth of almost blinding evidence. The mind sees all the logical relations of being with an apparent subtlety and instantaneity to which its normal consciousness offers no parallel; only as sobriety returns, the feeling of insight fades, and one is left staring vacantly at a few disjointed words and phrases, as one stares at a cadaverous-looking snow-peak from which the sunset glow has just fled, or at the black cinder left by an extinguished brand.

The immense emotional sense of *reconciliation* which characterizes the 'maudlin' stage of alcoholic drunkenness, — a stage which seems silly to lookers-on, but the subjective rapture of which probably constitutes a chief part of the temptation to the vice, — is well known. The centre and periphery of things seem to come together. The ego and its objects, the *meum* and the *tuum*, are one. Now this, only a thousandfold enhanced, was the effect upon me of the gas: and its first result was to make peal through me with unutterable power the conviction that Hegelism was true after all, and that the deepest convictions of my intellect hitherto were wrong. Whatever idea or representation occurred to the mind was seized by the same logical forceps, and served to illustrate the same truth; and that truth was that every opposition, among whatsoever things, vanishes in a higher unity in which it is based; that all contradictions, so-called, are but differences; that all differences are of degree; that all degrees are of a common kind; that unbroken continuity is of the essence of being; and that we are literally in the midst of *an infinite*, to perceive the existence of which is the utmost we can attain. Without the *same* as a basis, how could strife occur? Strife presupposes something to be striven about; and in this common topic, the same for both parties, the differences merge. From the hardest contradiction to the tenderest diversity of verbiage differences evaporate; *yes* and *no* agree at least in being assertions; a denial of a statement is but another mode of stating the same, contradiction can only occur of the same thing, — all opinions are thus synonyms, are synonymous, are the same. But the same phrase by difference of emphasis is two; and here again difference and no-difference merge in one.

It is impossible to convey an idea of the torrential character of the identification of opposites as it streams through the mind in this experience. I have sheet after sheet of phrases dictated or written during the intoxication, which to the sober reader seem meaningless drivel, but which at the moment of transcribing were fused in the fire of infinite rationality. God and devil, good and evil, life and death, I and thou, sober and drunk, matter and form, black and white, quantity and quality, shiver of ecstasy and shudder of horror, vomiting and swallowing, inspiration and expiration, fate and reason, great and small, extent and intent, joke and earnest, tragic and comic, and fifty other contrasts figure in these pages in the same monotonous way. The mind saw how each term *belonged* to its contrast through a knife-edge moment of transition which *it* effected, and which, perennial and eternal, was the *nunc stans* of life. The thought of mutual implication of the parts in the bare form of a judgment of opposition, as ' nothing — but,' ' no more — than,' ' only — if,' etc., produced a perfect delirium of theoretic rapture. And at last, when definite ideas to work on came slowly, the mind went through the mere *form* of recognizing sameness in identity by contrasting the same word with itself, differently emphasized, or shorn of its initial letter. Let me transcribe a few sentences:

What's mistake but a kind of take?
What's nausea but a kind of -ausea?
Sober, drunk, -*unk*, astonishment.
Everything can become the subject of criticism — how criticise without something *to* criticise?
Agreement — disagreement!!
Emotion — motion!!!
Die away from, *from*, die away (without the *from*).
Reconciliation of opposites; sober, drunk, all the same!
Good and evil reconciled in a laugh!
It escapes, it escapes!
But ——
What escapes, WHAT escapes?
Emphasis, EMphasis; there must be some emphasis in order for there to be a phasis.
No verbiage can give it, because the verbiage is *other*.
*In*coherent, coherent — same.
And it fades! And it's infinite! AND it's infinite!
If it was n't *going*, why should you hold on to it?
Don't you see the difference, don't you see the identity?
Constantly opposites united!
The same me telling you to write and not to write!
Extreme — extreme, extreme! Within the *ex*tensity that ' extreme' contains is contained the ' *extreme*' of *in*tensity.
Something, and *other* than that thing!
Intoxication, and *otherness* than intoxication.
Every attempt at betterment, — every attempt at otherment, — is a ——.
It fades forever and forever as we move.

There *is* a reconciliation !

Reconciliation — *e*conciliation !

By God, how that hurts ! By God, how it *does n't* hurt !
Reconciliation of two extremes.

By George, nothing but *oth*ing !

That sounds like nonsense, but it is pure *on*sense !

Thought deeper than speech —— !

Medical school; divinity school, *school!* SCHOOL ! Oh my
God, oh God, oh God !

The most coherent and articulate sentence which came was
this : —

There are no differences but differences of degree between
different degrees of difference and no difference.

This phrase has the true Hegelian ring, being in fact a regular *sich als sich auf sich selbst beziehende Negativität.* And
true Hegelians will *überhaupt* be able to read between the
lines and feel, at any rate, what *possible* ecstasies of cognitive
emotion might have bathed these tattered fragments of thought
when they were alive. But for the assurance of a certain
amount of respect from them, I should hardly have ventured to
print what must be such caviare to the general.

But now comes the reverse of the medal. What is the
principle of unity in all this monotonous rain of instances ?
Although I did not see it at first, I soon found that it was in
each case nothing but the abstract *genus* of which the conflicting terms were opposite species. In other words, although the
flood of ontologic *emotion* was Hegelian through and through,
the *ground* for it was nothing but the world-old principle that
things are the same only so far and no farther than they *are*
the same, or partake of a common nature, — the principle that
Hegel most tramples under foot. At the same time the rapture
of beholding a process that was infinite, changed (as the nature
of the infinitude was realized by the mind) into the sense of a
dreadful and ineluctable fate, with whose magnitude every finite
effort is incommensurable and in the light of which whatever
happens is indifferent. This instantaneous revulsion of mood
from rapture to horror is, perhaps, the strongest emotion I have
ever experienced. I got it repeatedly when the inhalation was
continued long enough to produce incipient nausea ; and I cannot but regard it as the normal and inevitable outcome of the

intoxication, if sufficiently prolonged. A pessimistic fatalism, depth within depth of impotence and indifference, reason and silliness united, not in a higher synthesis, but in the fact that whichever you choose it is all one, — this is the upshot of a revelation that began so rosy bright.

Even when the process stops short of this ultimatum, the reader will have noticed from the phrases quoted how often it ends by losing the clue. Something 'fades,' 'escapes;' and the feeling of insight is changed into an intense one of bewilderment, puzzle, confusion, astonishment. I know no more singular sensation than this intense bewilderment, with nothing particular left to be bewildered at save the bewilderment itself. It seems, indeed, a *causa sui*, or 'spirit become its own object.'

My conclusion is that the togetherness of things in a common world, the law of sharing, of which I have said so much, may, when perceived, engender a very powerful emotion; that Hegel was so unusually susceptible to this emotion throughout his life that its gratification became his supreme end, and made him tolerably unscrupulous as to the means he employed; that *indifferentism* is the true outcome of every view of the world which makes infinity and continuity to be its essence, and that pessimistic or optimistic attitudes pertain to the mere accidental subjectivity of the moment; finally, that the identification of contradictories, so far from being the self-developing process which Hegel supposes, is really a self-consuming process, passing from the less to the more abstract, and terminating either in a laugh at the ultimate nothingness, or in a mood of vertiginous amazement at a meaningless infinity.

WHAT PSYCHICAL RESEARCH HAS ACCOMPLISHED.[1]

" THE great field for new discoveries," said a scientific friend to me the other day, " is always the unclassified residuum." Round about the accredited and orderly facts of every science there ever floats a sort of dust-cloud of exceptional observations, of occurrences minute and irregular and seldom met with, which it always proves more easy to ignore than to attend to. The ideal of every science is that of a closed and completed system of truth. The charm of most sciences to their more passive disciples consists in their appearing, in fact, to wear just this ideal form. Each one of our various *ologies* seems to offer a definite head of classification for every possible phenomenon of the sort which it professes to cover; and so far from free is most men's fancy, that, when a consistent and organized scheme of this sort has once been comprehended and assimilated, a different scheme is unimaginable. No alternative, whether to whole or parts, can any longer be conceived as possible. Phenomena unclassifiable within the system are therefore paradoxical absurdi-

---

[1] This Essay is formed of portions of an article in Scribner's Magazine for March, 1890, of an article in the Forum for July, 1892, and of the President's Address before the Society for Psychical Research, published in the Proceedings for June, 1896, and in Science.

ties, and must be held untrue. When, moreover, as
so often happens, the reports of them are vague and
indirect; when they come as mere marvels and od-
dities rather than as things of serious moment, — one
neglects or denies them with the best of scientific
consciences. Only the born geniuses let themselves
be worried and fascinated by these outstanding exceptions, and get no peace till they are brought
within the fold. Your Galileos, Galvanis, Fresnels,
Purkinjes, and Darwins are always getting confounded
and troubled by insignificant things. Any one will
renovate his science who will steadily look after the
irregular phenomena. And when the science is re-
newed, its new formulas often have more of the voice
of the exceptions in them than of what were supposed
to be the rules.

No part of the unclassified residuum has usually
been treated with a more contemptuous scientific
disregard than the mass of phenomena generally
called *mystical*. Physiology will have nothing to
do with them. Orthodox psychology turns its back
upon them. Medicine sweeps them out; or, at most,
when in an anecdotal vein, records a few of them as
'effects of the imagination,' — a phrase of mere dis-
missal, whose meaning, in this connection, it is impossible to make precise. All the while, however, the
phenomena are there, lying broadcast over the surface
of history. No matter where you open its pages,
you find things recorded under the name of divinations, inspirations, demoniacal possessions, apparitions,
trances, ecstasies, miraculous healings and productions of disease, and occult powers possessed by
peculiar individuals over persons and things in their
neighborhood. We suppose that 'mediumship' origi-

nated in Rochester, N. Y., and animal magnetism with Mesmer; but once look behind the pages of official history, in personal memoirs, legal documents, and popular narratives and books of anecdote, and you will find that there never was a time when these things were not reported just as abundantly as now. We college-bred gentry, who follow the stream of cosmopolitan culture exclusively, not infrequently stumble upon some old-established journal, or some voluminous native author, whose names are never heard of in *our* circle, but who number their readers by the quarter-million. It always gives us a little shock to find this mass of human beings not only living and ignoring us and all our gods, but actually reading and writing and cogitating without ever a thought of our canons and authorities. Well, a public no less large keeps and transmits from generation to generation the traditions and practices of the occult; but academic science cares as little for its beliefs and opinions as you, gentle reader, care for those of the readers of the Waverley and the Fireside Companion. To no one type of mind is it given to discern the totality of truth. Something escapes the best of us, — not accidentally, but systematically, and because we have a twist. The scientific-academic mind and the feminine-mystical mind shy from each other's facts, just as they fly from each other's temper and spirit. Facts are there only for those who have a mental affinity with them. When once they are indisputably ascertained and admitted, the academic and critical minds are by far the best fitted ones to interpret and discuss them, — for surely to pass from mystical to scientific speculations is like passing from lunacy to sanity; but on the other hand if there is anything which human history demonstrates, it is the extreme slowness with which the ordinary academic and critical mind acknowledges facts to exist which present themselves as wild facts, with no stall or pigeon-hole, or as facts which threaten to break up the accepted system. In psychology, physiology, and medicine, wherever a debate between the mystics and the scientifics has been once for all decided, it is the mystics who have usually proved to be right about the *facts*, while the scientifics had the better of it in respect to the theories. The most recent and flagrant example of this is ' animal magnetism,' whose facts were stoutly dismissed as a pack of lies by academic medical science the world over, until the non-mystical theory of ' hypnotic suggestion ' was found for them, — when they were admitted to be so excessively and dangerously common that special penal laws, forsooth, must be passed to keep all persons unequipped with medical diplomas from taking part in their production. Just so stigmatizations, invulnerabilities, instantaneous cures, inspired discourses, and demoniacal possessions, the records of which were shelved in our libraries but yesterday in the alcove headed ' superstitions,' now, under the brandnew title of ' cases of hystero-epilepsy,' are republished, reobserved, and reported with an even too credulous avidity.

Repugnant as the mystical style of philosophizing may be (especially when self-complacent), there is no sort of doubt that it goes with a gift for meeting with certain kinds of phenomenal experience. The writer of these pages has been forced in the past few years to this admission; and he now believes that he who will pay attention to facts of the sort dear to mystics, while reflecting upon them in academic-scientific ways, will be in the best possible position to help philosophy. It is a circumstance of good augury that certain scientifically trained minds in all countries seem drifting to the same conclusion. The Society for Psychical Research has been one means of bringing science and the occult together in England and America; and believing that this Society fulfils a function which, though limited, is destined to be not unimportant in the organization of human knowledge, I am glad to give a brief account of it to the uninstructed reader.

According to the newspaper and drawing-room myth, soft-headedness and idiotic credulity are the bond of sympathy in this Society, and general wonder-sickness its dynamic principle. A glance at the membership fails, however, to corroborate this view. The president is Prof. Henry Sidgwick,[1] known by his other deeds as the most incorrigibly and exasperatingly critical and sceptical mind in England. The hard-headed Arthur Balfour is one vice-president, and the hard-headed Prof. J. P. Langley, secretary of the Smithsonian Institution, is another. Such men as Professor Lodge, the eminent English physicist, and Professor Richet, the eminent French physiologist, are among the most active contributors to the Society's Proceedings; and through the catalogue of membership are sprinkled names honored throughout the world for their scientific capacity. In fact, were I asked to point to a scientific journal where hard-headedness and never-sleeping suspicion of sources of error might be seen in their full bloom,

[1] Written in 1891. Since then, Mr. Balfour, the present writer, and Professor William Crookes have held the presidential office.

I think I should have to fall back on the Proceedings of the Society for Psychical Research. The common run of papers, say on physiological subjects, which one finds in other professional organs, are apt to show a far lower level of critical consciousness. Indeed, the rigorous canons of evidence applied a few years ago to testimony in the case of certain 'mediums' led to the secession from the Society of a number of spiritualists. Messrs. Stainton Moses and A. R. Wallace, among others, thought that no experiences based on mere eyesight could ever have a chance to be admitted as true, if such an impossibly exacting standard of proof were insisted on in every case.

The S. P. R., as I shall call it for convenience, was founded in 1882 by a number of gentlemen, foremost among whom seem to have been Professors Sidgwick, W. F. Barrett, and Balfour Stewart, and Messrs. R. H. Hutton, Hensleigh Wedgwood, Edmund Gurney, and F. W. H. Myers. Their purpose was twofold, — first, to carry on systematic experimentation with hypnotic subjects, mediums, clairvoyants, and others; and, secondly, to collect evidence concerning apparitions, haunted houses, and similar phenomena which are incidentally reported, but which, from their fugitive character, admit of no deliberate control. Professor Sidgwick, in his introductory address, insisted that the divided state of public opinion on all these matters was a scandal to science, — absolute disdain on à priori grounds characterizing what may be called professional opinion, while indiscriminate credulity was too often found among those who pretended to have a first-hand acquaintance with the facts.

As a sort of weather-bureau for accumulating

reports of such meteoric phenomena as apparitions, the S. P. R. has done an immense amount of work. As an experimenting body, it cannot be said to have completely fulfilled the hopes of its founders. The reasons for this lie in two circumstances: first, the clairvoyant and other subjects who will allow themselves to be experimented upon are few and far between; and, secondly, work with them takes an immense amount of time, and has had to be carried on at odd intervals by members engaged in other pursuits. The Society has not yet been rich enough to control the undivided services of skilled experimenters in this difficult field. The loss of the lamented Edmund Gurney, who more than any one else had leisure to devote, has been so far irreparable. But were there no experimental work at all, and were the S. P. R. nothing but a weather-bureau for catching sporadic apparitions, etc., in their freshness, I am disposed to think its function indispensable in the scientific organism. If any one of my readers, spurred by the thought that so much smoke must needs betoken fire, has ever looked into the existing literature of the supernatural for proof, he will know what I mean. This literature is enormous, but it is practically worthless for evidential purposes. Facts enough are cited, indeed; but the records of them are so fallible and imperfect that at most they lead to the opinion that it may be well to keep a window open upon that quarter in one's mind.

In the S. P. R.'s Proceedings, on the contrary, a different law prevails. Quality, and not mere quantity, is what has been mainly kept in mind. The witnesses, where possible, have in every reported case been cross-examined personally, the collateral facts have been looked up, and the story appears with its precise coefficient of evidential worth stamped on it, so that all may know just what its weight as proof may be. Outside of these Proceedings, I know of no systematic attempt to *weigh* the evidence for the supernatural. This makes the value of the volumes already published unique; and I firmly believe that as the years go on and the ground covered grows still wider, the Proceedings will more and more tend to supersede all other sources of information concerning phenomena traditionally deemed occult. Collections of this sort are usually best appreciated by the rising generation. The young anthropologists and psychologists who will soon have full occupancy of the stage will feel how great a scientific scandal it has been to leave a great mass of human experience to take its chances between vague tradition and credulity on the one hand and dogmatic denial at long range on the other, with no body of persons extant who are willing and competent to study the matter with both patience and rigor. If the Society lives long enough for the public to become familiar with its presence, so that any apparition, or house or person infested with unaccountable noises or disturbances of material objects, will as a matter of course be reported to its officers, we shall doubtless end by having a mass of facts concrete enough to theorize upon. Its sustainers, therefore, should accustom themselves to the idea that its first duty is simply to exist from year to year and perform this recording function well, though no conclusive results of any sort emerge at first. All our learned societies have begun in some such modest way.

But one cannot by mere outward organization make much progress in matters scientific. Societies can

back men of genius, but can never take their place.
The contrast between the parent Society and the
American Branch illustrates this. In England, a little
group of men with enthusiasm and genius for the
work supplied the nucleus; in this country, Mr.
Hodgson had to be imported from Europe before
any tangible progress was made. What perhaps more
than anything else has held the Society together in
England is Professor Sidgwick's extraordinary gift of
inspiring confidence in diverse sorts of people. Such
tenacity of interest in the result and such absolute
impartiality in discussing the evidence are not once
in a century found in an individual. His obstinate
belief that there is something yet to be brought to
light communicates patience to the discouraged; his
constitutional inability to draw any precipitate conclusion reassures those who are afraid of being dupes.
Mrs. Sidgwick — a sister, by the way, of the great
Arthur Balfour — is a worthy ally of her husband in
this matter, showing a similarly rare power of holding her judgment in suspense, and a keenness of
observation and capacity for experimenting with
human subjects which are rare in either sex.

The *worker* of the Society, as originally constituted,
was Edmund Gurney. Gurney was a man of the
rarest sympathies and gifts. Although, like Carlyle,
he used to groan under the burden of his labors, he
yet exhibited a colossal power of dispatching business
and getting through drudgery of the most repulsive
kind. His two thick volumes on 'Phantasms of the
Living,' collected and published in three years, are a
proof of this. Besides this, he had exquisite artistic
instincts, and his massive volume on 'The Power of
Sound' was, when it appeared, the most important

work on æsthetics in the English language. He had also the tenderest heart and a mind of rare metaphysical power, as his volumes of essays, 'Tertium Quid,' will prove to any reader. Mr. Frederic Myers, already well known as one of the most brilliant of English essayists, is the *ingenium præfervidum* of the S. P. R. Of the value of Mr. Myers's theoretic writings I will say a word later. Dr. Hodgson, the American secretary, is distinguished by a balance of mind almost as rare in its way as Sidgwick's. He is persuaded of the reality of many of the phenomena called spiritualistic, but he also has uncommon keenness in detecting error; and it is impossible to say in advance whether it will give him more satisfaction to confirm or to smash a given case offered to his examination.

It is now time to cast a brief look upon the actual contents of these Proceedings. The first two years were largely taken up with experiments in thought-transference. The earliest lot of these were made with the daughters of a clergyman named Creery, and convinced Messrs. Balfour Stewart, Barrett, Myers, and Gurney that the girls had an inexplicable power of guessing names and objects thought of by other persons. Two years later, Mrs. Sidgwick and Mr. Gurney, recommencing experiments with the same girls, detected them signalling to each other. It is true that for the most part the conditions of the earlier series had excluded signalling, and it is also possible that the cheating may have grafted itself on what was originally a genuine phenomenon. Yet Gurney was wise in abandoning the entire series to the scepticism of the reader. Many critics of the S. P. R. seem out of all its labors to have heard only of this case. But there are experiments recorded with upwards of thirty other subjects. Three were experimented upon at great length during the first two years: one was Mr. G. A. Smith; the other two were young ladies in Liverpool in the employment of Mr. Malcolm Guthrie.

It is the opinion of all who took part in these latter experiments that sources of conscious and unconscious deception were sufficiently excluded, and that the large percentage of correct reproductions by the subjects of words, diagrams, and sensations occupying other persons' consciousness were entirely inexplicable as results of chance. The witnesses of these performances were in fact all so satisfied of the genuineness of the phenomena, that 'telepathy' has figured freely in the papers of the Proceedings and in Gurney's book on Phantasms as a *vera causa* on which additional hypotheses might be built. No mere reader can be blamed, however, if he demand, for so revolutionary a belief, a more overwhelming bulk of testimony than has yet been supplied. Any day, of course, may bring in fresh experiments in successful picture-guessing. But meanwhile, and lacking that, we can only point out that the present data are strengthened in the flank, so to speak, by all observations that tend to corroborate the possibility of other kindred phenomena, such as telepathic impression, clairvoyance, or what is called 'test-mediumship.' The wider genus will naturally cover the narrower species with its credit.

Gurney's papers on hypnotism must be mentioned next. Some of them are less concerned with establishing new facts than with analyzing old ones. But omitting these, we find that in the line of pure observation Gurney claims to have ascertained in more than one subject the following phenomenon: The subject's hands are thrust through a blanket, which screens the operator from his eyes, and his mind is absorbed in conversation with a third person. The operator meanwhile points with his finger to one of the fingers of the subject, which finger alone responds to this silent selection by becoming stiff or anæsthetic, as the case may be. The interpretation is difficult, but the phenomenon, which I have myself witnessed, seems authentic.

Another observation made by Gurney seems to prove the possibility of the subject's mind being directly influenced by the operator's. The hypnotized subject responds, or fails to respond, to questions asked by a third party according to the operator's silent permission or refusal. Of course, in these experiments all obvious sources of deception were excluded. But Gurney's most important contribution to our knowledge of hypnotism was his series of experiments on the automatic writing of subjects who had received post-hypnotic suggestions. For example, a subject during trance is told that he will poke the fire in six minutes after waking. On being waked he has no memory of the order, but while he is engaged in conversation his hand is placed on a *planchette*, which immediately writes the sentence, " P., you will poke the fire in six minutes." Experiments like this, which were repeated in great variety, seem to prove that below the upper consciousness the hypnotic consciousness persists, engrossed with the suggestion and able to express itself through the involuntarily moving hand.

Gurney shares, therefore, with Janet and Binet, the

credit of demonstrating the simultaneous existence of
two different strata of consciousness, ignorant of each
other, in the same person. The ' extra-consciousness,'
as one may call it, can be kept on tap, as it were, by the
method of automatic writing. This discovery marks
a new era in experimental psychology, and it is impossible to overrate its importance. But Gurney's greatest piece of work is his laborious ' Phantasms of the
Living.' As an example of the drudgery stowed away
in the volumes, it may suffice to say that in looking
up the proofs for the alleged physical phenomena of
witchcraft, Gurney reports a careful search through
two hundred and sixty books on the subject, with the
result of finding no first-hand evidence recorded in
the trials except the confessions of the victims themselves; and these, of course, are presumptively due
to either torture or hallucination. This statement,
made in an unobtrusive note, is only one instance of
the care displayed throughout the volumes. In the
course of these, Gurney discusses about seven hundred cases of apparitions which he collected. A large
number of these were ' veridical,' in the sense of coin-
ciding with some calamity happening to the person
who appeared. Gurney's explanation is that the mind
of the person undergoing the calamity was at that
moment able to impress the mind of the percipient
with an hallucination.

Apparitions, on this ' telepathic ' theory, may be
called ' objective ' facts, although they are not ' material' facts. In order to test the likelihood of such
veridical hallucinations being due to mere chance,
Gurney instituted the ' census of hallucinations,' which
has been continued with the result of obtaining answers from over twenty-five thousand persons, asked

at random in different countries whether, when in good health and awake, they had ever heard a voice, seen a form, or felt a touch which no material presence could account for. The result seems to be, roughly speaking, that in England about one adult in ten has had such an experience at least once in his life, and that of the experiences themselves a large number coincide with some distant event. The question is, Is the frequency of these latter cases too great to be deemed fortuitous, and must we suppose an occult connection between the two events? Mr. and Mrs. Sidgwick have worked out this problem on the basis of the English returns, seventeen thousand in number, with a care and thoroughness that leave nothing to be desired. Their conclusion is that the cases where the apparition of a person is seen on the day of his death are four hundred and forty times too numerous to be ascribed to chance. The reasoning employed to calculate this number is simple enough. If there be only a fortuitous connection between the death of an individual and the occurrence of his apparition to some one at a distance, the death is no more likely to fall on the same day as the apparition than it is to occur on the same day with any other event in nature. But the chance-probability that any individual's death will fall on any given day marked in advance by some other event is just equal to the chance-probability that the individual will die at all on any specified day; and the national death-rate gives that probability as one in nineteen thousand. If, then, when the death of a person coincides with an apparition of the same person, the coincidence be merely fortuitous, it ought not to occur oftener than once in nineteen thousand cases. As a matter of fact, however, it does occur (according to the census) once in forty-three cases, a number (as aforesaid) four hundred and forty times too great. The American census. of some seven thousand answers, gives a remarkably similar result. Against this conclusion the only rational answer that I can see is that the data are still too few; that the net was not cast wide enough; and that we need, to get fair averages, far more than twenty-four thousand answers to the census question. This may, of course, be true, though it seems exceedingly unlikely; and in our own twenty-four thousand answers veridical cases may possibly have heaped themselves unduly.

The next topic worth mentioning in the Proceedings is the discussion of the physical phenomena of mediumship (slate-writing, furniture-moving, and so forth) by Mrs. Sidgwick, Mr. Hodgson, and 'Mr. Davey.' This, so far as it goes, is destructive of the claims of all the mediums examined. 'Mr. Davey' himself produced fraudulent slate-writing of the highest order, while Mr. Hodgson, a 'sitter' in his confidence, reviewed the written reports of the series of his other sitters, — all of them intelligent persons, — and showed that in every case they failed to see the essential features of what was done before their eyes. This Davey-Hodgson contribution is probably the most damaging document concerning eye-witnesses' evidence that has ever been produced. Another substantial bit of work based on personal observation is Mr. Hodgson's report on Madame Blavatsky's claims to physical mediumship. This is adverse to the lady's pretensions; and although some of Madame Blavatsky's friends make light of it, it is a stroke from which her reputation will not recover.

Physical mediumship in all its phases has fared hard in the Proceedings. The latest case reported on is that of the famous Eusapia Paladino, who being detected in fraud at Cambridge, after a brilliant career of success on the continent, has, according to the draconian rules of method which govern the Society, been ruled out from a further hearing. The case of Stainton Moses, on the other hand, concerning which Mr. Myers has brought out a mass of unpublished testimony, seems to escape from the universal condemnation, and appears to force upon us what Mr. Andrew Lang calls the choice between a moral and a physical miracle.

In the case of Mrs. Piper, not a physical but a trance medium, we seem to have no choice offered at all. Mr. Hodgson and others have made prolonged study of this lady's trances, and are all convinced that supernormal powers of cognition are displayed therein. These are *primâ facie* due to ' spirit-control.' But the conditions are so complex that a dogmatic decision either for or against the spirit-hypothesis must as yet be postponed.

One of the most important experimental contributions to the Proceedings is the article of Miss X. on ' Crystal Vision.' Many persons who look fixedly into a crystal or other vaguely luminous surface fall into a kind of daze, and see visions. Miss X. has this susceptibility in a remarkable degree, and is, moreover, an unusually intelligent critic. She reports many visions which can only be described as apparently clairvoyant, and others which beautifully fill a vacant niche in our knowledge of subconscious mental operations. For example, looking into the crystal before breakfast one morning she reads in printed characters of the

death of a lady of her acquaintance, the date and other
circumstances all duly appearing in type. Startled by
this, she looks at the 'Times' of the previous day for
verification, and there among the deaths are the identical words which she has seen. On the same page
of the Times are other items which she remembers
reading the day before; and the only explanation
seems to be that her eyes then inattentively observed, so to speak, the death-item, which forthwith
fell into a special corner of her memory, and came
out as a visual hallucination when the peculiar modification of consciousness induced by the crystal-
gazing set in.

Passing from papers based on observation to papers
based on narrative, we have a number of ghost stories,
etc., sifted by Mrs. Sidgwick and discussed by Messrs.
Myers and Podmore. They form the best ghost literature I know of from the point of view of emotional
interest. As to the conclusions drawn, Mrs. Sidgwick is rigorously non-committal, while Mr. Myers
and Mr. Podmore show themselves respectively hos-
pitable and inhospitable to the notion that such stories
have a basis of objectivity dependent on the continued existence of the dead.

I must close my gossip about the Proceedings by
naming what, after all, seems to me the most important part of its contents. This is the long series of
articles by Mr. Myers on what he now calls the 'subliminal self,' or what one might designate as ultra-
marginal consciousness. The result of Myers's learned
and ingenious studies in hypnotism, hallucinations,
automatic writing, mediumship, and the whole series
of allied phenomena is a conviction which he expresses in the following terms:

" Each of us is in reality an abiding psychical entity far more extensive than he knows, — an individuality which can never express itself completely through any corporeal manifestation. The self manifests itself through the organism ; but there is always some part of the self unmanifested, and always, as it seems, some power of organic expression in abeyance or reserve."

The ordinary consciousness Mr. Myers likens to the visible part of the solar spectrum ; the total consciousness is like that spectrum prolonged by the inclusion of the ultra-red and ultra-violet rays. In the psychic spectrum the ' ultra ' parts may embrace a far wider range, both of physiological and of psychical activity, than is open to our ordinary consciousness and memory. At the lower end we have the *physiological* extension, mind-cures, ' stigmatization ' of ecstatics, etc. ; in the upper, the hyper-normal cognitions of the medium-trance. Whatever the judgment of the future may be on Mr. Myers's speculations, the credit will always remain to them of being the first attempt in any language to consider the phenomena of hallucination, hypnotism, automatism, double personality, and mediumship as connected parts of one whole subject. All constructions in this field must be provisional, and it is as something provisional that Mr. Myers offers us his formulations. But, thanks to him, we begin to see for the first time what a vast interlocked and graded system these phenomena, from the rudest motor-automatisms to the most startling sensory-apparition, form. Quite apart from Mr. Myers's conclusions, his methodical treatment of them by classes and series is the first great step toward overcoming the distaste of orthodox science to look at them at all.

One's reaction on hearsay testimony is always determined by one's own experience. Most men who have once convinced themselves, by what seems to them a careful examination, that any one species of the supernatural exists, begin to relax their vigilance as to evidence, and throw the doors of their minds more or less wide open to the supernatural along its whole extent. To a mind that has thus made its *salto mortale*, the minute work over insignificant cases and quiddling discussion of 'evidential values,' of which the Society's reports are full, seems insufferably tedious. And it is so; few species of literature are more truly dull than reports of phantasms. Taken simply by themselves, as separate facts to stare at, they appear so devoid of meaning and sweep, that, even were they certainly true, one would be tempted to leave them out of one's universe for being so idiotic. Every other sort of fact has some context and continuity with the rest of nature. These alone are contextless and discontinuous.

Hence I think that the sort of loathing — no milder word will do — which the very words ' psychical research ' and ' psychical researcher ' awaken in so many honest scientific breasts is not only natural, but in a sense praiseworthy. A man who is unable himself to conceive of any *orbit* for these mental meteors can only suppose that Messrs. Gurney, Myers, & Co.'s mood in dealing with them must be that of silly marvelling at so many detached prodigies. And such prodigies! So science simply falls back on her general *non-possumus ;* and most of the would-be critics of the Proceedings have been contented to oppose to the phenomena recorded the simple presumption that in some way or other the reports *must* be fallacious, — for so far as the order of nature has been subjected to really scientific scrutiny, it always has been proved to run the other way. But the oftener one is forced to reject an alleged sort of fact by the use of this mere presumption, the weaker does the presumption itself get to be; and one might in course of time use up one's presumptive privileges in this way, even though one started (as our anti-telepathists do) with as good a case as the great induction of psychology that all our knowledge comes by the use of our eyes and ears and other senses. And we must remember also that this undermining of the strength of a presumption by reiterated report of facts to the contrary does not logically require that the facts in question should all be well proved. A lot of rumors in the air against a business man's credit, though they might all be vague, and no one of them amount to proof that he is unsound, would certainly weaken the *presumption* of his soundness. And all the more would they have this effect if they formed what Gurney called a fagot and not a chain, — that is, if they were independent of one another, and came from different quarters. Now, the evidence for telepathy, weak and strong, taken just as it comes, forms a fagot and not a chain. No one item cites the content of another item as part of its own proof. But taken together the items have a certain general consistency; there is a method in their madness, so to speak. So each of them adds presumptive value to the lot; and cumulatively, as no candid mind can fail to see, they subtract presumptive force from the orthodox belief that there can be nothing in any one's intellect that has not come in through ordinary experiences of sense.

But it is a miserable thing for a question of truth

to be confined to mere presumption and counter-presumption, with no decisive thunderbolt of fact to clear the baffling darkness. And, sooth to say, in talking so much of the merely presumption-weakening value of our records, I have myself been wilfully taking the point of view of the so-called 'rigorously scientific' disbeliever, and making an *ad hominem* plea. My own point of view is different. For me the thunderbolt *has* fallen, and the orthodox belief has not merely had its presumption weakened, but the truth itself of the belief is decisively overthrown. If I may employ the language of the professional logic-shop, a universal proposition can be made untrue by a particular instance. If you wish to upset the law that all crows are black, you must not seek to show that no crows are; it is enough if you prove one single crow to be white. My own white crow is Mrs. Piper. In the trances of this medium, I cannot resist the conviction that knowledge appears which she has never gained by the ordinary waking use of her eyes and ears and wits. What the source of this knowledge may be I know not, and have not the glimmer of an explanatory suggestion to make; but from admitting the fact of such knowledge I can see no escape. So when I turn to the rest of the evidence, ghosts and all, I cannot carry with me the irreversibly negative bias of the 'rigorously scientific' mind, with its presumption as to what the true order of nature ought to be. I feel as if, though the evidence be flimsy in spots, it may nevertheless collectively carry heavy weight. The rigorously scientific mind may, in truth, easily overshoot the mark. Science means, first of all, a certain dispassionate method. To suppose that it means a certain set of results that one should pin one's faith upon and hug forever is sadly to mistake its genius, and degrades the scientific body to the status of a sect.

We all, scientists and non-scientists, live on some inclined plane of credulity. The plane tips one way in one man, another way in another; and may he whose plane tips in no way be the first to cast a stone! As a matter of fact, the trances I speak of have broken down for my own mind the limits of the admitted order of nature. Science, so far as science denies such exceptional occurrences, lies prostrate in the dust for me; and the most urgent intellectual need which I feel at present is that science be built up again in a form in which such things may have a positive place. Science, like life, feeds on its own decay. New facts burst old rules; then newly divined conceptions bind old and new together into a reconciling law.

And here is the real instructiveness of Messrs. Myers and Gurney's work. They are trying with the utmost conscientiousness to find a reconciling conception which shall subject the old laws of nature to the smallest possible strain. Mr. Myers uses that method of gradual approach which has performed such wonders in Darwin's hands. When Darwin met a fact which seemed a poser to his theory, his regular custom, as I have heard an able colleague say, was to fill in all round it with smaller facts, as a wagoner might heap dirt round a big rock in the road, and thus get his team over without upsetting. So Mr. Myers, starting from the most ordinary facts of inattentive consciousness, follows this clue through a long series which terminates in ghosts, and seeks to show that these are but extreme manifestations of a common truth, — the truth that the invisible segments of our minds are susceptible, under rarely realized conditions, of acting and being acted upon by the invisible segments of other conscious lives. This may not be ultimately true (for the theosophists, with their astral bodies and the like, may, for aught I now know, prove to be on the correcter trail), but no one can deny that it is in good scientific form, — for science always takes a known kind of phenomenon, and tries to extend its range.

I have myself, as American agent for the census, collected hundreds of cases of hallucination in healthy persons. The result is to make me feel that we all have potentially a ' subliminal' self, which may make at any time irruption into our ordinary lives. At its lowest, it is only the depository of our forgotten memories; at its highest, we do not know what it is at all. Take, for instance, a series of cases. During sleep, many persons have something in them which measures the flight of time better than the waking self does. It wakes them at a preappointed hour; it acquaints them with the moment when they first awake. It may produce an hallucination, — as in a lady who informs me that at the instant of waking she has a vision of her watch-face with the hands pointing (as she has often verified) to the exact time. It may be the feeling that some physiological period has elapsed; but, whatever it is, it is subconscious.

A subconscious something may also preserve experiences to which we do not openly attend. A lady taking her lunch in town finds herself without her purse. Instantly a sense comes over her of rising from the breakfast-table and hearing her purse drop upon the floor. On reaching home she finds noth-

ing under the table, but summons the servant to
say where she has put the purse. The servant produces it, saying: "How did you know where it was?
You rose and left the room as if you did n't know
you 'd dropped it." The same subconscious something may recollect what we have forgotten. A lady
accustomed to taking salicylate of soda for muscular
rheumatism wakes one early winter morning with an
aching neck. In the twilight she takes what she supposes to be her customary powder from a drawer, dissolves it in a glass of water, and is about to drink it
down, when she feels a sharp slap on her shoulder and
hears a voice in her ear saying, " Taste it ! " On examination, she finds she has got a morphine powder
by mistake. The natural interpretation is that a sleeping memory of the morphine powders awoke in this
quasi-explosive way. A like explanation offers itself
as most plausible for the following case : A lady, with
little time to catch the train, and the expressman
about to call, is excitedly looking for the lost key of a
packed trunk. Hurrying upstairs with a bunch of
keys, proved useless, in her hand, she hears an
' objective' voice distinctly say, "Try the key of the
cake-box." Being tried, it fits. This also may well
have been the effect of forgotten experience.

Now, the effect is doubtless due to the same hallu-
cinatory mechanism; but the source is less easily as-
signed as we ascend the scale of cases. A lady, for
instance, goes after breakfast to see about one of her
servants who has become ill over night. She is
startled at distinctly reading over the bedroom door
in gilt letters the word ' small-pox.' The doctor is
sent for, and ere long pronounces small-pox to be
the disease, although the lady says, " The thought of

the girl's having small-pox never entered my mind till I saw the apparent inscription." Then come other cases of warning; for example, that of a youth sitting in a wagon under a shed, who suddenly hears his dead mother's voice say, " Stephen, get away from here quick! " and jumps out just in time to see the shed-roof fall.

After this come the experiences of persons appearing to distant friends at or near the hour of death. Then, too, we have the trance-visions and utterances, which may appear astonishingly profuse and continuous, and maintain a fairly high intellectual level. For all these higher phenomena, it seems to me that while the proximate mechanism is that of 'hallucination,' it is straining an hypothesis unduly to name any ordinary subconscious mental operation — such as expectation, recollection, or inference from inattentive perception — as the ultimate cause that starts it up. It is far better tactics, if you wish to get rid of mystery, to brand the narratives themselves as unworthy of trust. The trustworthiness of most of them is to my own mind far from proved. And yet in the light of the medium-trance, which *is* proved, it seems as if they might well all be members of a natural kind of fact of which we do not yet know the full extent.

Thousands of sensitive organizations in the United States to-day live as steadily in the light of these experiences, and are as indifferent to modern science, as if they lived in Bohemia in the twelfth century. They are indifferent to science, because science is so callously indifferent to their experiences. Although in its essence science only stands for a method and for no fixed belief, yet as habitually taken, both by its votaries and outsiders, it is identified with a certain fixed belief, — the belief that the hidden order of nature is mechanical exclusively, and that non-mechanical categories are irrational ways of conceiving and explaining even such things as human life. Now, this mechanical rationalism, as one may call it, makes, if it becomes one's only way of thinking, a violent breach with the ways of thinking that have played the greatest part in human history. Religious thinking, ethical thinking, poetical thinking, teleological, emotional, sentimental thinking, what one might call the personal view of life to distinguish it from the impersonal and mechanical, and the romantic view of life to distinguish it from the rationalistic view, have been, and even still are, outside of well-drilled scientific circles, the dominant forms of thought. But for mechanical rationalism, personality is an insubstantial illusion. The chronic belief of mankind, that events may happen for the sake of their personal significance, is an abomination; and the notions of our grandfathers about oracles and omens, divinations and apparitions, miraculous changes of heart and wonders worked by inspired persons, answers to prayer and providential leadings, are a fabric absolutely baseless, a mass of sheer *un*truth.

Now, of course, we must all admit that the excesses to which the romantic and personal view of nature may lead, if wholly unchecked by impersonal rationalism, are direful. Central African Mumbo-jumboism is one of unchecked romanticism's fruits. One ought accordingly to sympathize with that abhorrence of romanticism as a sufficient world-theory; one ought to understand that lively intolerance of the least grain of romanticism in the views of life of other people, which are such characteristic marks of those who follow the scientific professions to-day. Our debt to science is literally boundless, and our gratitude for what is positive in her teachings must be correspondingly immense. But the S. P. R.'s Proceedings have, it seems to me, conclusively proved one thing to the candid reader; and that is that the verdict of pure insanity, of gratuitous preference for error, of superstition without an excuse, which the scientists of our day are led by their intellectual training to pronounce upon the entire thought of the past, is a most shallow verdict. The personal and romantic view of life has other roots besides wanton exuberance of imagination and perversity of heart. It is perennially fed by *facts of experience*, whatever the ulterior interpretation of those facts may prove to be; and at no time in human history would it have been less easy than now — at most times it would have been much more easy — for advocates with a little industry to collect in its favor an array of contemporary documents as good as those which our publications present. These documents all relate to real experiences of persons. These experiences have three characters in common: They are capricious, discontinuous, and not easily controlled; they require peculiar persons for their production; their significance seems to be wholly for personal life. Those who preferentially attend to them, and still more those who are individually subject to them, not only easily may find, but are logically bound to find, in them valid arguments for their romantic and personal conception of the world's course. Through my slight participation in the investigations of the S. P. R. I have become acquainted with numbers of persons of this sort, for whom the very word 'science' has become a name of reproach, for reasons that I now both understand

and respect. It is the intolerance of science for such
phenomena as we are studying, her peremptory denial
either of their existence or of their significance (except as proofs of man's absolute innate folly), that has
set science so apart from the common sympathies of
the race. I confess that it is on this, its humanizing
mission, that the Society's best claim to the gratitude
of our generation seems to me to depend. It has
restored continuity to history. It has shown some
reasonable basis for the most superstitious aberrations
of the foretime. It has bridged the chasm, healed
the hideous rift that science, taken in a certain narrow
way, has shot into the human world.

I will even go one step farther. When from our
present advanced standpoint we look back upon the
past stages of human thought, whether it be scientific
thought or theological thought, we are amazed that a
universe which appears to us of so vast and mysterious a complication should ever have seemed to
any one so little and plain a thing. Whether it be
Descartes's world or Newton's, whether it be that of
the materialists of the last century or that of the
Bridgewater treatises of our own, it always looks the
same to us, — incredibly perspectiveless and short.
Even Lyell's, Faraday's, Mill's, and Darwin's consciousness of their respective subjects are already
beginning to put on an infantile and innocent look.
Is it then likely that the science of our own day will
escape the common doom; that the minds of its
votaries will never look old-fashioned to the grand-
children of the latter? It would be folly to suppose
so. Yet if we are to judge by the analogy of the
past, when our science once becomes old-fashioned,
it will be more for its omissions of fact, for its igno-

rance of whole ranges and orders of complexity in the phenomena to be explained, than for any fatal lack in its spirit and principles. The spirit and principles of science are mere affairs of method; there is nothing in them that need hinder science from dealing successfully with a world in which personal forces are the starting-point of new effects. The only form of thing that we directly encounter, the only experience that we concretely have, is our own personal life. The only complete category of our thinking, our pro fessors of philosophy tell us, is the category of personality, every other category being one of the abstract elements of that. And this systematic denial on science's part of personality as a condition of events, this rigorous belief that in its own essential and innermost nature our world is a strictly impersonal world, may, conceivably, as the whirligig of time goes round, prove to be the very defect that our descendants will be most surprised at in our own boasted science, the omission that to their eyes will most tend to make *it* look perspectiveless and short.

INDEX.

HUMAN IMMORTALITY

two supposed objections to the doctrine

by William James

Dover Publications, Inc., New York

THE INGERSOLL LECTURESHIP

Extract from the will of Miss Caroline Haskell Ingersoll, who died in Keene, County of Cheshire, New Hampshire, Jan. 26, 1893.

First. In carrying out the wishes of my late beloved father, George Goldthwait Ingersoll, as declared by him in his last will and testament, I give and bequeath to Harvard University in Cambridge, Mass., where my late father was graduated, and which he always held in love and honor, the sum of Five thousand dollars ($5,000) as a fund for the establishment of a Lectureship on a plan somewhat similar to that of the Dudleian lecture, that is — one lecture to be delivered each year, on any convenient day between the last day of May and the first day of December, on this subject, "the Immortality of Man," said lecture not to form a part of the usual college course, nor to be delivered by any Professor or Tutor as part of his usual routine of instruction, though any such Professor or Tutor may be appointed to such service. The choice of said lecturer is not to be limited to any one religious denomination, nor to any one profession, but may be that of either clergyman or layman, the appointment to take place at least six months before the delivery of said lecture. The above sum to be safely invested and three fourths of the annual interest thereof to be paid to the lecturer for his services and the remaining fourth to be expended in the publishment and gratuitous distribution of the lecture, a copy of which is always to be furnished by the lecturer for such purpose. The same lecture to be named and known as "the Ingersoll lecture on the Immortality of Man."

PREFACE TO SECOND EDITION

O many critics have made one and the same objection to the doorway to immortality which my lecture claims to be left open by the "transmission-theory" of cerebral action, that I feel tempted, as the book is again going to press, to add a word of explanation.

If our finite personality here below, the objectors say, be due to the transmission through the brain of portions of a preëxisting larger consciousness, all that can remain after the brain expires is the larger consciousness itself as such, with which we should thenceforth be perforce reconfounded, the only means of our existence in finite personal form having ceased.

But this, the critics continue, is the

pantheistic idea of immortality, survival, namely, in the soul of the world ; not the Christian idea of immortality, which means survival in strictly personal form.

In showing the possibility of a mental life after the brain's death, they conclude, the lecture has thus at the same time shown the impossibility of its identity with the personal life, which is the brain's function.

Now I am myself anything but a pantheist of the monistic pattern ; yet for simplicity's sake I did in the lecture speak of the "mother-sea" in terms that must have sounded pantheistic, and suggested that I thought of it myself as a unit. On page 30, I even added that future lecturers might prove the loss of some of our personal limitations after death not to be matter for absolute regret. The interpretation of my critics was therefore not unnatural ; and I ought to have been more careful to guard against its being made.

In note 5 on page 58 I partially guarded

against it by saying that the "mother-
sea" from which the finite mind is supposed to be strained by the brain, need
not be conceived of in pantheistic terms
exclusively.   There might be, I said, many
minds behind the scenes as well as one.
The plain truth is that *one may conceive the
mental world behind the veil in as individualistic a form as one pleases, without any
detriment to the general scheme by which
the brain is represented as a transmissive
organ.*

If the extreme individualistic view were
taken, one's finite mundane consciousness
would be an extract from one's larger,
truer personality, the latter having even
now some sort of reality behind the
scenes.   And in transmitting it — to keep
to our extremely mechanical metaphor,
which confessedly throws no light on the
actual *modus operandi* — one's brain would
also leave effects upon the part remaining
behind the veil ; for when a thing is torn,
both fragments feel the operation.

And just as (to use a very coarse figure) the stubs remain in a check-book whenever a check is used, to register the transaction, so these impressions on the transcendent self might constitute so many vouchers of the finite experiences of which the brain had been the mediator; and ultimately they might form that collection within the larger self of memories of our earthly passage, which is all that, since Locke's day, the continuance of our personal identity beyond the grave has by psychology been recognized to mean.

It is true that all this would seem to have affinities rather with preëxistence and with possible re-incarnations than with the Christian notion of immortality. But my concern in the lecture was not to discuss immortality in general. It was confined to showing it to be *not incompatible* with the brain-function theory of our present mundane consciousness. I hold that it is so compatible, and compatible moreover in fully individualized form. The reader would be in accord with everything that the text of my lecture intended to say, were he to assert that every memory and affection of his present life is to be preserved, and that he shall never *in sæcula sæculorum* cease to be able to say to himself : " I am the same personal being who in old times upon the earth had those experiences."

HUMAN IMMORTALITY

T is a matter unfortunately too often seen in history to call for much remark, that when a living want of mankind has got itself officially protected and organized in an institution, one of the things which the institution most surely tends to do is to stand in the way of the natural gratification of the want itself. We see this in laws and courts of justice; we see it in ecclesiasticisms; we see it in academies of the fine arts, in the medical and other professions, and we even see it in the universities themselves.

Too often do the place-holders of such institutions frustrate the spiritual purpose to which they were appointed to minister, by the technical light which soon becomes

the only light in which they seem able to
see the purpose, and the narrow way which
is the only way in which they can work in
its service.

I confess that I thought of this for a
moment when the Corporation of our University invited me last spring to give this
Ingersoll lecture. Immortality is one of
the great spiritual needs of man. The
churches have constituted themselves the
official guardians of the need, with the result that some of them actually pretend to
accord or to withhold it from the individual by their conventional sacraments, —
withhold it at least in the only shape in
which it can be an object of desire. And
now comes the Ingersoll lectureship. Its
high-minded founder evidently thought that
our University might serve the cause he
had at heart more liberally than the
churches do, because a university is a body
so much less trammeled by traditions and
by impossibilities in regard to choice of
persons. And yet one of the first things

which the university does is to appoint a
man like him who stands before you, certainly not because he is known as an en-
thusiastic messenger of the future life,
burning to publish the good tidings to his
fellow-men, but apparently because he is
a university official.

Thinking in this way, I felt at first as if
I ought to decline the appointment. The
whole subject of immortal life has its prime
roots in personal feeling. I have to confess that my own personal feeling about
immortality has never been of the keenest
order, and that, among the problems that
give my mind solicitude, this one does not
take the very foremost place. Yet there
are individuals with a real passion for the
matter, men and women for whom a life
hereafter is a pungent craving, and the
thought of it an obsession; and in whom
keenness of interest has bred an insight
into the relations of the subject that no one
less penetrated with the mystery of it can
attain. Some of these people are known

to me. They are not official personages ;
they do not speak as the scribes, but as
having direct authority. And surely, if
anywhere a prophet clad in goatskins, and
not a uniformed official, should be called to
give inspiration, assurance, and instruction,
it would seem to be here, on such a theme.
Office, at any rate, ought not to displace
spiritual calling.

And yet, in spite of these reflections,
which I could not avoid making, I am
here to-night, all uninspired and official as
I am. I am sure that prophets clad in
goatskins, or, to speak less figuratively, laymen inspired with emotional messages on
the subject, will often enough be invited
by our Corporation to give the Ingersoll
lecture hereafter.   Meanwhile, all negative
and deadening as the remarks of a mere
professional psychologist like myself may
be in comparison with the vital lessons they
will give, I am sure, upon mature reflection, that those who have the responsibility
of administering the Ingersoll foundation

are in duty bound to let the most various kinds of official personages take their turn as well. The subject is really an enormous subject. At the back of Mr. Alger's 'Critical History of the Doctrine of a Future Life,' there is a bibliography of more than five thousand titles of books in which it is treated. Our Corporation cannot think only of the single lecture: it must think of the whole series of lectures *in futuro*. Single lectures, however emotionally inspired and inspiring they may be, will not be enough. The lectures must remedy each other, so that out of the series there shall emerge a collective literature worthy of the importance of the theme. This unquestionably was what the founder had in mind. He wished the subject to be turned over in all possible aspects, so that at last results might ponderate harmoniously in the true direction. Seen in this long perspective, the Ingersoll foundation calls for nothing so much as for minute division of labor. Orators must take their turn, and prophets ; but narrow specialists as well. The ologians of every creed, metaphysicians, anthropologists, and psychologists must alternate with biologists and physicists and psychical researchers,— even with mathematicians. If any one of them presents a grain of truth, seen from his point of view, that will remain and accrete with truths brought by the others, his will have been a good appointment.

In the hour that lies before us, then, I shall seek to justify my appointment by offering what seem to me two such grains of truth, two points well fitted, if I am not mistaken, to combine with anything that other lecturers may bring.

These points are both of them in the nature of replies to objections, to difficulties which our modern culture finds in the old notion of a life hereafter, — difficulties that I am sure rob the notion of much of its old power to draw belief, in the scientifically cultivated circles to which this audience belong.

The first of these difficulties is relative to the absolute dependence of our spiritual life, as we know it here, upon the brain. One hears not only physiologists, but numbers of laymen who read the popular science books and magazines, saying all about us, How can we believe in life hereafter when Science has once for all attained to proving, beyond possibility of escape, that our inner life is a function of that famous material, the so-called 'gray matter' of our cerebral convolutions? How can the function possibly persist after its organ has undergone decay?

Thus physiological psychology is what is supposed to bar the way to the old faith. And it is now as a physiological psychologist that I ask you to look at the question with me a little more closely.

It is indeed true that physiological science has come to the conclusion cited; and we must confess that in so doing she has only carried out a little farther the common belief of mankind. Every one

knows that arrests of brain development
occasion imbecility, that blows on the
head abolish memory or consciousness, and
that brain-stimulants and poisons change
the quality of our ideas. The anatomists,
physiologists, and pathologists have only
shown this generally admitted fact of a
dependence to be detailed and minute.
What the laboratories and hospitals have
lately been teaching us is not only that
thought in general is one of the brain's
functions, but that the various special
forms of thinking are functions of special
portions of the brain. When we are thinking of things seen, it is our occipital convolutions that are active; when of things
heard, it is a certain portion of our temporal lobes; when of things to be spoken,
it is one of our frontal convolutions. Professor Flechsig of Leipzig (who perhaps
more than any one may claim to have
made the subject his own) considers that
in other special convolutions those processes of association go on, which permit

the more abstract processes of thought, to take place. I could easily show you these regions if I had here a picture of the brain.[1] Moreover, the diminished or exaggerated associations of what this author calls the *Körperfühlsphäre* with the other regions, accounts, according to him, for the complexion of our emotional life, and eventually decides whether one shall be a callous brute or criminal, an unbalanced sentimentalist, or a character accessible to feeling, and yet well poised. Such special opinions may have to be corrected; yet so firmly established do the main positions worked out by the anatomists, physiologists, and pathologists of the brain appear, that the youth of our medical schools are everywhere taught unhesitatingly to believe them. The assurance that observation will go on to establish them ever more and more minutely is the inspirer of all contemporary research. And almost any of our young psychologists will tell you that only a few belated scholastics, or pos-

sibly some crack - brained theosophist or
psychical researcher, can be found holding back, and still talking as if mental
phenomena might exist as independent
variables in the world.

For the purposes of my argument, now,
I wish to adopt this general doctrine as
if it were established absolutely, with no
possibility of restriction. During this hour
I wish you also to accept it as a postulate,
whether you think it incontrovertibly established or not ; so I beg you to agree
with me to-day in subscribing to the great
psycho-physiological formula : *Thought is
a function of the brain.*

The question is, then, Does this doctrine
logically compel us to disbelieve in immortality ?   Ought it to force every truly consistent thinker to sacrifice his hopes of an
hereafter to what he takes to be his duty
of accepting all the consequences of a scientific truth ?

Most persons imbued with what one may
call the puritanism of science would feel

themselves bound to answer this question with a yes. If any medically or psychologically bred young scientists feel otherwise, it is probably in consequence of that incoherency of mind of which the majority of mankind happily enjoy the privilege. At one hour scientists, at another they are Christians or common men, with the will to live burning hot in their breasts; and, holding thus the two ends of the chain, they are careless of the intermediate connection. But the more radical and uncompromising disciple of science makes the sacrifice, and, sorrowfully or not, according to his temperament, submits to giving up his hopes of heaven.[2]

This, then, is the objection to immortality; and the next thing in order for me is to try to make plain to you why I believe that it has in strict logic no deterrent power. I must show you that the fatal consequence is not coercive, as is commonly imagined; and that, even though our soul's life (as here below it is revealed to us) may be in literal strictness the function of a brain that perishes, yet it is not at all impossible, but on the contrary quite possible, that the life may still continue when the brain itself is dead.

The supposed impossibility of its continuing comes from too superficial a look at the admitted fact of functional dependence. The moment we inquire more closely into the notion of functional dependence, and ask ourselves, for example, how many kinds of functional dependence there may be, we immediately perceive that there is one kind at least that does not exclude a life hereafter at all. The fatal conclusion of the physiologist flows from his assuming offhand another kind of functional dependence, and treating it as the only imaginable kind.[3]

When the physiologist who thinks that his science cuts off all hope of immortality pronounces the phrase, " Thought is a function of the brain," he thinks of the matter just as he thinks when he says,

"Steam is a function of the tea-kettle," "Light is a function of the electric circuit," "Power is a function of the moving waterfall." In these latter cases the several material objects have the function of inwardly creating or engendering their effects, and their function must be called *productive* function. Just so, he thinks, it must be with the brain. Engendering consciousness in its interior, much as it engenders cholesterin and creatin and carbonic acid, its relation to our soul's life must also be called productive function. Of course, if such production be the function, then when the organ perishes, since the production can no longer continue, the soul must surely die. Such a conclusion as this is indeed inevitable from that particular conception of the facts.[4]

But in the world of physical nature productive function of this sort is not the only kind of function with which we are familiar. We have also releasing or permissive function; and we have transmissive function.

The trigger of a crossbow has a releasing function : it removes the obstacle that holds the string, and lets the bow fly back to its natural shape. So when the hammer falls upon a detonating compound. By knocking out the inner molecular obstructions, it lets the constituent gases resume their normal bulk, and so permits the explosion to take place.

In the case of a colored glass, a prism, or a refracting lens, we have transmissive function. The energy of light, no matter how produced, is by the glass sifted and limited in color, and by the lens or prism determined to a certain path and shape. Similarly, the keys of an organ have only a transmissive function. They open successively the various pipes and let the wind in the air-chest escape in various ways. The voices of the various pipes are constituted by the columns of air trembling as they emerge. But the air is not engendered in the organ. The organ proper, as distinguished from its air-chest, is only an apparatus for letting portions of it loose upon the world in these peculiarly limited shapes.

My thesis now is this : that, when we think of the law that thought is a function of the brain, we are not required to think of productive function only ; *we are entitled also to consider permissive or transmissive function.* And this the ordinary psycho-physiologist leaves out of his account.

Suppose, for example, that the whole universe of material things — the furniture of earth and choir of heaven — should turn out to be a mere surface-veil of phenomena, hiding and keeping back the world of genuine realities. Such a supposition is foreign neither to common sense nor to philosophy. Common sense believes in realities behind the veil even too superstitiously ; and idealistic philosophy declares the whole world of natural experience, as we get it, to be but a time-mask, shattering or refracting the one infinite Thought which is the sole reality into those millions of finite streams of consciousness known to us as our private selves.

> "Life, like a dome of many-colored glass,
> Stains the white radiance of eternity."

Suppose, now, that this were really so, and suppose, moreover, that the dome, opaque enough at all times to the full super-solar blaze, could at certain times and places grow less so, and let certain beams pierce through into this sublunary world. These beams would be so many finite rays, so to speak, of consciousness, and they would vary in quantity and quality as the opacity varied in degree. Only at particular times and places would it seem that, as a matter of fact, the veil of nature can grow thin and rupturable enough for such effects to occur. But in those places gleams, however finite and unsatisfying, of the absolute life of the universe, are from time to time vouchsafed. Glows of feeling, glimpses of insight, and streams of knowledge and perception float into our finite world.

Admit now that *our brains* are such thin

and half - transparent places in the veil. What will happen? Why, as the white radiance comes through the dome, with all sorts of staining and distortion imprinted on it by the glass, or as the air now comes through my glottis determined and limited in its force and quality of its vibrations by the peculiarities of those vocal chords which form its gate of egress and shape it into my personal voice, even so the genuine matter of reality, the life of souls as it is in its fullness, will break through our several brains into this world in all sorts of restricted forms, and with all the imperfections and queernesses that characterize our finite individualities here below.

According to the state in which the brain finds itself, the barrier of its obstructiveness may also be supposed to rise or fall. It sinks so low, when the brain is in full activity, that a comparative flood of spiritual energy pours over. At other times, only such occasional waves of thought as heavy sleep permits get by. And when finally a brain stops acting altogether, or decays, that special stream of consciousness which it subserved will vanish entirely from this natural world. But the sphere of being that supplied the consciousness would still be intact ; and in that more real world with which, even whilst here, it was continuous, the consciousness might, in ways unknown to us, continue still.

You see that, on all these suppositions, our soul's life, as we here know it, would none the less in literal strictness be the function of the brain. The brain would be the independent variable, the mind would vary dependently on it. But such dependence on the brain for this natural life would in no wise make immortal life impossible, — it might be quite compatible with supernatural life behind the veil hereafter.

As I said, then, the fatal consequence is not coercive, the conclusion which materialism draws being due solely to its one-sided way of taking the word 'function.'

And, whether we care or not for immortality in itself, we ought, as mere critics doing police duty among the vagaries of mankind, to insist on the illogicality of a denial based on the flat ignoring of a palpable alternative. How much more ought we to insist, as lovers of truth, when the denial is that of such a vital hope of mankind!

In strict logic, then, the fangs of cerebralistic materialism are drawn. My words ought consequently already to exert a releasing function on your hopes. You *may* believe henceforward, whether you care to profit by the permission or not. But, as this is a very abstract argument, I think it will help its effect to say a word or two about the more concrete conditions of the case.

All abstract hypotheses sound unreal; and the abstract notion that our brains are colored lenses in the wall of nature, admitting light from the super-solar source, but at the same time tingeing and restricting it, has a thoroughly fantastic sound. What

is it, you may ask, but a foolish metaphor?
And how can such a function be imagined? Is n't the common materialistic
notion vastly simpler? Is not consciousness really more comparable to a sort of
steam, or perfume, or electricity, or nerve-
glow, generated on the spot in its own
peculiar vessel? Is it not more rigorously
scientific to treat the brain's function as
function of production?

The immediate reply is, that, if we are
talking of science positively understood,
function can mean nothing more than bare
concomitant variation. When the brain-
activities change in one way, consciousness changes in another; when the currents pour through the occipital lobes,
consciousness *sees* things ; when through
the lower frontal region, consciousness
says things to itself ; when they stop, she
goes to sleep, etc. In strict science, we
can only write down the bare fact of con-
comitance ; and all talk about either production or transmission, as the mode of

taking place, is pure superadded hypothesis, and metaphysical hypothesis at that,
for we can frame no more notion of the
details on the one alternative than on
the other. Ask for any indication of the
exact process either of transmission or
of production, and Science confesses her
imagination to be bankrupt. She has, so
far, not the least glimmer of a conjecture
or suggestion, — not even a bad verbal
metaphor or pun to offer. *Ignoramus,
ignorabimus,* is what most physiologists, in
the words of one of their number, will say
here. The production of such a thing as
consciousness in the brain, they will reply
with the late Berlin professor of physiology, is the absolute world-enigma, — something so paradoxical and abnormal as to be
a stumbling block to Nature, and almost a
self-contradiction. Into the mode of production of steam in a tea-kettle we have
conjectural insight, for the terms that
change are physically homogeneous one
with another, and we can easily imagine

the case to consist of nothing but altera-
tions of molecular motion. But in the
production of consciousness by the brain,
the terms are heterogeneous natures altogether; and as far as our understanding
goes, it is as great a miracle as if we said,
Thought is 'spontaneously generated,' or
' created out of nothing.'

The theory of production is therefore
not a jot more simple or credible in itself
than any other conceivable theory. It is
only a little more popular. All that one
need do, therefore, if the ordinary materialist should challenge one to explain how
the brain *can* be an organ for limiting and
determining to a certain form a consciousness elsewhere produced, is to retort with
a *tu quoque,* asking him in turn to explain how it can be an organ for producing
consciousness out of whole cloth. For
polemic purposes, the two theories are thus
exactly on a par.

But if we consider the theory of transmission in a wider way, we see that it has

certain positive superiorities, quite apart from its connection with the immortality question.

Just how the process of transmission may be carried on, is indeed unimaginable; but the outer relations, so to speak, of the process, encourage our belief. Consciousness in this process does not have to be generated *de novo* in a vast number of places. It exists already, behind the scenes, coeval with the world. The transmission-theory not only avoids in this way multiplying miracles, but it puts itself in touch with general idealistic philosophy better than the production-theory does. It should always be reckoned a good thing when science and philosophy thus meet.[5]

It puts itself also in touch with the conception of a 'threshold,' — a word with which, since Fechner wrote his book called 'Psychophysik,' the so-called 'new Psychology' has rung. Fechner imagines as the condition of consciousness a certain kind of psycho-physical movement, as he terms it. Before consciousness can come, a certain degree of activity in the movement must be reached. This requisite degree is called the 'threshold;' but the height of the threshold varies under different circumstances: it may rise or fall. When it falls, as in states of great lucidity, we grow conscious of things of which we should be unconscious at other times; when it rises, as in drowsiness, consciousness sinks in amount. This rising and lowering of a psycho-physical threshold exactly conforms to our notion of a permanent obstruction to the transmission of consciousness, which obstruction may, in our brains, grow alternately greater or less.[6]

The transmission-theory also puts itself in touch with a whole class of experiences that are with difficulty explained by the production-theory. I refer to those obscure and exceptional phenomena reported at all times throughout human history, which the 'psychical-researchers,' with

Mr. Frederic Myers at their head, are doing so much to rehabilitate; [7] such phenomena, namely, as religious conversions,
providential leadings in answer to prayer,
instantaneous healings, premonitions, apparitions at time of death, clairvoyant visions or impressions, and the whole range
of mediumistic capacities, to say nothing
of still more exceptional and incomprehen-
sible things. If all our human thought be
a function of the brain, then of course, if
any of these things are facts, — and to my
own mind some of them are facts, — we may
not suppose that they can occur without
preliminary brain-action. But the ordinary
production-theory of consciousness is knit
up with a peculiar notion of how brain-
action *can* occur, — that notion being that
all brain-action, without exception, is due to
a prior action, immediate or remote, of the
bodily sense-organs *on* the brain. Such
action makes the brain produce sensations
and mental images, and out of the sensations
and images the higher forms of thought and

knowledge in their turn are framed.   As
transmissionists, we also must admit this to
be the condition of all our usual thought.
Sense-action is what lowers the brain-bar-
rier.   My voice and aspect, for instance,
strike upon your ears and eyes ; your brain
thereupon becomes more pervious, and
an awareness on your part of what I say
and who I am slips into this world from the
world behind the veil.   But, in the mysterious phenomena to which I allude, it is
often hard to see where the sense-organs
can come in.   A medium, for example, will
show knowledge of his sitter's private affairs which it seems impossible he should
have acquired through sight or hearing, or
inference therefrom.   Or you will have an
apparition of some one who is now dying
hundreds of miles away.   On the production - theory one does not see from what
sensations such odd bits of knowledge are
produced.   On the transmission - theory,
they don't have to be 'produced,' — they
exist ready - made in the transcendental

world, and all that is needed is an abnormal lowering of the brain-threshold to let them through. In cases of conversion, in providential leadings, sudden mental healings, etc., it seems to the subjects themselves of the experience as if a power from without, quite different from the ordinary action of the senses or of the sense-led mind, came into their life, as if the latter suddenly opened into that greater life in which it has its source. The word 'influx,' used in Swedenborgian circles, well describes this impression of new insight, or new willingness, sweeping over us like a tide. All such experiences, quite paradoxical and meaningless on the production-theory, fall very naturally into place on the other theory. We need only suppose the continuity of our consciousness with a mother sea, to allow for exceptional waves occasionally pouring over the dam. Of course the causes of these odd lowerings of the brain's threshold still remain a mystery on any terms.

Add, then, this advantage to the transmission-theory, — an advantage which I am
well aware that some of you will not rate
very high, — and also add the advantage of
not conflicting with a life hereafter, and I
hope you will agree with me that it has
many points of superiority to the more
familiar theory. It is a theory which, in
the history of opinion on such matters,
has never been wholly left out of account,
though never developed at any great length.
In the great orthodox philosophic tradition,
the body is treated as an essential condition
to the soul's life in this world of sense ; but
after death, it is said, the soul is set free,
and becomes a purely intellectual and non-
appetitive being. Kant expresses this idea
in terms that come singularly close to those
of our transmission-theory. The death of
the body, he says, may indeed be the end
of the sensational use of our mind, but only
the beginning of the intellectual use. " The
body," he continues, " would thus be, not
the cause of our thinking, but merely a

condition restrictive thereof, and, although essential to our sensuous and animal consciousness, it may be regarded as an impeder of our pure spiritual life.[8] And in a recent book of great suggestiveness and power, less well-known as yet than it deserves, — I mean 'Riddles of the Sphinx,' by Mr. F. C. S. Schiller of Oxford, late of Cornell University, — the transmission-theory is defended at some length.[9]

But still, you will ask, in what positive way does this theory help us to realize our immortality in imagination? What we all wish to keep is just these individual restrictions, these selfsame tendencies and peculiarities that define us to ourselves and others, and constitute our identity, so called. Our finitenesses and limitations seem to be our personal essence; and when the finiting organ drops away, and our several spirits revert to their original source and resume their unrestricted condition, will they then be anything like those sweet streams of feeling which we know, and which even now our brains are sifting out from the great reservoir for our enjoyment here below? Such questions are truly living questions, and surely they must be seriously discussed by future lecturers upon this Ingersoll foundation. I hope, for my part, that more than one such lecturer will penetratingly discuss the conditions of our immortality, and tell us how much we may lose, and how much we may possibly gain, if its finiting outlines should be changed? If all determination is negation, as the philosophers say, it might well prove that the loss of some of the particular determinations which the brain imposes would not appear a matter for such absolute regret.

But into these higher and more transcendental matters I refuse to enter upon this occasion ; and I proceed, during the remainder of the hour, to treat of my second point. Fragmentary and negative it is, as my first one has been. Yet, between them, they do give to our belief in immortality a freer wing.

My second point is relative to the incredible and intolerable number of beings which, with our modern imagination, we must believe to be immortal, if immortality be true. I cannot but suspect that this, too, is a stumbling-block to many of my present audience. And it is a stumbling-block which I should thoroughly like to clear away.

It is, I fancy, a stumbling-block of altogether modern origin, due to the strain upon the quantitative imagination which recent scientific theories, and the moral feelings consequent upon them, have brought in their train.

For our ancestors the world was a small, and — compared with our modern sense of it — a comparatively snug affair. Six thousand years at most it had lasted. In its history a few particular human heroes, kings, ecclesiarchs, and saints stood forth very prominent, overshadowing the imagination with their claims and merits, so that not only they, but all who were associated familiarly with them, shone with a glamour which even the Almighty, it was supposed, must recognize and respect. These prominent personages and their associates were the nucleus of the immortal group; the minor heroes and saints of minor sects came next, and people without distinction formed a sort of background and filling in. The whole scene of eternity (so far, at least, as Heaven and not the nether place was concerned in it) never struck to the believer's fancy as an overwhelmingly large or inconveniently crowded stage. One might call this an aristocratic view of immortality; the immortals — I speak of Heaven exclusively, for an immortality of torment need not now concern us — were always an élite, a select and manageable number.

But, with our own generation, an entirely new quantitative imagination has swept over our western world. The theory of evolution now requires us to suppose a far vaster scale of times, spaces, and numbers

than our forefathers ever dreamed the cosmic process to involve. Human history
grows continuously out of animal history,
and goes back possibly even to the tertiary
epoch. From this there has emerged in-
sensibly a democratic view, instead of the
old aristocratic view, of immortality. For
our minds, though in one sense they may
have grown a little cynical, in another they
have been made sympathetic by the evolutionary perspective. Bone of our bone and
flesh of our flesh are these half-brutish pre-
historic brothers. Girdled about with the
immense darkness of this mysterious universe even as we are, they were born and
died, suffered and struggled. Given over
to fearful crime and passion, plunged in the
blackest ignorance, preyed upon by hideous and grotesque delusions, yet steadfastly
serving the profoundest of ideals in their
fixed faith that existence in any form is
better than non-existence, they ever rescued trimphantly from the jaws of ever-im-
minent destruction the torch of life, which,

thanks to them, now lights the world
for us.   How small indeed seem individual distinctions when we look back on
these overwhelming numbers of human
beings panting and straining under the
pressure of that vital want!   And how
inessential in the eyes of God must be
the small surplus of the individual's merit,
swamped as it is in the vast ocean of the
common merit of mankind, dumbly and
undauntedly doing the fundamental duty
and living the heroic life!   We grow humble and reverent as we contemplate the
prodigious spectacle.   Not our differences
and distinctions, — we feel — no, but our
common animal essence of patience under
suffering and enduring effort must be what
redeems us in the Deity's sight.   An immense compassion and kinship fill the
heart.   An immortality from which these
inconceivable billions of fellow - strivers
should be excluded becomes an irrational
idea for us.   That our superiority in personal refinement or in religious creed

should constitute a difference between ourselves and our messmates at life's banquet,
fit to entail such a consequential difference
of destiny as eternal life for us, and for
them torment hereafter, or death with the
beasts that perish, is a notion too absurd
to be considered serious. Nay, more, the
very beasts themselves — the wild ones
at any rate — are leading the heroic life
at all times. And a modern mind, ex-
panded as some minds are by cosmic emotion, by the great evolutionist vision of
universal continuity, hesitates to draw the
line even at man. If any creature lives
forever, why not all? — why not the patient brutes? So that a faith in immortality, if we are to indulge it, demands of us
nowadays a scale of representation so stu-
pendous that our imagination faints before
it, and our personal feelings refuse to rise
up and face the task. The supposition we
are swept along to is too vast, and, rather
than face the conclusion, we abandon the
premise from which it starts. We give up

our own immortality sooner than believe
that all the hosts of Hottentots and Aus-
tralians that have been, and shall ever be,
should share it with us *in secula seculorum.*
Life is a good thing on a reasonably copious scale ; but the very heavens themselves,
and the cosmic times and spaces, would
stand aghast, we think, at the notion of
preserving eternally such an ever-swelling
plethora and glut of it.

Having myself, as a recipient of modern
scientific culture, gone through a subjective experience like this, I feel sure that
it must also have been the experience of
many, perhaps of most, of you who listen
to my words.　But I have also come to see
that it harbors a tremendous fallacy ; and,
since the noting of the fallacy has set my
own mind free again, I have felt that one
service I might render to my listeners to-
night would be to point out where it lies.

It is the most obvious fallacy in the
world, and the only wonder is that all the
world should not see through it.　It is the

result of nothing but an invincible blindness from which we suffer, an insensibility to the inner significance of alien lives, and a conceit that would project our own incapacity into the vast cosmos, and measure the wants of the Absolute by our own puny needs. Our christian ancestors dealt with the problem more easily than we do. We, indeed, lack sympathy ; but they had a positive antipathy for these alien human creatures, and they naïvely supposed the Deity to have the antipathy, too. Being, as they were, 'heathen,' our forefathers felt a certain sort of joy in thinking that their Creator made them as so much mere fuel for the fires of hell. Our culture has humanized us beyond that point, but we cannot yet conceive them as our comrades in the fields of heaven. We have, as the phrase goes, *no use for them*, and it oppresses us to think of their survival. Take, for instance, all the Chinamen. Which of you here, my friends, sees any fitness in their eternal perpetuation unre-

duced in numbers? Surely not one of you.
At most, you might deem it well to keep a
few chosen specimens alive to represent an
interesting and peculiar variety of humanity; but as for the rest, what comes in such
surpassing numbers, and what you can
only imagine in this abstract summary
collective manner, must be something of
which the units, you are sure, can have no
individual preciousness. God himself, you
think, can have no use for them. An immortality of every separate specimen must
be to him and to the universe as indigestible a load to carry as it is to you. So,
engulfing the whole subject in a sort of
mental giddiness and nausea, you drift
along, first doubting that the mass can be
immortal, then losing all assurance in the
immortality of your own particular person,
precious as you all the while feel and realize the latter to be. This, I am sure, is
the attitude of mind of some of you before
me.

But is not such an attitude due to the

veriest lack and dearth of your imagination? You take these swarms of alien
kinsmen as they are *for you:* an external
picture painted on your retina, representing a crowd oppressive by its vastness and
confusion. As they are for you, so you
think they positively and absolutely are. *I*
feel no call for them, you say; therefore
there *is* no call for them. But all the
while, beyond this externality which is
your way of realizing them, they realize
themselves with the acutest internality,
with the most violent thrills of life. 'T is
you who are dead, stone-dead and blind
and senseless, in your way of looking on.
You open your eyes upon a scene of which
you miss the whole significance. Each of
these grotesque or even repulsive aliens is
animated by an inner joy of living as hot
or hotter than that which you feel beating
in your private breast. The sun rises and
beauty beams to light his path. To miss
the inner joy of him, as Stevenson says, is
to miss the whole of him.[10] Not a being

of the countless throng is there whose continued life is not called for, and called for
intensely, by the consciousness that animates the being's form. That *you* neither
realize nor understand nor call for it, that
you have no use for it, is an absolutely
irrelevant circumstance. That you have
a saturation-point of interest tells us nothing of the interests that absolutely are.
The Universe, with every living entity
which her resources create, creates at the
same time a call for that entity, and an
appetite for its continuance, — creates it,
if nowhere else, at least within the heart of
the entity itself. It is absurd to suppose,
simply because our private power of sympathetic vibration with other lives gives
out so soon, that in the heart of infinite
being itself there can be such a thing as
plethora, or glut, or supersaturation. It
is not as if there were a bounded room
where the minds in possession had to
move up or make place and crowd together
to accommodate new occupants. Each new

mind brings its own edition of the universe
of space along with it, its own room to inhabit ; and these spaces never crowd each
other, — the space of my imagination, for
example, in no way interferes with yours.
The amount of possible consciousness
seems to be governed by no law analogous
to that of the so-called conservation of energy in the material world. When one
man wakes up, or one is born, another does
not have to go to sleep, or die, in order to
keep the consciousness of the universe a
constant quantity. Professor Wundt, in
fact, in his 'System of Philosophy,' has
formulated a law of the universe which he
calls the law of increase of spiritual energy, and which he expressly opposes to
the law of conservation of energy in physical things.[11] There seems no formal limit
to the positive increase of being in spiritual respects ; and since spiritual being,
whenever it comes, affirms itself, expands
and craves continuance, we may justly and
literally say, regardless of the defects of

our own private sympathy, that the supply of individual life in the universe can never possibly, however immeasurable it may become, exceed the demand. The demand for that supply is there the moment the supply itself comes into being, for the beings supplied demand their own continuance.

I speak, you see, from the point of view of all the other individual beings, realizing and enjoying inwardly their own existence. If we are pantheists, we can stop there. We need, then, only say that through them, as through so many diversified channels of expression, the eternal Spirit of the Universe affirms and realizes its own infinite life. But if we are theists, we can go farther without altering the result. God, we can then say, has so inexhaustible a capacity for love that his call and need is for a literally endless accumulation of created lives. He can never faint or grow weary, as we should, under the increasing supply. His scale is infinite in all things. His sympathy can never know satiety or glut.

I hope now that you agree with me that the tiresomeness of an over-peopled Heaven is a purely subjective and illusory notion, a sign of human incapacity, a remnant of the old narrow-hearted aristocratic creed. " Revere the Maker, lift thine eye up to his style and manners of the sky," and you will believe that this is indeed a democratic universe, in which your paltry exclusions play no regulative part. Was your taste consulted in the peopling of this globe ? How, then, should it be consulted as to the peopling of the vast City of God ? Let us put our hand over our mouth, like Job, and be thankful that in our personal littleness we ourselves are here at all. The Deity that suffers us, we may be sure, can suffer many another queer and wondrous and only half-delightful thing.

For my own part, then, so far as logic goes, I am willing that every leaf that ever grew in this world's forests and rustled in the breeze should become immortal. It is purely a question of fact : are the leaves so, or not ? Abstract quantity, and the abstract needlessness in our eyes of so much reduplication of things so much alike, have no connection with the subject. For bigness and number and generic similarity are only manners of our finite way of thinking ; and, considered in itself and apart from our imagination, one scale of dimensions and of numbers for the Universe is no more miraculous or inconceivable than another, the moment you grant to a universe the liberty to be at all, in place of the Non-entity that might conceivably have reigned.

The heart of being can have no exclusions akin to those which our poor little hearts set up. The inner significance of other lives exceeds all our powers of sympathy and insight. If we feel a significance in our own life which would lead us spontaneously to claim its perpetuity, let us be at least tolerant of like claims made by other lives, however numerous, however unideal they may seem to us to be. Let us at any rate not decide adversely on our own claim, whose grounds we feel directly, because we cannot decide favorably on the alien claims, whose grounds we cannot feel at all. That would be letting blindness lay down the law to sight.

NOTES

Note 1, page 9.

The gaps between the centres first recognized as motor and sensory — gaps which form in man two thirds of the surface of the hemispheres — are thus positively interpreted by Flechsig as intellectual centres strictly so called. [Compare his *Gehirn und Seele*, 2te Ausgabe, 1896, p. 23.] They have, he considers, a common type of microscopic structure; and the fibres connected with them are a month later in gaining their medullary sheath than are the fibres connected with the other centres. When disordered, they are the starting-point of the insanities, properly so called. Already Wernicke had defined insanity as disease of the organ of association, without so definitely pretending to circumscribe the latter — compare his *Grundriss der Psychiatrie*, 1894, p. 7. Flechsig goes so far as to say that he finds a difference of symptoms in general paralytics according as their frontal or their more posterior association-centres are diseased. Where it is the frontal centres, the patient's consciousness of self is more deranged than is his perception of purely objective relations. Where the posterior associative regions suffer, it is rather the patient's system of objective ideas that undergoes disintegration (*loc. cit.* pp. 89–91). In rodents Flechsig thinks there is a complete absence of association-centres, — the sensory centres touch each other. In carnivora and the lower monkeys the latter centres still exceed the association - centres in volume. Only in the katarhinal apes do we begin to find anything like the human type (p. 84).

In his little pamphlet, *Die Grenzen geistiger Gesundheit und Krankheit,* Leipzig, 1896, Flechsig ascribes the moral insensibility which is found in certain criminals to a diminution of internal pain-feeling due to degeneration of the ' Körperfühlsphäre,' that extensive anterior region first so named by Munk, in which he lays the seat of all the emotions and of the consciousness of self [*Gehirn und Seele*, pp. 62–68; *die Grenzen*, etc., pp. 31–39, 48]. — I give these references to Flechsig for concreteness' sake, not because his views are irreversibly made out.

NOTE 2, page 11.

So widespread is this conclusion in positivistic circles, so abundantly is it expressed in conversa-

tion, and so frequently implied in things that are
written, that I confess that my surprise was great
when I came to look into books for a passage
explicitly denying immortality on physiological
grounds, which I might quote to make my text
more concrete. I was unable to find anything
blunt and distinct enough to serve. I looked
through all the books that would naturally suggest
themselves, with no effect; and I vainly asked various psychological colleagues. And yet I should almost have been ready to take oath that I had read
several such passages of the most categoric sort
within the last decade. Very likely this is a false
impression, and it may be with this opinion as with
many others. The atmosphere is full of them;
many a writer's pages logically presuppose and
involve them; yet, if you wish to refer a student
to an express and radical statement that he may
employ as a text to comment on, you find almost
nothing that will do. In the present case there
are plenty of passages in which, in a general way,
mind is said to be conterminous with brain-function, but hardly one in which the author thereupon
explicitly denies the possibility of immortality.
The best one I have found is perhaps this: " Not
only consciousness, but every stirring of life, depends on functions that go out like a flame when
nourishment is cut off. . . . The phenomena of

consciousness correspond, element for element, to
the operations of special parts of the brain. . . .
The destruction of any piece of the apparatus involves the loss of some one or other of the vital
operations; and the consequence is that, as far as
life extends, we have before us only an organic
function, not a *Ding-an-sich*, or an expression of
that imaginary entity the Soul. This fundamental
proposition . . . carries with it the denial of the
immortality of the soul, since, where no soul exists,
its mortality or immortality cannot be raised as
a question. . . . The function fills its time, — the
flame illuminates and therein gives out its whole
being. That is all; and verily that is enough. . . .
Sensation has its definite organic conditions, and,
as these decay with the natural decay of life, it is
quite impossible for a mind accustomed to deal
with realities to suppose any capacity of sensation
as surviving when the machinery of our natural
existence has stopped." [*E. Duhring: der Werth
des Lebens*, 3d edition, pp. 48, 168.]

NOTE 3, page 12.

The philosophically instructed reader will notice
that I have all along been placing myself at the
ordinary dualistic point of view of natural science
and of common sense. From this point of view
mental facts like feelings are made of one kind of

stuff or substance, physical facts of another. An
absolute phenomenism, not believing such a dualism to be ultimate, may possibly end by solving
some of the problems that are insoluble when pro-
pounded in dualistic terms. Meanwhile, since the
physiological objection to immortality has arisen
on the ordinary dualistic plane of thought, and
since absolute phenomenism has as yet said nothing
articulate enough to count about the matter, it is
proper that my reply to the objection should be
expressed in dualistic terms — leaving me free, of
course, on any later occasion to make an attempt,
if I wish, to transcend them and use different categories.

Now, on the dualistic assumption, one cannot see
more than two really different sorts of dependence
of our mind on our brain: Either

(1) The brain brings into being the very stuff
of consciousness of which our mind consists; or
else

(2) Consciousness preëxists as an entity, and the
various brains give to it its various special forms.

If supposition 2 be the true one, and the stuff of
mind preëxists, there are, again, only two ways of
conceiving that our brain confers upon it the specifically human form. It may exist

(a) In disseminated particles; and then our brains
are organs of concentration, organs for combining

and massing these into resultant minds of personal form. Or it may exist

(*b*) In vaster unities (absolute 'world-soul,' or something less); and then our brains are organs for separating it into parts and giving them finite form.

There are thus three possible theories of the brain's function, and no more. We may name them, severally, —

1. The theory of production;

2*a*. The theory of combination;

2*b*. The theory of separation.

In the text of the lecture, theory number 2*b* (specified more particularly as the transmission-theory) is defended against theory number 1. Theory 2*a*, otherwise known as the mind-dust or mind-stuff theory, is left entirely unnoticed for lack of time. I also leave it uncriticised in these notes, having already considered it, as fully as the so-far published forms of it may seem to call for, in my work, *The Principles of Psychology*, New York, Holt & Co., 1892, chapter VI. I may say here, however, that Professor W. K. Clifford, one of the ablest champions of the combination-theory, and originator of the useful term 'mind-stuff,' considers that theory incompatible with individual immortality, and in his review of Stewart's and Tait's book, *The Unseen Universe*, thus expresses his conviction : —

" The laws connecting consciousness with changes in the brain are very definite and precise, and their necessary consequences are not to be evaded. . . . Consciousness is a complex thing made up of elements, a stream of feelings. The action of the brain is also a complex thing made up of elements, a stream of nerve-messages. For every feeling in consciousness there is at the same time a nerve-message in the brain. . . . Consciousness is not a simple thing, but a complex ; it is the combination of feelings into a stream. It exists at the same time with the combination of nerve-messages into a stream. If individual feeling always goes with individual nerve-message, if combination or stream of feelings always goes with stream of nerve-messages, does it not follow that, when the stream of nerve-messages is broken up, the stream of feelings will be broken up also, will no longer form a consciousness ? Does it not follow that, when the messages themselves are broken up, the individual feelings will be resolved into still simpler elements? The force of this evidence is not to be weakened by any number of spiritual bodies. Inexorable facts connect our consciousness with this body that we know ; and that not merely as a whole, but the parts of it are connected severally with parts of our brain-action. If there is any similar connection with a spiritual body, it only follows that the spirit-

ual body must die at the same time with the natural one." [*Lectures and Essays*, vol. i. p. 247–49.
Compare also passages of similar purport in vol. ii.
pp. 65–70.]

Note 4, page 13.

The theory of production, or materialistic theory, seldom ventures to formulate itself very distinctly. Perhaps the following passage from Ca-
banis is as explicit as anything one can find : —

"To acquire a just idea of the operations from
which thought results, we must consider the brain
as a particular organ specially destined to produce
it; just as the stomach and intestines are destined
to operate digestion, the liver to filter bile, the pa-
rotid and maxillary glands to prepare the salivary
juices. The impressions, arriving in the brain,
force it to enter into activity; just as the alimen-
tary materials, falling into the stomach, excite it to
a more abundant secretion of gastric juice, and to
the movements which result in their own solution.
The function proper to the first organ is that of re-
ceiving [*percevoir*] each particular impression, of
attaching signs to it, of combining the different impressions, of comparing them with each other, of
drawing from them judgments and resolves; just
as the function of the other organ is to act upon
the nutritive substances whose presence excites it,

to dissolve them, and to assimilate their juices to
our nature.

"Do you say that the organic movements by
which the brain exercises these functions are unknown? I reply that the action by which the
nerves of the stomach determine the different operations which constitute digestion, and the manner
in which they confer so active a solvent power upon
the gastric juice, are equally hidden from our scrutiny. We see the food-materials fall into this viscus with their own proper qualities; we see them
emerge with new qualities, and we infer that the
stomach is really the author of this alteration.
Similarly we see the impressions reaching the brain
by the intermediation of the nerves; they then are
isolated and without coherence. The viscus enters into action; it acts upon them, and soon it
emits [*renvoie*] them metamorphosed into ideas,
to which the language of physiognomy or gesture,
or the signs of speech and writing, give an outward
expression. We conclude, then, with an equal
certitude, that the brain digests, as it were, the impressions; that it performs organically the secretion of thought." [*Rapports du Physique et du
Moral*, 8th edition, 1844, p. 137.]

It is to the ambiguity of the word 'impression'
that such an account owes whatever plausibility it
may seem to have. More recent forms of the pro-

duction-theory have shown a tendency to liken
thought to a 'force' which the brain exerts, or to a
'state' into which it passes. Herbert Spencer, for
instance, writes : —

"The law of metamorphosis, which holds among
the physical forces, holds equally between them
and the mental forces. . . . How this metamorphosis takes place; how a force existing as motion, heat, or light can become a mode of consciousness ; how it is possible for aerial vibrations
to generate the sensation we call sound, or for the
forces liberated by chemical changes in the brain
to give rise to emotion, — these are mysteries
which it is impossible to fathom. But they are
not profounder mysteries than the transformations
of the physical forces into each other." [*First
Principles, 2nd Edition*, p. 217.]

So Büchner says : "Thinking must be regarded
as a special mode of general natural motion, which
is as characteristic of the substance of the central
nervous elements as the motion of contraction is
of the nerve-substance, or the motion of light is of
the universal-ether. . . . That thinking is and must
be a mode of motion is not merely a postulate of
logic, but a proposition which has of late been
demonstrated experimentally. . . . Various ingenious experiments have proved that the swiftest
thought that we are able to evolve occupies at least

the eighth or tenth part of a second." [*Force and Matter*, New York, 1891, p. 241.]

Heat and light, being modes of motion, 'phosphorescence' and 'incandescence' are phenomena to which consciousness has been likened by the production-theory: "As one sees a metallic rod, placed in a glowing furnace, gradually heat itself, and — as the undulations of the caloric grow more and more frequent — pass successively from the shades of bright red to dark red (*sic*), to white, and develope, as its temperature rises, heat and light, — so the living sensitive cells, in presence of the incitations that solicit them, exalt themselves progressively as to their most interior sensibility, enter into a phase of erethism, and at a certain number of vibrations, set free (*dégagent*) pain as a physiological expression of this same sensibility superheated to a red-white." [J. Luys: *le Cerveau*, p. 91.]

In a similar vein Mr. Percival Lowell writes: "When we have, as we say, an idea, what happens inside of us is probably something like this: the neural current of molecular change passes up the nerves, and through the ganglia reaches at last the cortical cells. . . . When it reaches the cortical cells, it finds a set of molecules which are not so accustomed to this special change. The current encounters resistance, and in overcoming this

resistance it causes the cells to glow. This white-
heating of the cells we call consciousness. Consciousness, in short, is probably nerve-glow." [*Occult Japan*, Boston, 1895, p. 311.]

NOTE 5, page 23.

The transmission - theory connects itself very
naturally with that whole tendency of thought
known as transcendentalism. Emerson, for example, writes: "We lie in the lap of immense intelligence, which makes us receivers of its truth and
organs of its activity. When we discern justice,
when we discern truth, we do nothing of ourselves,
but allow a passage to its beams." [*Self-Reliance,
p. 56.] But it is not necessary to identify the consciousness postulated in the lecture, as preëxisting
behind the scenes, with the Absolute Mind of transcendental Idealism, although, indeed, the notion of
it might lead in that direction. The absolute Mind
of transcendental Idealism is one integral Unit, one
single World-mind. For the purposes of my lecture, however, there might be many minds behind
the scenes as well as one. All that the transmission-theory absolutely requires is that they should
transcend *our* minds, — which thus come from
something mental that pre-exists, and is larger
than themselves.

NOTE 6, page 24.

Fechner's conception of a 'psycho - physical threshold' as connected with his 'wave-scheme' is little known to English readers. I accordingly subjoin it, in his own words, abridged : —

"The psychically one is connected with a physically many ; the physically many contract psychically into a one, a simple, or at least a more simple. Otherwise expressed : the psychically unified and simple are resultants of physical multiplicity ; the physically manifold gives unified or simple results. . . .

"The facts which are grouped together under these expressions, and which give them their meaning, are as follows : . . . With our two hemispheres we think singly ; with the identical parts of our two retinæ we see singly. . . . The simplest sensation of light or sound in us is connected with processes which, since they are started and kept up by outer oscillations, must themselves be somehow of an oscillatory nature, although we are wholly unaware of the separate phases and oscillations. . . .

"It is certain, then, that some unified or simple psychic resultants depend on physical multiplicity. But, on the other hand, it is equally certain that the multiplicities of the physical world do not always combine into a simple psychical resultant,

— no, not even when they are compounded in a single bodily system. Whether they may not nevertheless combine into a *unified* resultant is a matter for opinion, since one is always free to ask whether the entire world, as such, may not have some unified psychic resultant. But of any such resultant we at least have no consciousness. . . .

"For brevity's sake, let us distinguish *psychophysical continuity* and *discontinuity* from each other. Continuity, let us say, takes place so far as a physical manifold gives a unified or simple psychic resultant; discontinuity, so far as it gives a distinguishable multiplicity of such resultants. Inasmuch, however, as, within the unity of a more general consciousness or phenomenon of consciousness, there still may be a multiplicity distinguished, the continuity of a more general consciousness does not exclude the discontinuity of particular phenomena.

"One of the most important problems and tasks of Psycho-physics now is this : to determine the conditions (*Gesichtspunkte*) under which the cases of continuity and of discontinuity occur.

"Whence comes it that different organisms have separate consciousnesses, although their bodies are just as much connected by general Nature as the parts of a single organism are with each other, and these latter give a single conscious resultant? Of course we can say that the connection is more intimate between the parts of an organism than between the organisms of Nature. But what do we mean by a more intimate connection? Can an absolute difference of result depend on anything so relative? And does not Nature as a whole show as strict a connection as any organism does, — yea, one even more indissoluble? And the same questions come up within each organism. How comes it that, with different nerve-fibres of touch and sight, we distinguish different space-points, but with one fibre distinguish nothing, although the different fibres are connected in the brain just as much as the parts are in the single fibre? We may again call the latter connection the more *intimate*, but then the same sort of question will arise again.

" Unquestionably the problem which here lies before Psycho - physics cannot be *sharply* answered; but we may establish a general point of view for its treatment, consistently with what we laid down in a former chapter on the relations of more general with more particular phenomena of consciousness."

[The earlier passage is here inserted:] " The essential principle is this: That human psycho-physical activity must exceed a certain intensity for any waking consciousness at all to occur, and

that during the waking state any particular specification of the said activity (whether spontaneous or
due to stimulation), which is capable of occasion-
ing a particular specification of consciousness, must
exceed in its turn a certain further degree of intensity for the consciousness actually to arise. . . .

" This state of things (in itself a mere fact need-
ing no picture) may be made clearer by an image
or scheme, and also more concisely spoken of.
Imagine the whole psycho-physical activity of man
to be a wave, and the degree of this activity to be
symbolized by the height of the wave above a hori-
zontal basal line or surface, to which every psycho-
physically active point contributes an ordinate. . . .
The whole form and evolution of the consciousness will then depend on the rising and falling of
this wave; the intensity of the consciousness at
any time on the wave's height at that time; and
the height must always *somewhere* exceed a certain
limit, which we will call a *threshold*, if waking consciousness is to exist at all.

" Let us call this wave the *total wave*, and the
threshold in question the *principal threshold*."

[Since our various states of consciousness recur,
some in long, some in short periods], "we may
represent such a long period as that of the slowly
fluctuating condition of our general wakefulness and
the general direction of our attention as a wave

that slowly changes the place of its summit. If we call this the *under-wave*, then the movements of shorter period, on which the more special conscious states depend, can be symbolized by wavelets superposed upon the under-wave, and we can call these *over-waves*. They will cause all sorts of modifications of the under-wave's surface, and the total wave will be the resultant of both sets of waves.

"The greater, now, the strength of the movements of short period, the amplitude of the oscillations of the psycho-physical activity, the higher will the crests of the wavelets that represent them rise above, and the lower will their valleys sink below the surface of the under-wave that bears them. And these heights and depressions must exceed a certain limit of quantity which we may call the *upper threshold*, before the special mental state which is correlated with them can appear in consciousness " [pp. 454–456].

" So far now as we symbolize any system of psycho-physical activity, to which a generally unified or principal consciousness corresponds, by the image of a total wave rising with its crest above a certain 'threshold,' we have a means of schematizing in a single diagram the physical solidarity of all these psycho-physical systems throughout Nature, together with their pyscho-physical discontinuity.

For we need only draw all the waves so that they run into each other below the threshold, whilst above it they appear distinct, as in the figure below.

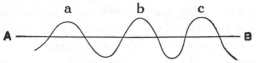

a   b   c

A   B

" In this figure *a, b, c* stand for three organisms, or rather for the total waves of psycho-physical activity of three organisms, whilst A B represents the threshold. In each wave the part that rises above the threshold is an integrated thing, and is connected with a single consciousness. Whatever lies below the threshold, being unconscious, separates the conscious crests, although it is still the means of physical connection.

" In general terms: wherever a psycho-physical total wave is continuous with itself above the threshold, there we find the unity or identity of a consciousness, inasmuch as the connection of the psychical phenomena which correspond to the parts of the wave also appears in consciousness. Whenever, on the contrary, total waves are disconnected, or connected only underneath the threshold, the corresponding consciousness is broken, and no connection between its several parts appears. More briefly: consciousness is continuous or discontinu-

ous, unified or discrete, according as the psycho-
physical total waves that subserve it are themselves continuous or discontinuous above the
threshold. . . .

" If, in the diagram, we should raise the entire
line of waves so that not only the crests but the
valleys appeared above the threshold, then these
latter would appear only as depressions in one
great continuous wave above the threshold, and the
discontinuity of the consciousness would be con-
verted into continuity. We of course cannot bring
this about. We might also squeeze the wave together so that the valleys should be pressed up,
and the crests above the threshold flow into a line ;
then the discretely-feeling organisms would have
become a singly - feeling organism. This, again,
Man cannot voluntarily bring about, but it is
brought about in Man's nature. His two halves,
the right one and the left one, are thus united ; and
the number of segments of radiates and articulates
show that more than two parts can be thus psycho-
physically conjoined. One need only cut them
asunder, *i. e.* interpolate another part of nature
between them under the threshold, and they break
into two separately conscious beings." . . . [*Ele-
mente der Psychophysik*, 1860, vol. ii. pp. 526–
530.]

One sees easily how, on Fechner's wave-scheme,

a world-soul may be expressed. All psycho-physical activity being continuous 'below the threshold,' the consciousness might also become continuous if the threshold sank low enough to uncover
all the waves. The threshold throughout nature
in general is, however, very high, so the consciousness that gets over it is of the discontinuous form.

NOTE 7, page 25.

See the long series of articles by Mr. Myers in the
Proceedings of the Society for Psychical Research,
beginning in the third volume with automatic writing, and ending in the latest volumes with the
higher manifestations of knowledge by mediums.
Mr. Myers's theory of the whole range of phenomena is, that our normal consciousness is in continuous connection with a greater consciousness
of which we do not know the extent, and to which
he gives, in its relation to the particular person,
the not very felicitous name — though no better one
has been proposed — of his or her 'subliminal' self.

NOTE 8, page 29.

See *Kritik der reinen Vernunft*, second edition,
p. 809.

NOTE 9, page 29.

I subjoin a few extracts from Mr. Schiller's
work: " Matter is an admirably calculated machin-

ery for regulating, limiting, and restraining the
consciousness which it encases. . . . If the material encasement be coarse and simple, as in the
lower organisms, it permits only a little intelligence
to permeate through it; if it is delicate and complex, it leaves more pores and exits, as it were,
for the manifestations of consciousness. . . . On
this analogy, then, we may say that the lower animals are still entranced in the lower stage of brute
lethargy, while we have passed into the higher
phase of *somnambulism*, which already permits us
strange glimpses of a lucidity that divines the realities of a transcendent world. And this gives the
final answer to Materialism: it consists in showing
in detail . . . that Materialism is a hysteron prote-
ron, a putting of the cart before the horse, which
may be rectified by just inverting the connection
between Matter and Consciousness. Matter is not
that which *produces* Consciousness, but that which
limits it, and confines its intensity within certain
limits: material organization does not construct
consciousness out of arrangements of atoms, but
contracts its manifestation within the sphere which
it permits. This explanation . . . admits the connection of Matter and Consciousness, but contends
that the course of interpretation must proceed in
the contrary direction. Thus it will fit the facts
alleged in favor of Materialism equally well, be-

sides enabling us to understand facts which Materialism rejected as 'supernatural.' It explains the lower by the higher, Matter by Spirit, instead of *vice versa*, and thereby attains to an explanation which is ultimately tenable, instead of one which is ultimately absurd. And it is an explanation the possibility of which no evidence in favor of Materialism can possibly affect. For if, *e. g.*, a man loses consciousness as soon as his brain is injured, it is clearly as good an explanation to say the injury to the brain destroyed the mechanism by which the manifestation of the consciousness was rendered possible, as to say that it destroyed the seat of consciousness. On the other hand, there are facts which the former theory suits far better. If, *e. g.*, as sometimes happens, the man, after a time, more or less, recovers the faculties of which the injury to his brain had deprived him, and that not in consequence of a renewal of the injured part, but in consequence of the inhibited functions being performed by the vicarious action of other parts, the easiest explanation certainly is that, after a time, consciousness constitutes the remaining parts into a mechanism capable of acting as a substitute for the lost parts. And again, if the body is a mechanism for inhibiting consciousness, for preventing the full powers of the Ego from being prematurely actualized, it will be necessary to invert also our ordinary ideas on the subject of memory, and to account for forgetfulness instead of for memory. It will be during life that we drink the bitter cup of Lethe, it will be with our brain that we are enabled to forget. And this will serve to explain not only the extraordinary memories of the drowning and the dying generally, but also the curious hints which experimental psychology occasionally affords us that nothing is ever forgotten wholly and beyond recall." [*Riddles of the Sphinx*, London, Swan Sonnenschein, 1891, p. 293 ff.]

Mr. Schiller's conception is much more complex in its relations than the simple 'theory of transmission' postulated in my lecture, and to do justice to it the reader should consult the original work.

NOTE 10, page 39.

I beg the reader to peruse R. L. Stevenson's magnificent little essay entitled 'The Lantern Bearers,' reprinted in the collection entitled *Across the Plains*. The truth is that we are doomed, by the fact that we are practical beings with very limited tasks to attend to, and special ideals to look after, to be absolutely blind and insensible to the inner feelings, and to the whole inner significance of lives that are different from our own. Our opinion of the worth of such lives is absolutely wide of the mark, and unfit to be counted at all.

NOTE II, page 41.

W. Wundt: *System der Philosophie*, Leipzig, Engelmann, 1889, p. 315.

THE END.

CATALOGUE OF DOVER BOOKS

Philosophy, Religion

GUIDE TO PHILOSOPHY, C. E. M. Joad. A modern classic which examines many crucial problems which man has pondered through the ages: Does free will exist? Is there plan in the universe? How do we know and validate our knowledge? Such opposed solutions as subjective idealism and realism, chance and teleology, vitalism and logical positivism, are evaluated and the contributions of the great philosophers from the Greeks to moderns like Russell, Whitehead, and others, are considered in the context of each problem. "The finest introduction," BOSTON TRANSCRIPT. Index. Classified bibliography. 592pp. 5⅜ x 8.
T297 Paperbound **$2.00**

HISTORY OF ANCIENT PHILOSOPHY, W. Windelband. One of the clearest, most accurate comprehensive surveys of Greek and Roman philosophy. Discusses ancient philosophy in general, intellectual life in Greece in the 7th and 6th centuries B.C., Thales, Anaximander, Anaximenes, Heraclitus, the Eleatics, Empedocles, Anaxagoras, Leucippus, the Pythagoreans, the Sophists, Socrates, Democritus (20 pages), Plato (50 pages), Aristotle (70 pages), the Peripatetics, Stoics, Epicureans, Sceptics, Neo-platonists, Christian Apologists, etc. 2nd German edition translated by H. E. Cushman. xv + 393pp. 5⅜ x 8.
T357 Paperbound **$1.85**

ILLUSTRATIONS OF THE HISTORY OF MEDIEVAL THOUGHT AND LEARNING, R. L. Poole. Basic analysis of the thought and lives of the leading philosophers and ecclesiastics from the 8th to the 14th century—Abailard, Ockham, Wycliffe, Marsiglio of Padua, and many other great thinkers who carried the torch of Western culture and learning through the "Dark Ages": political, religious, and metaphysical views. Long a standard work for scholars and one of the best introductions to medieval thought for beginners. Index. 10 Appendices. xiii + 327pp. 5⅜ x 8.
T674 Paperbound **$2.00**

PHILOSOPHY AND CIVILIZATION IN THE MIDDLE AGES, M. de Wulf. This semi-popular survey covers aspects of medieval intellectual life such as religion, philosophy, science, the arts, etc. It also covers feudalism vs. Catholicism, rise of the universities, mendicant orders, monastic centers, and similar topics. Unabridged. Bibliography. Index. viii + 320pp. 5⅜ x 8.
T284 Paperbound **$1.85**

AN INTRODUCTION TO SCHOLASTIC PHILOSOPHY, Prof. M. de Wulf. Formerly entitled SCHOLASTICISM OLD AND NEW, this volume examines the central scholastic tradition from St. Anselm, Albertus Magnus, Thomas Aquinas, up to Suarez in the 17th century. The relation of scholasticism to ancient and medieval philosophy and science in general is clear and easily followed. The second part of the book considers the modern revival of scholasticism, the Louvain position, relations with Kantianism and Positivism. Unabridged. xvi + 271pp. 5⅜ x 8.
T296 Clothbound **$3.50**
T283 Paperbound **$1.75**

A HISTORY OF MODERN PHILOSOPHY, H. Höffding. An exceptionally clear and detailed coverage of western philosophy from the Renaissance to the end of the 19th century. Major and minor men such as Pomponazzi, Bodin, Boehme, Telesius, Bruno, Copernicus, da Vinci, Kepler, Galileo, Bacon, Descartes, Hobbes, Spinoza, Leibniz, Wolff, Locke, Newton, Berkeley, Hume, Erasmus, Montesquieu, Voltaire, Diderot, Rousseau, Lessing, Kant, Herder, Fichte, Schelling, Hegel, Schopenhauer, Comte, Mill, Darwin, Spencer, Hartmann, Lange, and many others, are discussed in terms of theory of knowledge, logic, cosmology, and psychology. Index. 2 volumes, total of 1159pp. 5⅜ x 8.
T117 Vol. 1, Paperbound **$2.25**
T118 Vol. 2, Paperbound **$2.25**

ARISTOTLE, A. E. Taylor. A brilliant, searching non-technical account of Aristotle and his thought written by a foremost Platonist. It covers the life and works of Aristotle; classification of the sciences; logic; first philosophy; matter and form; causes; motion and eternity; God; physics; metaphysics; and similar topics. Bibliography. New Index compiled for this edition. 128pp. 5⅜ x 8.
T280 Paperbound **$1.00**

THE SYSTEM OF THOMAS AQUINAS, M. de Wulf. Leading Neo-Thomist, one of founders of University of Louvain, gives concise exposition to central doctrines of Aquinas, as a means toward determining his value to modern philosophy, religion. Formerly "Medieval Philosophy Illustrated from the System of Thomas Aquinas." Trans. by E. Messenger. Introduction. 151pp. 5⅜ x 8.
T568 Paperbound **$1.25**

LEIBNIZ, H. W. Carr. Most stimulating middle-level coverage of basic philosophical thought of Leibniz. Easily understood discussion, analysis of major works: "Theodicy," "Principles of Nature and Grace," "Monadology"; Leibniz's influence; intellectual growth; correspondence; disputes with Bayle, Malebranche, Newton; importance of his thought today, with reinterpretation in modern terminology. "Power and mastery," London Times. Bibliography. Index. 226pp. 5⅜ x 8.
T624 Paperbound **$1.35**

THE SENSE OF BEAUTY, G. Santayana. A revelation of the beauty of language as well as an important philosophic treatise, this work studies the "why, when, and how beauty appears, what conditions an object must fulfill to be beautiful, what elements of our nature make us sensible of beauty, and what the relation is between the constitution of the object and the excitement of our susceptibility." "It is doubtful if a better treatment of the subject has since been published," PEABODY JOURNAL. Index. ix + 275pp. 5⅜ x 8.
T238 Paperbound **$1.00**

PROBLEMS OF ETHICS, Moritz Schlick. The renowned leader of the "Vienna Circle" applies the logical positivist approach to a wide variety of ethical problems: the source and means of attaining knowledge, the formal and material characteristics of the good, moral norms and principles, absolute vs. relative values, free will and responsibility, comparative importance of pleasure and suffering as ethical values, etc. Disarmingly simple and straightforward despite complexity of subject. First English translation, authorized by author before his death, of a thirty-year old classic. Translated and with an introduction by David Rynin. Index. Foreword by Prof. George P. Adams. xxi + 209pp. 5⅜ x 8. T946 Paperbound **$1.60**

AN INTRODUCTION TO EXISTENTIALISM, Robert G. Olson. A new and indispensable guide to one of the major thought systems of our century, the movement that is central to the thinking of some of the most creative figures of the past hundred years. Stresses Heidegger and Sartre, with careful and objective examination of the existentialist position, values—freedom of choice, individual dignity, personal love, creative effort—and answers to the eternal questions of the human condition. Scholarly, unbiased, analytic, unlike most studies of this difficult subject, Prof. Olson's book is aimed at the student of philosophy as well as at the reader with no formal training who is looking for an absorbing, accessible, and thorough introduction to the basic texts. Index. xv + 221pp. 5⅜ x 8½. T55 Paperbound **$1.65**

SYMBOLIC LOGIC, C. I. Lewis and C. H. Langford. Since first publication in 1932, this has been among most frequently cited works on symbolic logic. Still one of the best introductions both for beginners and for mathematicians, philosophers. First part covers basic topics which easily lend themselves to beginning study. Second part is rigorous, thorough development of logistic method, examination of some of most difficult and abstract aspects of symbolic logic, including modal logic, logical paradoxes, many-valued logic, with Prof. Lewis' own contributions. 2nd revised (corrected) edition. 3 appendixes, one new to this edition. 524pp. 5⅜ x 8. S170 Paperbound **$2.00**

WHITEHEAD'S PHILOSOPHY OF CIVILIZATION, A. H. Johnson. A leading authority on Alfred North Whitehead synthesizes the great philosopher's thought on civilization, scattered throughout various writings, into unified whole. Analysis of Whitehead's general definition of civilization, his reflections on history and influences on its development, his religion, including his analysis of Christianity, concept of solitariness as first requirement of personal religion, and so on. Other chapters cover views on minority groups, society, civil liberties, education. Also critical comments on Whitehead's philosophy. Written with general reader in mind. A perceptive introduction to important area of the thought of a leading philosopher of our century. Revised index and bibliography. xii + 211pp. 5⅜ x 8½.
T996 Paperbound **$1.50**

WHITEHEAD'S THEORY OF REALITY, A. H. Johnson. Introductory outline of Whitehead's theory of actual entities, the heart of his philosophy of reality, followed by his views on nature of God, philosophy of mind, theory of value (truth, beauty, goodness and their opposites), analyses of other philosophers, attitude toward science. A perspicacious lucid introduction by author of dissertation on Whitehead, written under the subject's supervision at Harvard. Good basic view for beginning students of philosophy and for those who are simply interested in important contemporary ideas. Revised index and bibliography. xiii + 267pp. 5⅜ x 8½.
T989 Paperbound **$1.50**

MIND AND THE WORLD-ORDER, C. I. Lewis. Building upon the work of Peirce, James, and Dewey, Professor Lewis outlines a theory of knowledge in terms of "conceptual pragmatism." Dividing truth into abstract mathematical certainty and empirical truth, the author demonstrates that the traditional understanding of the a priori must be abandoned. Detailed analyses of philosophy, metaphysics, method, the "given" in experience, knowledge of objects, nature of the a priori, experience and order, and many others. Appendices. xiv + 446pp. 5⅜ x 8. T359 Paperbound **$2.25**

SCEPTICISM AND ANIMAL FAITH, G. Santayana. To eliminate difficulties in the traditional theory of knowledge, Santayana distinguishes between the independent existence of objects and the essence our mind attributes to them. Scepticism is thereby established as a form of belief, and animal faith is shown to be a necessary condition of knowledge. Belief, classical idealism, intuition, memory, symbols, literary psychology, and much more, discussed with unusual clarity and depth. Index. xii + 314pp. 5⅜ x 8. T235 Clothbound **$3.50**
T236 Paperbound **$1.75**

LANGUAGE AND MYTH, E. Cassirer. Analyzing the non-rational thought processes which go to make up culture, Cassirer demonstrates that beneath both language and myth there lies a dominant unconscious "grammar" of experience whose categories and canons are not those of logical thought. His analyses of seemingly diverse phenomena such as Indian metaphysics, the Melanesian "mana," the Naturphilosophie of Schelling, modern poetry, etc., are profound without being pedantic. Introduction and translation by Susanne Langer. Index. x + 103pp. 5⅜ x 8. T51 Paperbound **$1.25**

AN ESSAY CONCERNING HUMAN UNDERSTANDING, John Locke. Edited by A. C. Fraser. Unabridged reprinting of definitive edition; only complete edition of "Essay" in print. Marginal analyses of almost every paragraph; hundreds of footnotes; authoritative 140-page biographical, critical, historical prolegomena. Indexes. 1170pp. 5⅜ x 8.

T530 Vol. 1 (Books 1, 2) Paperbound **$2.50**
T531 Vol. 2 (Books 3, 4) Paperbound **$2.50**
2 volume set **$5.00**

THE PHILOSOPHY OF HISTORY, G. W. F. Hegel. One of the great classics of western thought which reveals Hegel's basic principle: that history is not chance but a rational process, the realization of the Spirit of Freedom. Ranges from the oriental cultures of subjective thought to the classical subjective cultures, to the modern absolute synthesis where spiritual and secular may be reconciled. Translation and introduction by J. Sibree. Introduction by C. Hegel. Special introduction for this edition by Prof. Carl Friedrich. xxxix + 447pp. 5⅜ x 8.

T112 Paperbound **$2.25**

THE PHILOSOPHY OF HEGEL, W. T. Stace. The first detailed analysis of Hegel's thought in English, this is especially valuable since so many of Hegel's works are out of print. Dr. Stace examines Hegel's debt to Greek idealists and the 18th century and then proceeds to a careful description and analysis of Hegel's first principles, categories, reason, dialectic method, his logic, philosophy of nature and spirit, etc. Index. Special 14 x 20 chart of Hegelian system. x + 526pp. 5⅜ x 8.

T254 Paperbound **$2.45**

THE WILL TO BELIEVE and HUMAN IMMORTALITY, W. James. Two complete books bound as one. THE WILL TO BELIEVE discusses the interrelations of belief, will, and intellect in man; chance vs. determinism, free will vs. determinism, free will vs. fate, pluralism vs. monism; the philosophies of Hegel and Spencer, and more. HUMAN IMMORTALITY examines the question of survival after death and develops an unusual and powerful argument for immortality. Two prefaces. Index. Total of 429pp. 5⅜ x 8.

T291 Paperbound **$2.00**

THE WORLD AND THE INDIVIDUAL, Josiah Royce. Only major effort by an American philosopher to interpret nature of things in systematic, comprehensive manner. Royce's formulation of an absolute voluntarism remains one of the original and profound solutions to the problems involved. Part One, Four Historical Conceptions of Being, inquires into first principles, true meaning and place of individuality. Part Two, Nature, Man, and the Moral Order, is application of first principles to problems concerning religion, evil, moral order. Introduction by J. E. Smith, Yale Univ. Index. 1070pp. 5⅜ x 8.

T561 Vol. 1 Paperbound **$2.75**
T562 Vol. 2 Paperbound **$2.75**
Two volume set **$5.50**

THE PHILOSOPHICAL WRITINGS OF PEIRCE, edited by J. Buchler. This book (formerly THE PHILOSOPHY OF PEIRCE) is a carefully integrated exposition of Peirce's complete system composed of selections from his own work. Symbolic logic, scientific method, theory of signs, pragmatism, epistemology, chance, cosmology, ethics, and many other topics are treated by one of the greatest philosophers of modern times. This is the only inexpensive compilation of his key ideas. xvi + 386pp. 5⅜ x 8.

T217 Paperbound **$2.00**

EXPERIENCE AND NATURE, John Dewey. An enlarged, revised edition of the Paul Carus lectures which Dewey delivered in 1925. It covers Dewey's basic formulation of the problem of knowledge, with a full discussion of other systems, and a detailing of his own concepts of the relationship of external world, mind, and knowledge. Starts with a thorough examination of the philosophical method; examines the interrelationship of experience and nature; analyzes experience on basis of empirical naturalism, the formulation of law, role of language and social factors in knowledge; etc. Dewey's treatment of central problems in philosophy is profound but extremely easy to follow. ix + 448pp. 5⅜ x 8.

T471 Paperbound **$2.00**

THE PHILOSOPHICAL WORKS OF DESCARTES. The definitive English edition of all the major philosophical works and letters of René Descartes. All of his revolutionary insights, from his famous "Cogito ergo sum" to his detailed account of contemporary science and his astonishingly fruitful concept that all phenomena of the universe (except mind) could be reduced to clear laws by the use of mathematics. An excellent source for the thought of men like Hobbes, Arnauld, Gassendi, etc., who were Descarte's contemporaries. Translated by E. S. Haldane and G. Ross. Introductory notes. Index. Total of 842pp. 5⅜ x 8.

T71 Vol. 1, Paperbound **$2.00**
T72 Vol. 2, Paperbound **$2.00**

THE CHIEF WORKS OF SPINOZA. An unabridged reprint of the famous Bohn edition containing all of Spinoza's most important works: Vol. I: The Theologico-Political Treatise and the Political Treatise. Vol. II: On The Improvement Of Understanding, The Ethics, Selected Letters. Profound and enduring ideas on God, the universe, pantheism, society, religion, the state, democracy, the mind, emotions, freedom and the nature of man, which influenced Goethe, Hegel, Schelling, Coleridge, Whitehead, and many others. Introduction. 2 volumes. 826pp. 5⅜ x 8.

T249 Vol. I, Paperbound **$1.50**
T250 Vol. II, Paperbound **$1.50**

THE ANALYSIS OF MATTER, Bertrand Russell. A classic which has retained its importance in understanding the relation between modern physical theory and human perception. Logical analysis of physics, prerelativity physics, causality, scientific inference, Weyl's theory, tensors, invariants and physical interpretations, periodicity, and much more is treated with Russell's usual brilliance. "Masterly piece of clear thinking and clear writing," NATION AND ATHENAEUM. "Most thorough treatment of the subject," THE NATION. Introduction. Index. 8 figures. viii + 408pp. 5⅜ x 8.   S231 Paperbound **$1.95**

CONCEPTUAL THINKING (A LOGICAL INQUIRY), S. Körner. Discusses origin, use of general concepts on which language is based, and the light they shed on basic philosophical questions. Rigorously examines how different concepts are related; how they are linked to experience; problems in the field of contact between exact logical, mathematical, and scientific concepts, and the inexactness of everyday experience (studied at length). This work elaborates many new approaches to the traditional problems of philosophy—epistemology, value theories, metaphysics, aesthetics, morality. "Rare originality . . . brings a new rigour into philosophical argument," Philosophical Quarterly. New corrected second edition. Index. vii + 301pp. 5⅜ x 8   T516 Paperbound **$1.75**

INTRODUCTION TO SYMBOLIC LOGIC, S. Langer. No special knowledge of math required — probably the clearest book ever written on symbolic logic, suitable for the layman, general scientist, and philosopher. You start with simple symbols and advance to a knowledge of the Boole-Schroeder and Russell-Whitehead systems. Forms, logical structure, classes, the calculus of propositions, logic of the syllogism, etc., are all covered. "One of the clearest and simplest introductions," MATHEMATICS GAZETTE. Second enlarged, revised edition. 368pp. 5⅜ x 8.   S164 Paperbound **$1.85**

LANGUAGE, TRUTH AND LOGIC, A. J. Ayer. A clear, careful analysis of the basic ideas of Logical Positivism. Building on the work of Schlick, Russell, Carnap, and the Viennese School, Mr. Ayer develops a detailed exposition of the nature of philosophy, science, and metaphysics; the Self and the World; logic and common sense, and other philosophic concepts. An aid to clarity of thought as well as the first full-length development of Logical Positivism in English. Introduction by Bertrand Russell. Index. 160pp. 5⅜ x 8.   T10 Paperbound **$1.25**

ESSAYS IN EXPERIMENTAL LOGIC, J. Dewey. Based upon the theory that knowledge implies a judgment which in turn implies an inquiry, these papers consider the inquiry stage in terms of: the relationship of thought and subject matter, antecedents of thought, data and meanings. 3 papers examine Bertrand Russell's thought, while 2 others discuss pragmatism and a final essay presents a new theory of the logic of values. Index. viii + 444pp. 5⅜ x 8.
T73 Paperbound **$2.25**

TRAGIC SENSE OF LIFE, M. de Unamuno. The acknowledged masterpiece of one of Spain's most influential thinkers. Between the despair at the inevitable death of man and all his works and the desire for something better, Unamuno finds that "saving incertitude" that alone can console us. This dynamic appraisal of man's faith in God and in himself has been called "a masterpiece" by the ENCYCLOPAEDIA BRITANNICA. xxx + 332pp. 5⅜ x 8.
T257 Paperbound **$2.00**

HISTORY OF DOGMA, A. Harnack. Adolph Harnack, who died in 1930, was perhaps the greatest Church historian of all time. In this epoch-making history, which has never been surpassed in comprehensiveness and wealth of learning, he traces the development of the authoritative Christian doctrinal system from its first crystallization in the 4th century down through the Reformation, including also a brief survey of the later developments through the Infallibility decree of 1870. He reveals the enormous influence of Greek thought on the early Fathers, and discusses such topics as the Apologists, the great councils, Manichaeism, the historical position of Augustine, the medieval opposition to indulgences, the rise of Protestantism, the relations of Luther's doctrines with modern tendencies of thought, and much more. "Monumental work; still the most valuable history of dogma . . . luminous analysis of the problems . . . abounds in suggestion and stimulus and can be neglected by no one who desires to understand the history of thought in this most important field," Dutcher's Guide to Historical Literature. Translated by Neil Buchanan. Index. Unabridged reprint in 4 volumes. Vol I: Beginnings to the Gnostics and Marcion. Vol II & III: 2nd century to the 4th century Fathers. Vol IV & V: 4th century Councils to the Carlovingian Renaissance. Vol VI & VII: Period of Clugny (c. 1000) to the Reformation, and after. Total of cii + 2407pp. 5⅜ x 8.

T904 Vol I	Paperbound	**$2.50**
T905 Vol II & III	Paperbound	**$2.75**
T906 Vol IV & V	Paperbound	**$2.75**
T907 Vol VI & VII	Paperbound	**$2.75**
	The set	**$10.75**

THE GUIDE FOR THE PERPLEXED, Maimonides. One of the great philosophical works of all time and a necessity for everyone interested in the philosophy of the Middle Ages in the Jewish, Christian, and Moslem traditions. Maimonides develops a common meeting-point for the Old Testament and the Aristotelian thought which pervaded the medieval world. His ideas and methods predate such scholastics as Aquinas and Scotus and throw light on the entire problem of philosophy or science vs. religion. 2nd revised edition. Complete unabridged Friedländer translation. 55 page introduction to Maimonides's life, period, etc., with an important summary of the GUIDE. Index. lix + 414pp. 5⅜ x 8.   T351 Paperbound **$2.00**

Orientalia

ORIENTAL RELIGIONS IN ROMAN PAGANISM, F. Cumont. A study of the cultural meeting of east and west in the Early Roman Empire. It covers the most important eastern religions of the time from their first appearance in Rome, 204 B.C., when the Great Mother of the Gods was first brought over from Syria. The ecstatic cults of Syria and Phrygia — Cybele, Attis, Adonis, their orgies and mutilatory rites; the mysteries of Egypt — Serapis, Isis, Osiris, the dualism of Persia, the elevation of cosmic evil to equal stature with the deity, Mithra; worship of Hermes Trismegistus; Ishtar, Astarte; the magic of the ancient Near East, etc. Introduction. 55pp. of notes; extensive bibliography. Index. xxiv + 298pp. 5⅜ x 8.
T321 Paperbound **$2.00**

THE MYSTERIES OF MITHRA, F. Cumont. The definitive coverage of a great ideological struggle between the west and the orient in the first centuries of the Christian era. The origin of Mithraism, a Persian mystery religion, and its association with the Roman army is discussed in detail. Then utilizing fragmentary monuments and texts, in one of the greatest feats of scholarly detection, Dr. Cumont reconstructs the mystery teachings and secret doctrines, the hidden organization and cult of Mithra. Mithraic art is discussed, analyzed, and depicted in 70 illustrations. 239pp. 5⅜ x 8.
T323 Paperbound **$1.85**

CHRISTIAN AND ORIENTAL PHILOSOPHY OF ART, A. K. Coomaraswamy. A unique fusion of philosopher, orientalist, art historian, and linguist, the author discusses such matters as: the true function of aesthetics in art, the importance of symbolism, intellectual and philosophic backgrounds, the role of traditional culture in enriching art, common factors in all great art, the nature of medieval art, the nature of folklore, the beauty of mathematics, and similar topics. 2 illustrations. Bibliography. 148pp. 5⅜ x 8.
T378 Paperbound **$1.35**

TRANSFORMATION OF NATURE IN ART, A. K. Coomaraswamy. Unabridged reissue of a basic work upon Asiatic religious art and philosophy of religion. The theory of religious art in Asia and Medieval Europe (exemplified by Meister Eckhart) is analyzed and developed. Detailed consideration is given to Indian medieval aesthetic manuals, symbolic language in philosophy, the origin and use of images in India, and many other fascinating and little known topics. Glossaries of Sanskrit and Chinese terms. Bibliography. 41pp. of notes. 245pp. 5⅜ x 8.
T368 Paperbound **$1.75**

BUDDHIST LOGIC, F.Th. Stcherbatsky. A study of an important part of Buddhism usually ignored by other books on the subject: the Mahayana buddhistic logic of the school of Dignaga and his followers. First vol. devoted to history of Indian logic with Central Asian continuations, detailed exposition of Dignaga system, including theory of knowledge, the sensible world (causation, perception, ultimate reality) and mental world (judgment, inference, logical fallacies, the syllogism), reality of external world, and negation (law of contradiction, universals, dialectic). Vol. II contains translation of Dharmakirti's Nyayabindu with Dharmamottara's commentary. Appendices cover translations of Tibetan treatises on logic, Hindu attacks on Buddhist logic, etc. The basic work, one of the products of the great St. Petersburg school of Indian studies. Written clearly and with an awareness of Western philosophy and logic; meant for the Asian specialist and for the general reader with only a minimum of background. Vol. I, xii + 559pp. Vol. II, viii + 468pp. 5⅜ x 8½.
T955 Vol. I Paperbound **$2.50**
T956 Vol. II Paperbound **$2.50**
The set **$5.00**

THE TEXTS OF TAOISM. The first inexpensive edition of the complete James Legge translations of the Tao Te King and the writings of Chinese mystic Chuang Tse. Also contains several shorter treatises: the T'ai Shang Tractate of Actions and Their Retributions; the King Kang King, or Classic of Purity; the Yin Fu King, or Classic of the Harmony of the Seen and Unseen; the Yu Shu King, or Classic of the Pivot of Jade; and the Hsia Yung King, or Classic of the Directory for a Day. While there are other translations of the Tao Te King, this is the only translation of Chuang Tse and much of other material. Extensive introduction discusses differences between Taoism, Buddhism, Confucianism; authenticity and arrangement of Tao Te King and writings of Chuang Tse; the meaning of the Tao and basic tenets of Taoism; historical accounts of Lao-tse and followers; other pertinent matters. Clarifying notes incorporated into text. Originally published as Volumes 39, 40 of SACRED BOOKS OF THE EAST series, this has long been recognized as an indispensable collection. Sinologists, philosophers, historians of religion will of course be interested and anyone with an elementary course in Oriental religion or philosophy will understand and profit from these writings. Index. Appendix analyzing thought of Chuang Tse. Vol. I, xxiii + 396pp. Vol. II, viii + 340pp. 5⅜ x 8½.
T990 Vol. I Paperbound **$2.25**
T991 Vol. II Paperbound **$2.25**

Americana

THE EYES OF DISCOVERY, J. Bakeless. A vivid reconstruction of how unspoiled America appeared to the first white men. Authentic and enlightening accounts of Hudson's landing in New York, Coronado's trek through the Southwest; scores of explorers, settlers, trappers, soldiers. America's pristine flora, fauna, and Indians in every region and state in fresh and unusual new aspects. "A fascinating view of what the land was like before the first highway went through," Time. 68 contemporary illustrations, 39 newly added in this edition. Index. Bibliography. x + 500pp. 5⅜ x 8. T761 Paperbound **$2.00**

AUDUBON AND HIS JOURNALS, J. J. Audubon. A collection of fascinating accounts of Europe and America in the early 1800's through Audubon's own eyes. Includes the Missouri River Journals —an eventful trip through America's untouched heartland, the Labrador Journals, the European Journals, the famous "Episodes", and other rare Audubon material, including the descriptive chapters from the original letterpress edition of the "Ornithological Studies", omitted in all later editions. Indispensable for ornithologists, naturalists, and all lovers of Americana and adventure. 70-page biography by Audubon's granddaughter. 38 illustrations. Index. Total of 1106pp. 5⅜ x 8. T675 Vol I Paperbound **$2.25**
T676 Vol II Paperbound **$2.25**
The set **$4.50**

TRAVELS OF WILLIAM BARTRAM, edited by Mark Van Doren. The first inexpensive illustrated edition of one of the 18th century's most delightful books is an excellent source of first-hand material on American geography, anthropology, and natural history. Many descriptions of early Indian tribes are our only source of information on them prior to the infiltration of the white man. "The mind of a scientist with the soul of a poet," John Livingston Lowes. 13 original illustrations and maps. Edited with an introduction by Mark Van Doren. 448pp. 5⅜ x 8. T13 Paperbound **$2.00**

GARRETS AND PRETENDERS: A HISTORY OF BOHEMIANISM IN AMERICA, A. Parry. The colorful and fantastic history of American Bohemianism from Poe to Kerouac. This is the only complete record of hoboes, cranks, starving poets, and suicides. Here are Pfaff, Whitman, Crane, Bierce, Pound, and many others. New chapters by the author and by H. T. Moore bring this thorough and well-documented history down to the Beatniks. "An excellent account," N. Y. Times. Scores of cartoons, drawings, and caricatures. Bibliography. Index. xxviii + 421pp. 5⅝ x 8⅜. T708 Paperbound **$1.95**

THE EXPLORATION OF THE COLORADO RIVER AND ITS CANYONS, J. W. Powell. The thrilling first-hand account of the expedition that filled in the last white space on the map of the United States. Rapids, famine, hostile Indians, and mutiny are among the perils encountered as the unknown Colorado Valley reveals its secrets. This is the only uncut version of Major Powell's classic of exploration that has been printed in the last 60 years. Includes later reflections and subsequent expedition. 250 illustrations, new map. 400pp. 5⅝ x 8⅜. T94 Paperbound **$2.25**

THE JOURNAL OF HENRY D. THOREAU, Edited by Bradford Torrey and Francis H. Allen. Henry Thoreau is not only one of the most important figures in American literature and social thought; his voluminous journals (from which his books emerged as selections and crystallizations) constitute both the longest, most sensitive record of personal internal development and a most penetrating description of a historical moment in American culture. This present set, which was first issued in fourteen volumes, contains Thoreau's entire journals from 1837 to 1862, with the exception of the lost years which were found only recently. We are reissuing it, complete and unabridged, with a new introduction by Walter Harding, Secretary of the Thoreau Society. Fourteen volumes reissued in two volumes. Foreword by Henry Seidel Canby. Total of 1888pp. 8⅜ x 12¼. T312-3 Two volume set, Clothbound **$20.00**

GAMES AND SONGS OF AMERICAN CHILDREN, collected by William Wells Newell. A remarkable collection of 190 games with songs that accompany many of them; cross references to show similarities, differences among them; variations; musical notation for 38 songs. Textual discussions show relations with folk-drama and other aspects of folk tradition. Grouped into categories for ready comparative study: Love-games, histories, playing at work, human life, bird and beast, mythology, guessing-games, etc. New introduction covers relations of songs and dances to timeless heritage of folklore, biographical sketch of Newell, other pertinent data. A good source of inspiration for those in charge of groups of children and a valuable reference for anthropologists, sociologists, psychiatrists. Introduction by Carl Withers. New indexes of first lines, games. 5⅜ x 8½. xii + 242pp. T354 Paperbound **$1.75**

GARDNER'S PHOTOGRAPHIC SKETCH BOOK OF THE CIVIL WAR, Alexander Gardner. The first published collection of Civil War photographs, by one of the two or three most famous photographers of the era, outstandingly reproduced from the original positives. Scenes of crucial battles: Appomattox, Manassas, Mechanicsville, Bull Run, Yorktown, Fredericksburg, etc. Gettysburg immediately after retirement of forces. Battle ruins at Richmond, Petersburg, Gaines'Mill. Prisons, arsenals, a slave pen, fortifications, headquarters, pontoon bridges, soldiers, a field hospital. A unique glimpse into the realities of one of the bloodiest wars in history, with an introductory text to each picture by Gardner himself. Until this edition, there were only five known copies in libraries, and fewer in private hands, one of which sold at auction in 1952 for $425. Introduction by E. F. Bleiler. 100 full page 7 x 10 photographs (original size). 224pp. 8½ x 10¾. T476 Clothbound **$6.00**

A BIBLIOGRAPHY OF NORTH AMERICAN FOLKLORE AND FOLKSONG, Charles Haywood, Ph.D. The only book that brings together bibliographic information on so wide a range of folklore material. Lists practically everything published about American folksongs, ballads, dances, folk beliefs and practices, popular music, tales, similar material—more than 35,000 titles of books, articles, periodicals, monographs, music publications, phonograph records. Each entry complete with author, title, date and place of publication, arranger and performer of particular examples of folk music, many with Dr. Haywood's valuable criticism, evaluation. Volume I, "The American People," is complete listing of general and regional studies, titles of tales and songs of Negro and non-English speaking groups and where to find them, Occupational Bibliography including sections listing sources of information, folk material on cowboys, riverboat men, 49ers, American characters like Mike Fink, Frankie and Johnnie, John Henry, many more. Volume II, "The American Indian," tells where to find information on dances, myths, songs, ritual of more than 250 tribes in U.S., Canada. A monumental product of 10 years' labor, carefully classified for easy use. "All students of this subject . . . will find themselves in debt to Professor Haywood," Stith Thompson, in American Anthropologist. ". . . a most useful and excellent work," Duncan Emrich, Chief Folklore Section, Library of Congress, in "Notes." Corrected, enlarged republication of 1951 edition. New Preface. New index of composers, arrangers, performers. General index of more than 15,000 items. Two volumes. Total of 1301pp. 6⅛ x 9¼. T797-798 Clothbound **$12.50**

INCIDENTS OF TRAVEL IN YUCATAN, John L. Stephens. One of first white men to penetrate interior of Yucatan tells the thrilling story of his discoveries of 44 cities, remains of once-powerful Maya civilization. Compelling text combines narrative power with historical significance as it takes you through heat, dust, storms of Yucatan; native festivals with brutal bull fights; great ruined temples atop man-made mounds. Countless idols, sculptures, tombs, examples of Mayan taste for rich ornamentation, from gateways to personal trinkets, accurately illustrated, discussed in text. Will appeal to those interested in ancient civilizations, and those who like stories of exploration, discovery, adventure. Republication of last (1843) edition. 124 illustrations by English artist, F. Catherwood. Appendix on Mayan architecture, chronology. Two volume set. Total of xxviii + 927pp.

Vol I T926 Paperbound **$2.00**
Vol II T927 Paperbound **$2.00**
The set **$4.00**

A GENIUS IN THE FAMILY, Hiram Percy Maxim. Sir Hiram Stevens Maxim was known to the public as the inventive genius who created the Maxim gun, automatic sprinkler, and a heavier-than-air plane that got off the ground in 1894. Here, his son reminisces—this is by no means a formal biography—about the exciting and often downright scandalous private life of his brilliant, eccentric father. A warm and winning portrait of a prankish, mischievous, impious personality, a genuine character. The style is fresh and direct, the effect is unadulterated pleasure. "A book of charm and lasting humor . . . belongs on the 'must read' list of all fathers," New York Times. "A truly gorgeous affair," New Statesman and Nation. 17 illustrations, 16 specially for this edition. viii + 108pp. 5⅜ x 8½. T948 Paperbound **$1.00**

HORSELESS CARRIAGE DAYS, Hiram P. Maxim. The best account of an important technological revolution by one of its leading figures. The delightful and rewarding story of the author's experiments with the exact combustibility of gasoline, stopping and starting mechanisms, carriage design, and engines. Captures remarkably well the flavor of an age of scoffers and rival inventors not above sabotage; of noisy, uncontrollable gasoline vehicles and incredible mobile steam kettles. ". . . historic information and light humor are combined to furnish highly entertaining reading," New York Times. 56 photographs, 12 specially for this edition. xi + 175pp. 5⅜ x 8½. T964 Paperbound **$1.35**

BODY, BOOTS AND BRITCHES: FOLKTALES, BALLADS AND SPEECH FROM COUNTRY NEW YORK, Harold W. Thompson. A unique collection, discussion of songs, stories, anecdotes, proverbs handed down orally from Scotch-Irish grandfathers, German nurse-maids, Negro workmen, gathered from all over Upper New York State. Tall tales by and about lumbermen and pirates, canalers and injun-fighters, tragic and comic ballads, scores of sayings and proverbs all tied together by an informative, delightful narrative by former president of New York Historical Society. ". . . a sparkling homespun tapestry that every lover of Americana will want to have around the house," Carl Carmer, New York Times. Republication of 1939 edition. 20 line-drawings. Index. Appendix (Sources of material, bibliography). 530pp. 5⅜ x 8½. T411 Paperbound **$2.25**

Art, History of Art, Antiques, Graphic Arts, Handcrafts

ART STUDENTS' ANATOMY, E. J. Farris. Outstanding art anatomy that uses chiefly living objects for its illustrations. 71 photos of undraped men, women, children are accompanied by carefully labeled matching sketches to illustrate the skeletal system, articulations and movements, bony landmarks, the muscular system, skin, fasciae, fat, etc. 9 x-ray photos show movement of joints. Undraped models are shown in such actions as serving in tennis, drawing a bow in archery, playing football, dancing, preparing to spring and to dive. Also discussed and illustrated are proportions, age and sex differences, the anatomy of the smile, etc. 8 plates by the great early 18th century anatomic illustrator Siegfried Albinus are also included. Glossary. 158 figures, 7 in color. x + 159pp. 5⅝ x 8⅜.   T744 Paperbound **$1.50**

AN ATLAS OF ANATOMY FOR ARTISTS, F Schider. A new 3rd edition of this standard text enlarged by 52 new illustrations of hands, anatomical studies by Cloquet, and expressive life studies of the body by Barcsay. 189 clear, detailed plates offer you precise information of impeccable accuracy. 29 plates show all aspects of the skeleton, with closeups of special areas, while 54 full-page plates, mostly in two colors, give human musculature as seen from four different points of view, with cutaways for important portions of the body. 14 full-page plates provide photographs of hand forms, eyelids, female breasts, and indicate the location of muscles upon models. 59 additional plates show how great artists of the past utilized human anatomy. They reproduce sketches and finished work by such artists as Michelangelo, Leonardo da Vinci, Goya, and 15 others. This is a lifetime reference work which will be one of the most important books in any artist's library. "The standard reference tool," AMERICAN LIBRARY ASSOCIATION. "Excellent," AMERICAN ARTIST. Third enlarged edition. 189 plates, 647 illustrations. xxvi + 192pp. 7⅞ x 10⅝.   T241 Clothbound **$6.00**

AN ATLAS OF ANIMAL ANATOMY FOR ARTISTS, W. Ellenberger, H. Baum, H. Dittrich. The largest, richest animal anatomy for artists available in English. 99 detailed anatomical plates of such animals as the horse, dog, cat, lion, deer, seal, kangaroo, flying squirrel, cow, bull, goat, monkey, hare, and bat. Surface features are clearly indicated, while progressive beneath-the-skin pictures show musculature, tendons, and bone structure. Rest and action are exhibited in terms of musculature and skeletal structure and detailed cross-sections are given for heads and important features. The animals chosen are representative of specific families so that a study of these anatomies will provide knowledge of hundreds of related species. "Highly recommended as one of the very few books on the subject worthy of being used as an authoritative guide," DESIGN. "Gives a fundamental knowledge," AMERICAN ARTIST. Second revised, enlarged edition with new plates from Cuvier, Stubbs, etc. 288 illustrations. 153pp. 11⅜ x 9.   T82 Clothbound **$6.00**

THE HUMAN FIGURE IN MOTION, Eadweard Muybridge. The largest selection in print of Muybridge's famous high-speed action photos of the human figure in motion. 4789 photographs illustrate 162 different actions: men, women, children—mostly undraped—are shown walking, running, carrying various objects, sitting, lying down, climbing, throwing, arising, and performing over 150 other actions. Some actions are shown in as many as 150 photographs each. All in all there are more than 500 action strips in this enormous volume, series shots taken at shutter speeds of as high as 1/6000th of a second! These are not posed shots, but true stopped motion. They show bone and muscle in situations that the human eye is not fast enough to capture. Earlier, smaller editions of these prints have brought $40 and more on the out-of-print market. "A must for artists," ART IN FOCUS. "An unparalleled dictionary of action for all artists," AMERICAN ARTIST. 390 full-page plates, with 4789 photographs. Printed on heavy glossy stock. Reinforced binding with headbands. xxi + 390pp. 7⅞ x 10⅝.
T204 Clothbound **$10.00**

ANIMALS IN MOTION, Eadweard Muybridge. This is the largest collection of animal action photos in print. 34 different animals (horses, mules, oxen, goats, camels, pigs, cats, guanacos, lions, gnus, deer, monkeys, eagles—and 21 others) in 132 characteristic actions. The horse alone is shown in more than 40 different actions. All 3919 photographs are taken in series at speeds up to 1/6000th of a second. The secrets of leg motion, spinal patterns, head movements, strains and contortions shown nowhere else are captured. You will see exactly how a lion sets his foot down; how an elephant's knees are like a human's—and how they differ; the position of a kangaroo's legs in mid-leap; how an ostrich's head bobs; details of the flight of birds—and thousands of facets of motion only the fastest cameras can catch. Photographed from domestic animals and animals in the Philadelphia zoo, it contains neither semiposed artificial shots nor distorted telephoto shots taken under adverse conditions. Artists, biologists, decorators, cartoonists, will find this book indispensable for understanding animals in motion. "A really marvelous series of plates," NATURE (London). "The dry plate's most spectacular early use was by Eadweard Muybridge," LIFE. 3919 photographs; 380 full pages of plates. 440pp. Printed on heavy glossy paper. Deluxe binding with headbands. 7⅞ x 10⅝.   T203 Clothbound **$10.00**

METALWORK AND ENAMELLING, H. Maryon. This is probably the best book ever written on the subject. Prepared by Herbert Maryon, F.S.A., of the British Museum, it tells everything necessary for home manufacture of jewelry, rings, ear pendants, bowls, and dozens of other objects. Clearly written chapters provide precise information on such topics as materials, tools, soldering, filigree, setting stones, raising patterns, spinning metal, repoussé work, hinges and joints, metal inlaying, damascening, overlaying, niello, Japanese alloys, enamelling, cloisonné, painted enamels, casting, polishing, coloring, assaying, and dozens of other techniques. This is the next best thing to apprenticeship to a master metalworker. 363 photographs and figures. 374pp. 5½ x 8½.   T183 Clothbound **$8.50**

SILK SCREEN TECHNIQUES, J. I. Biegeleisen, Max A. Cohn. A complete-to-the-last-detail copiously illustrated home course in this fast growing modern art form. Full directions for building silk screen out of inexpensive materials; explanations of five basic methods of stencil preparation—paper, blockout, tusche, film, photographic—and effects possible: light and shade, washes, dry brush, oil paint type impastos, gouaches, pastels. Detailed coverage of multicolor printing, illustrated by proofs showing the stages of a 4 color print. Special section on common difficulties. 149 illustrations, 8 in color. Sources of supply. xiv + 187pp. 6⅛ x 9¼.   T433 Paperbound **$1.75**

A HANDBOOK OF WEAVES, G. H. Oelsner. Now back in print! Probably the most complete book of weaves ever printed, fully explained, differentiated, and illustrated. Includes plain weaves; irregular, double-stitched, and filling satins; derivative, basket, and rib weaves; steep, undulating, broken, offset, corkscrew, interlocking, herringbone, and fancy twills; honeycomb, lace, and crepe weaves; tricot, matelassé, and montagnac weaves; and much more. Translated and revised by S. S. Dale, with supplement on the analysis of weaves and fabrics. 1875 illustrations. vii + 402pp. 6 x 9¼.   T209 Clothbound **$5.00**

BASIC BOOKBINDING, A. W. Lewis. Enables the beginner and the expert to apply the latest and most simplified techniques to rebinding old favorites and binding new paperback books. Complete lists of all necessary materials and guides to the selection of proper tools, paper, glue, boards, cloth, leather, or sheepskin covering fabrics, lettering inks and pigments, etc. You are shown how to collate a book, sew it, back it, trim it, make boards and attach them in easy step-by-step stages. Author's preface. 261 illustrations with appendix. Index. xi + 144pp. 5⅜ x 8.   T169 Paperbound **$1.45**

BASKETRY, F. J. Christopher. Basic introductions cover selection of materials, use and care of tools, equipment. Easy-to-follow instructions for preparation of oval, oblong trays, lidded baskets, rush mats, tumbler holders, bicycle baskets, waste paper baskets, many other useful, beautiful articles made of coiled and woven reed, willow, rushes, raffia. Special sections present in clear, simple language and numerous illustrations all the how-to information you could need: linings, skein wire, varieties of stitching, simplified construction of handles, dying processes. For beginner and skilled craftsman alike. Edited by Majorie O'Shaugnessy. Bibliography. Sources of supply. Index. 112 illustrations. 108pp. 5 x 7¼.   T903 Paperbound **$1.00**

THE ART OF ETCHING, E. S. Lumsden. Everything you need to know to do etching yourself. First two sections devoted to technique of etching and engraving, covering such essentials as relative merits of zinc and copper, cleaning and grounding plates, gravers, acids, arrangement of etching-room, methods of biting, types of inks and oils, mounting, stretching and framing, preserving and restoring plates, size and color of printing papers, much more. A review of the history of the art includes separate chapters on Dürer and Lucas van Leyden, Rembrandt and Van Dyck, Goya, Meryon, Haden and Whistler, British masters of nineteenth century, modern etchers. Final section is a collection of prints by contemporary etchers with comments by the artists. Professional etchers and engravers will find this a highly useful source of examples. Beginners and teachers, students of art and printing will find it a valuable tool. Index. 208 illustrations. 384pp. 5⅜ x 8.
T49 Paperbound **$2.50**

WHITTLING AND WOODCARVING, E. J. Tangerman. What to make and how to make it for even a moderately handy beginner. One of the few works that bridge gap between whittling and serious carving. History of the art, background information on selection and use of woods, grips, types of strokes and cuts, handling of tools and chapters on rustic work, flat toys and windmills, puzzles, chains, ships in bottle, nested spheres, fans, more than 100 useful, entertaining objects. Second half covers carving proper: woodcuts, low relief, sculpture in the round, lettering, inlay and marquetry, indoor and outdoor decorations, pierced designs, much more. Final chapter describes finishing, care of tools. Sixth edition. Index. 464 illustrations. x + 239pp. 5½ x 8⅛.   T965 Paperbound **$1.75**

THE PRACTICE OF TEMPERA PAINTING, Daniel V. Thompson, Jr. A careful exposition of all aspects of tempera painting, including sections on many possible modern uses, propensities of various woods, choice of material for panel, making and applying the gesso, pigments and brushes, technique of the actual painting, gilding and so on—everything one need know to try a hand at this proven but neglected art. The author is unquestionably the world's leading authority on tempera methods and processes and his treatment is based on exhaustive study of manuscript material. Drawings and diagrams increase clarity of text. No one interested in tempera painting can afford to be without this book. Appendix, "Tempera Practice in Yale Art School," by Lewis E. York. 85 illustrations by York; 4 full-page plates. ix x 149pp. 5⅜ x 8½.   T343 Paperbound **$1.50**

SHAKER FURNITURE, E. D. Andrews and F. Andrews. The most illuminating study on what many scholars consider the best examples of functional furniture ever made. Includes the history of the sect and the development of Shaker style. The 48 magnificent plates show tables, chairs, cupboards, chests, boxes, desks, beds, woodenware, and much more, and are accompanied by detailed commentary. For all antique collectors and dealers, designers and decorators, historians and folklorists. "Distinguished in scholarship, in pictorial illumination, and in all the essentials of fine book making," Antiques. 3 Appendixes. Bibliography. Index. 192pp. 7⅞ x 10¾. T679 Paperbound **$2.00**

JAPANESE HOMES AND THEIR SURROUNDINGS, E. S. Morse. Every aspect of the purely traditional Japanese home, from general plan and major structural features to ceremonial and traditional appointments—tatami, hibachi, shoji, tokonoma, etc. The most exhaustive discussion in English, this book is equally honored for its strikingly modern conception of architecture. First published in 1886, before the contamination of the Japanese traditions, it preserves the authentic features of an ideal of construction that is steadily gaining devotees in the Western world. 307 illustrations by the author. Index. Glossary. xxxvi + 372pp. 5⅝ x 8⅜. T746 Paperbound **$2.25**

COLONIAL LIGHTING, Arthur H. Hayward. The largest selection of antique lamps ever illustrated anywhere, from rush light-holders of earliest settlers to 1880's—with main emphasis on Colonial era. Primitive attempts at illumination ("Betty" lamps, variations of open wick design, candle molds, reflectors, etc.), whale oil lamps, painted and japanned hand lamps, Sandwich glass candlesticks, astral lamps, Bennington ware and chandeliers of wood, iron, pewter, brass, crystal, bronze and silver. Hundreds of illustrations, loads of information on colonial life, customs, habits, place of acquisition of lamps illustrated. A unique, thoroughgoing survey of an interesting aspect of Americana. Enlarged (1962) edition. New Introduction by James R. Marsh. Supplement "Colonial Chandeliers," photographs with descriptive notes. 169 illustrations, 647 lamps. xxxi + 312pp. 5⅝ x 8¼. T975 Paperbound **$2.00**

CHINESE HOUSEHOLD FURNITURE, George N. Kates. The first book-length study of authentic Chinese domestic furniture in Western language. Summarises practically everything known about Chinese furniture in pure state, uninfluenced by West. History of style, unusual woods used, craftsmanship, principles of design, specific forms like wardrobes, chests and boxes, beds, chairs, tables, stools, cupboards and other pieces. Based on author's own investigation into scanty Chinese historical sources and surviving pieces in private collections and museums. Will reveal a new dimension of simple, beautiful work to all interior decorators, furniture designers, craftsmen. 123 illustrations; 112 photographs. Bibliography. xiii + 205pp. 5¼ x 7¾. T958 Paperbound **$1.50**

ART AND THE SOCIAL ORDER, Professor D. W. Gotshalk, University of Illinois. One of the most profound and most influential studies of aesthetics written in our generation, this work is unusual in considering art from the relational point of view, as a transaction consisting of creation-object-apprehension. Discussing material from the fine arts, literature, music, and related disciplines, it analyzes the aesthetic experience, fine art, the creative process, art materials, form, expression, function, art criticism, art and social life and living. Graceful and fluent in expression, it requires no previous background in aesthetics and will be read with considerable enjoyment by anyone interested in the theory of art. "Clear, interesting, the soundest and most penetrating work in recent years," C. J. Ducasse, Brown University. New preface by Professor Gotshalk. xvi + 248pp. 5⅝ x 8½.
T294 Paperbound **$1.65**

FOUNDATIONS OF MODERN ART, A. Ozenfant. An illuminating discussion by a great artist of the interrelationship of all forms of human creativity, from painting to science, writing to religion. The creative process is explored in all facets of art, from paleolithic cave painting to modern French painting and architecture, and the great universals of art are isolated. Expressing its countless insights in aphorisms accompanied by carefully selected illustrations, this book is itself an embodiment in prose of the creative process. Enlarged by 4 new chapters. 226 illustrations. 368pp. 6⅛ x 9¼. T215 Paperbound **$2.00**

VITRUVIUS: TEN BOOKS ON ARCHITECTURE. Book by 1st century Roman architect, engineer, is oldest, most influential work on architecture in existence; for hundreds of years his specific instructions were followed all over the world, by such men as Bramante, Michelangelo, Palladio, etc., and are reflected in major buildings. He describes classic principles of symmetry, harmony; design of treasury, prison, etc.; methods of durability; much more. He wrote in a fascinating manner, and often digressed to give interesting sidelights, making this volume appealing reading even to the non-professional. Standard English translation, by Prof. M. H. Morgan, Harvard U. Index. 6 illus. 334pp. 5⅜ x 8. T645 Paperbound **$2.00**

THE BROWN DECADES, Lewis Mumford. In this now classic study of the arts in America, Lewis Mumford resurrects the "buried renaissance" of the post-Civil War period. He demonstrates that it contained the seeds of a new integrity and power and documents his study with detailed accounts of the founding of modern architecture in the work of Sullivan, Richardson, Root, Roebling; landscape development of Marsh, Olmstead, and Eliot; the graphic arts of Homer, Eakins, and Ryder. 2nd revised enlarged edition. Bibliography. 12 illustrations. Index. xiv + 266pp. 5⅜ x 8. T200 Paperbound **$1.75**

THE AUTOBIOGRAPHY OF AN IDEA, Louis Sullivan. The pioneer architect whom Frank Lloyd Wright called "the master" reveals an acute sensitivity to social forces and values in this passionately honest account. He records the crystallization of his opinions and theories, the growth of his organic theory of architecture that still influences American designers and architects, contemporary ideas, etc. This volume contains the first appearance of 34 full-page plates of his finest architecture. Unabridged reissue of 1924 edition. New introduction by R. M. Line. Index. xiv + 335pp. 5⅜ x 8. T281 Paperbound **$2.00**

THE DRAWINGS OF HEINRICH KLEY. The first uncut republication of both of Kley's devastating sketchbooks, which first appeared in pre-World War I Germany. One of the greatest cartoonists and social satirists of modern times, his exuberant and iconoclastic fantasy and his extraordinary technique place him in the great tradition of Bosch, Breughel, and Goya, while his subject matter has all the immediacy and tension of our century. 200 drawings. viii + 128pp. 7¾ x 10¾. T24 Paperbound **$1.85**

MORE DRAWINGS BY HEINRICH KLEY. All the sketches from Leut' Und Viecher (1912) and Sammel-Album (1923) not included in the previous Dover edition of Drawings. More of the bizarre, mercilessly iconoclastic sketches that shocked and amused on their original publication. Nothing was too sacred, no one too eminent for satirization by this imaginative, individual and accomplished master cartoonist. A total of 158 illustrations. lv + 104pp. 7¾ x 10¾. T41 Paperbound **$1.85**

PINE FURNITURE OF EARLY NEW ENGLAND, R. H. Kettell. A rich understanding of one of America's most original folk arts that collectors of antiques, interior decorators, craftsmen, woodworkers, and everyone interested in American history and art will find fascinating and immensely useful. 413 illustrations of more than 300 chairs, benches, racks, beds, cupboards, mirrors, shelves, tables, and other furniture will show all the simple beauty and character of early New England furniture. 55 detailed drawings carefully analyze outstanding pieces. "With its rich store of illustrations, this book emphasizes the individuality and varied design of early American pine furniture. It should be welcomed," ANTIQUES. 413 illustrations and 55 working drawings. 475. 8 x 10¾. T145 Clothbound **$10.00**

THE HUMAN FIGURE, J. H. Vanderpoel. Every important artistic element of the human figure is pointed out in minutely detailed word descriptions in this classic text and illustrated as well in 430 pencil and charcoal drawings. Thus the text of this book directs your attention to all the characteristic features and subtle differences of the male and female (adults, children, and aged persons), as though a master artist were telling you what to look for at each stage. 2nd edition, revised and enlarged by George Bridgman. Foreword. 430 illustrations. 143pp. 6⅛ x 9¼. T432 Paperbound **$1.50**

LETTERING AND ALPHABETS, J. A. Cavanagh. This unabridged reissue of LETTERING offers a full discussion, analysis, illustration of 89 basic hand lettering styles — styles derived from Caslons, Bodonis, Garamonds, Gothic, Black Letter, Oriental, and many others. Upper and lower cases, numerals and common signs pictured. Hundreds of technical hints on make-up, construction, artistic validity, strokes, pens, brushes, white areas, etc. May be reproduced without permission! 89 complete alphabets; 72 lettered specimens. 121pp. 9¾ x 8. T53 Paperbound **$1.35**

STICKS AND STONES, Lewis Mumford. A survey of the forces that have conditioned American architecture and altered its forms. The author discusses the medieval tradition in early New England villages; the Renaissance influence which developed with the rise of the merchant class; the classical influence of Jefferson's time; the "Mechanicsvilles" of Poe's generation; the Brown Decades; the philosophy of the Imperial facade; and finally the modern machine age. "A truly remarkable book," SAT. REV. OF LITERATURE. 2nd revised edition. 21 illustrations. xvii + 228pp. 5⅜ x 8. T202 Paperbound **$1.65**

THE STANDARD BOOK OF QUILT MAKING AND COLLECTING, Marguerite Ickis. A complete easy-to-follow guide with all the information you need to make beautiful, useful quilts. How to plan, design, cut, sew, appliqué, avoid sewing problems, use rag bag, make borders, tuft, every other aspect. Over 100 traditional quilts shown, including over 40 full-size patterns. At-home hobby for fun, profit. Index. 483 illus. 1 color plate. 287pp. 6¾ x 9½. T582 Paperbound **$2.00**

THE BOOK OF SIGNS, Rudolf Koch. Formerly $20 to $25 on the out-of-print market, now only $1.00 in this unabridged new edition! 493 symbols from ancient manuscripts, medieval cathedrals, coins, catacombs, pottery, etc. Crosses, monograms of Roman emperors, astrological, chemical, botanical, runes, housemarks, and 7 other categories. Invaluable for handicraft workers, illustrators, scholars, etc., this material may be reproduced without permission. 493 illustrations by Fritz Kredel. 104pp. 6½ x 9¼. T162 Paperbound **$1.00**

PRIMITIVE ART, Franz Boas. This authoritative and exhaustive work by a great American anthropologist covers the entire gamut of primitive art. Pottery, leatherwork, metal work, stone work, wood, basketry, are treated in detail. Theories of primitive art, historical depth in art history, technical virtuosity, unconscious levels of patterning, symbolism, styles, literature, music, dance, etc. A must book for the interested layman, the anthropologist, artist, handicrafter (hundreds of unusual motifs), and the historian. Over 900 illustrations (50 ceramic vessels, 12 totem poles, etc.). 376pp. 5⅜ x 8. T25 Paperbound **$2.00**

History, Political Science

THE POLITICAL THOUGHT OF PLATO AND ARISTOTLE, E. Barker. One of the clearest and most accurate expositions of the corpus of Greek political thought. This standard source contains exhaustive analyses of the "Republic" and other Platonic dialogues and Aristotle's "Politics" and "Ethics," and discusses the origin of these ideas in Greece, contributions of other Greek theorists, and modifications of Greek ideas by thinkers from Aquinas to Hegel. "Must" reading for anyone interested in the history of Western thought. Index. Chronological Table of Events. 2 Appendixes. xxiv + 560pp. 5⅜ x 8. T521 Paperbound **$2.50**

THE IDEA OF PROGRESS, J. B. Bury. Practically unknown before the Reformation, the idea of progress has since become one of the central concepts of western civilization. Prof. Bury analyzes its evolution in the thought of Greece, Rome, the Middle Ages, the Renaissance, to its flowering in all branches of science, religion, philosophy, industry, art, and literature, during and following the 16th century. Introduction by Charles Beard. Index. xl + 357pp. 5⅜ x 8. T40 Paperbound **$2.00**

THE ANCIENT GREEK HISTORIANS, J. B. Bury. This well known, easily read work covers the entire field of classical historians from the early writers to Herodotus, Thucydides, Xenophon, through Poseidonius and such Romans as Tacitus, Cato, Caesar, Livy. Scores of writers are studied biographically, in style, sources, accuracy, structure, historical concepts, and influences. Recent discoveries such as the Oxyrhinchus papyri are referred to, as well as such great scholars as Nissen, Gomperz, Cornford, etc. "Totally unblemished by pedantry." Outlook. "The best account in English," Dutcher, A Guide to Historical Lit. Bibliography, Index. x + 281pp. 5⅜ x 8. T397 Paperbound **$1.65**

HISTORY OF THE LATER ROMAN EMPIRE, J. B. Bury. This standard work by the leading Byzantine scholar of our time discusses the later Roman and early Byzantine empires from 395 A.D. through the death of Justinian in 565, in their political, social, cultural, theological, and military aspects. Contemporary documents are quoted in full, making this the most complete reconstruction of the period and a fit successor to Gibbon's "Decline and Fall." "Most unlikely that it will ever be superseded," Glanville Downey, Dumbarton Oaks Research Lib. Geneological tables. 5 maps. Bibliography. Index. 2 volumes total of 965pp. 5⅜ x 8. T398, 399 Two volume set, Paperbound **$4.50**

A HISTORY OF ANCIENT GEOGRAPHY, E. H. Bunbury. Standard study, in English, of ancient geography; never equalled for scope, detail. First full account of history of geography from Greeks' first world picture based on mariners, through Ptolemy. Discusses every important map, discovery, figure, travel expedition, war, conjecture, narrative, bearing on subject. Chapters on Homeric geography, Herodotus, Alexander expedition, Strabo, Pliny, Ptolemy, would stand alone as exhaustive monographs. Includes minor geographers, men not usually regarded in this context: Hecataeus, Pytheas, Hipparchus, Artemidorus, Marinus of Tyre, etc. Uses information gleaned from military campaigns such as Punic Wars, Hannibal's passage of Alps, campaigns of Lucullus, Pompey, Caesar's wars, the Trojan War. New introduction by W. H. Stahl, Brooklyn College. Bibliography. Index. 20 maps. 1426pp. 5⅜ x 8. T570-1, clothbound, 2-volume set **$12.50**

POLITICAL PARTIES, Robert Michels. Classic of social science, reference point for all later work, deals with nature of leadership in social organization on government and trade union levels. Probing tendency of oligarchy to replace democracy, It studies need for leadership, desire for organization, psychological motivations, vested interests, hero worship, reaction of leaders to power, press relations, many other aspects. Trans. by E. & C. Paul. Introduction. 447pp. 5⅜ x 8. T569 Paperbound **$2.00**

A HISTORY OF HISTORICAL WRITING, Harry Elmer Barnes. Virtually the only adequate survey of the whole course of historical writing in a single volume. Surveys developments from the beginnings of historiographies in the ancient Near East and the Classical World, up through the Cold War. Covers major historians in detail, shows interrelationship with cultural background, makes clear individual contributions, evaluates and estimates importance; also enormously rich upon minor authors and thinkers who are usually passed over. Packed with scholarship and learning, clear, easily written. Indispensable to every student of history. Revised and enlarged up to 1961. Index and bibliography. xv + 442pp. 5⅜ x 8½. T104 Paperbound **$2.25**

Prices subject to change without notice.

Dover publishes books on art, music, philosophy, literature, languages, history, social sciences, psychology, handcrafts, orientalia, puzzles and entertainments, chess, pets and gardens, books explaining science, intermediate and higher mathematics, mathematical physics, engineering, biological sciences, earth sciences, classics of science, etc. Write to:

Dept. catrr.
Dover Publications, Inc.
180 Varick Street, N. Y. 14, N. Y.